Christopher Wilson is an English journalist, broadcaster and author. His authoritative account of the secret relationship between Prince Charles and Camilla Parker Bowles, *A Greater Love*, was made into a major TV documentary, transmitted in the UK, USA, Canada, Australia, Europe and Japan. He has been a columnist for *The Times*, the *Sunday Telegraph*, the *Daily Express* and *Today*.

Also by Christopher Wilson

*A Greater Love*
*By Invitation Only*
*Diana v Charles* (with James Whitaker)
*Fergie: Her True Story* (with Allan Starkie)

# *Absolutely ... Goldie*

## THE BIOGRAPHY

## Christopher Wilson

HarperCollins*Entertainment*
*An Imprint of* HarperCollins*Publishers*

HarperCollins*Entertainment*
An Imprint of HarperCollins*Publishers*
77–85 Fulham Palace Road,
Hammersmith, London W6 8JB

www.**fire**and**water**.com

This paperback edition 2000
1 3 5 7 9 8 6 4 2

First published in Great Britain by
HarperCollins*Entertainment* 1999

Copyright © Christopher Wilson 1999

The Author asserts the moral right to
be identified as the author of this work

ISBN 0 00 653085 0

Set in New Baskerville

Printed and bound in Great Britain by
Clays Ltd, St Ives plc

*To the*
*Richards of Cynwyd*
*their children and grandchildren*

# Contents

# Illustrations

The author and publisher are grateful to the following for use of photographic material:

SECTION ONE
1 © Thomas Bell Collection, Special Collections, Carnegie Mellon University Libraries, Pittsburgh, PA; 2 Courtesy of Herbert R. Hawn, Jr; 3, 4, 6, 7, 8, 17 Courtesy of Sylvia Colen Berman; 5, 9 Courtesy of Montgomery Blair High School; 10, 11, 14 Courtesy of Warren E. Burger Collection, Earl Gregg Swem Library, College of William and Mary, Williamsburg, VA; 13 Courtesy of Donegan Smith; 15 © The Moviestore Collection; 16 © Camera Press.

SECTION TWO
1, 4 The Ronald Grant Archive; 2 © The Kobal Collection; 3, 5, 6, 8, 12, 13 © Rex Features; 7 © Angeli Photo News Agency; 9, 14, 16 © The Moviestore Collection; 10 Courtesy of David Walsh; 11 © Famous; 15 © Phil Loftus.

# Acknowledgements

Despite a well-meaning campaign by some of those closest to Goldie Hawn to stifle this book many, many friends, lovers, neighbours, colleagues, classmates and members of her extended family helped in shaping this portrait. In the movie business, I had assistance from producers, directors, fellow actors, writers and others with functions too diverse to list and I gathered much encouragement from those people whose daily lives she touched and who were prepared to share their reminiscences.

The name of the game in Hollywood is domination; the powers-that-be like to control exactly how much, and what quality of information is allowed out to the general public. With this book I made a spirited attempt to break down those barriers, even by the smallest amount, for there were others I talked to who were too fearful to be quoted, and people who started conversations with me but, after a telephone call, changed their minds. In the end, the hush-campaign made little difference: what information is held by one person is usually held by others and by perseverance, and the help of the people whose names follow, this, the first comprehensive portrait of Hollywood's longest-lasting comic actress, was completed.

Goldie always claimed there were only three men in her life, her two husbands and her common-law husband Kurt Russell. But there were two significant others: Bruno Wintzell, with whom she had a passionate three-year affair after the breakdown of her first marriage, and Yves Renier, who fulfilled the same function after the end of her second marriage. To these, above all, I extend my thanks for sharing details of their intimate times with the woman whom both of them, at different times, believed would become their wife.

From those members of Goldie's extended family who were kind enough to speak to me I would single out Goldie's cousin Herbert R. Hawn Jr and aunt Mary Hawn, both of Little Rock, Arkansas, who graciously and tirelessly fielded endless questions. In researching Goldie's rich and fascinating background I had limitless help from Susan Melnick of the Historical Society of Western Pennsylvania and from Linda Tashbook, who plugged into her circle of acquaintances. Bernhard Blumenfeld and Eugene Litman recalled the good-old-bad-old days of Braddock, while Tony Buba, whose documentaries on Braddock and the steel towns of Pittsburgh are noteworthy, made a significant contribution. Mary Becker, director of the Braddock Carnegie Library, should not be forgotten.

In the wider trawls for historical lineage I would thank Herr Otfried Muller of Freckenfeld, Bavaria, and members of the staff of the Cultural Attaché at the German Embassy in London. Professor James Haw of Indiana University-Purdue University at Fort Wayne, Inez West of the Amelia Historical Committee, Virginia; Russell Baker of the Arkansas History Commission, Amy Blyth of the Charleston Area Convention Bureau, James Sweany of the US Library of Congress, Julian Falk of the Pennsylvania Genealogical Society, Barbara Lowry of the Connellsville Area Historical Society and Pat Hash of the South Carolina Historical Society all generously contributed to the family history. Ken McCrae, Palatine historian in Philadelphia, rounded off the voyage of the *Janet*.

In Takoma Park and surrounding areas I would first like to thank Margaret Hall for her ground-breaking research. Goldie's school-friend Sylvia Colen Berman took endless trouble in discovering small details and long-forgotten names, and Annie Groer also recalled her days with Goldie. Donna Wulken, who now owns Goldie's childhood home, and Art MacMurdie, a neighbour, gave fascinating insights. Stephanie Luciani, formerly of Silver Spring Intermediary, Richard Pioli, Goldie's drama teacher at Montgomery Blair High School, former teachers David Bridges and Ed Brakus, and Christine Grasso,

Montgomery Blair High School's principal's secretary, also gave great insights. Mark Levin of the Montgomery Blair alumni committee, Dorothy Bayer of the Takoma Park Historical Committee and Rusty Walner, curator of the Mount Lebanon cemetery, Adelphi, provided useful background. The musicians Joe Shifrin, Sy Green and Sam Scheiber, all old colleagues of Rut Hawn, added some charming grace notes, and I was delighted to speak with Judge John Chinen who presided at Goldie's first wedding in Hawaii in 1969.

The singular performance of *Romeo and Juliet* at Williamsburg, Virginia, which set Goldie's career on course, was brought alive again by its director Donegan Smith and Goldie's co-star Lee Smith, for which my grateful thanks; and I would especially applaud Nancy Hadley of the College of William and Mary, Williamsburg, for her tireless research, while Professor Howard Scammon recalled the great days of directing *The Common Glory*. Robert Forman of the American University, Washington DC, provided details of Goldie's fleeting studies there.

From Goldie's go-go days I would like to thank Bobby Van for his memories, also Goldie's first real boyfriend Spiro Venduras; as well as Darryl Shayne for her memories of Dudes'n'Dolls and the Copacabana. In Las Vegas I found Randall Wood and Fred Aaron most helpful; but it was Joe Delaney, entertainment editor of the *Las Vegas Sun*, who stunned me with his copious knowledge and elephantine memory. From Goldie's early days of stardom I would specially applaud Dee Dee Wood, Emmy-winning choreographer, and Billy Barnes, who wrote the original music for 'Laugh-In', 'Pure Goldie', her Las Vegas special and much more besides.

In New York I have special thanks for Jennifer Langham whose kindly interest ultimately opened many doors, and Phil Black, a legend in dance who first put Goldie on the stage. I raise my glass to the professionalism of Pulitzer-prizewinning Mike McGovern and to someone from whom I learn something new every time we speak, Richard Mineards. For the sheer pleasure of her company I thank Princess Kropotkin, and to my guide and mentor in the Apple, Dezia Restivo, I merely add her help to the growing debt I can never repay.

I could not have written the 'Laugh-In' chapter without the beguiling Judy Carne, who is laughing still, and from whose store of memories I borrowed liberally, and I am grateful to the resourceful British Film Institute for finding copies of that benchmark show. I wish I could say the same for the BBC but, under new management, its library resources have become a haystack in which biographers may search for their needle in vain. From the pre-'Laugh-In' memories I am grateful to Frankie Avalon and to Sam Denoff, creator of the long lamented 'Good Morning, World'. Recalling *Cactus Flower* I thank Allan Hunter, from *Soup* I salute the lovely Graham Stark as well as Nicky Henson, Roy Boulting, Barry Took and Terence Frisby, and from this period I also thank Patricia Maclaine. I am grateful to Alexandra Goudard for her eloquent translations, and in Paris I offer thanks to Michele Stouvenot, Jean-Pierre Lacomme and Serge Igor for their enthusiastic input.

I count it a privilege to be entrusted with the thoughts of some quite illustrious people in the motion picture industry including the Oscar-winning director John Schlesinger, the Oscar-winning actress and eminently sensible politician, Glenda Jackson MP, and one of the Italian film industry's most enduring stars, Giancarlo Giannini. No more charming character-reference could one ask for than that of the Oscar-nominated actress Eileen Brennan, one of Goldie's oldest friends. And I was grateful for the input of two writers, Erica Jong, author of *Fear of Flying*, and Callie Khouri whose Oscar-winning *Thelma and Louise* showed Hollywood women how to do it. Being a cinematographer on set makes you privy to many secrets but the following managed both to divulge essential information while withholding gossip, a remarkable acheivement and all the more so because it was a consistent performance from all: Petrus Schloemp (*Dollars*), David M. Walsh (*Foul Play, Private Benjamin, Seems Like Old Times*), Tak Fujimoto (*Swing Shift*), John A. Alonzo (*Overboard, Housesitter*), Bob Primes (*Bird On A Wire*), Jack N. Green (*Deceived*), Ivan Strasburg (*CrissCross*), Dean Cundey (*Death Becomes Her*). Charles Shyer, creator and co-producer of *Private Benjamin* and much else besides, was extremely generous with his time.

Cyndi Stivers, editor-in-chief of *Time Out NY*, wrote the much-quoted profile of Goldie for *Time* in the 1980s and helped me with her perspective from here and now, the *Los Angeles Times'* film critic Kenneth Turan provided a sagacious overview, as did Larry Gerbrandt of the motion picture analysts Paul Kagan Associates. I am grateful for the introductions of Sue Woodford (Lady Hollick), the Hon. Christopher Gilmour and Charles Glass. For their various assistances I thank Irv Margolis, London bureau chief of 'Entertainment Tonight', Simon Perry of the London bureau of *People* magazine, Stryker Maguire of *Newsweek*, Sean Piccoli of the Fort Lauderdale *Sun-Sentinel*, Naomi Graham of Naomi Graham International and Laker Airways, the staff of the Los Angeles Public Library and those of Winchester and Salisbury Public Libraries, William Rogers and Sally Clisby of Lloyd's Bank, and Fiona Perry; and Laurence Malden, who found me such a fitting environment in which to complete this book.

The eminently wise Alexander Walker, Gary Gilbert, Tim Ewbank, Geoffrey Levy, Garth Gibbs and Allan Hall all gave much-needed assistance and advice; and though journalists are generally regarded as takers, I remember with gratitude the selfless generosity of my former colleague Garth Pearce. Emma Baddeley's picture research was crucial.

Many organisations helped unstintingly, among them Tigress Productions, Screen International UK and LA, the Andy Griffith Museum, American Film Institute, National Camera Union, Directors Guild USA, American Society of Cinematographers, Screen Actors Guild USA, Writers Guild of America, Dimension Films, Honolulu Star and Advertiser, Las Vegas News Bureau, Jerusalem Post, Israeli Embassy, London, Japanese Embassy, London, Immigration Research centre, Philadelphia, Paramount Pictures and Miramax.

There are a number of people whom I am unable publicly to thank. This is because their modesty and, more often, fear required me to omit their names. That they should seek anonymity is less a mark of the information they divulged, more an indicator of the deplorably retributive nature of Hollywood, its studios and stars. To them I give thanks, to Hollywood I shake a stick. But to Elaine Kitt, whose late but welcome arrival allowed this project to assume extra dimensions and whose skill, energy and sunny nature threatened to overshadow those of its subject, I humbly doff my cap.

Finally I should like to thank Val Hudson, publishing director of HarperCollins, a unique and uplifting spirit, Andrea Henry, my sagacious editor; and my wife Carolyne Cullum, who cared and shared.

# Introduction

Hollywood is hardtown. Neither forgiving nor forgetting, it stands by and watches you fall. Unless you have some hidden resolve, some inner steel, you will not survive there long, be you shoeshine boy or superstar.

In Hollywood the road to success can be short but it is a narrow highway, one where accidents occur. To stay on that road and to move forward, especially if you are a woman, is a virtual impossibility. To continue your advance for thirty years or more is to arrive at the halls of the Hollywood immortals, for this is a business with a short history.

To live and survive, then, and to flourish, takes an extra special courage. Goldie Hawn's paternal ancestors walked the length of Germany and Holland to find a new life, braving Atlantic storms to come to the New World as pioneers. To escape starvation her maternal ancestors, Jews from Austria and Hungary, took sail to America and walked from New York to Pittsburgh. It is there, in America's industrial heartland, that the true fighting spirit of Goldie Hawn was forged.

Braddock, Pennsylvania, is a steel town that just won't lie down and die. In its 150-year history it barely ever raised itself above the poverty-line and today is designated by the state as a financially distressed community. Here among the grime and dust and perpetual daylight splaying from the steel-mills' noisy furnaces Goldie's mother, bereft of parents, struggled in the Depression years from early life to late teens, living in a town that looked like Hell with the lid off. On her escape to the dappled glades of Maryland she took with her an instinct for survival that served her all her life and infused in her youngest child a determination never to quit: no greater preparation could there be for Hollywood's depredations.

In so many ways Goldie Hawn is the realisation of those immigrants' aspirations: health, vitality, lasting good looks, recognition, wealth, family, achievement. She has reached the promised land that her forbears could only dream of, and has served them well by bringing joy and fun and laughter to countless millions, as if in repayment for the struggles of the ten generations which preceded her since her ancestors' exile from Bavaria in 1751. She named her production company Cherry Alley, after one of the meanest streets in Braddock: to Goldie, Cherry Alley is a place in her mind, a place where her folks still live.

To the outside world she is a force for good. No other public figure in her generation has delivered such unalloyed pleasure, so consistently, for so long. The infectious laugh, the unlined face, the girlish figure, the unassailable *joie de vivre,* have permitted millions to grow older with her, comfortable in the belief that, if she still looks *that* good, maybe the ageing process is not such a painful business after all. After *Private Benjamin* was released, *Newsweek* magazine complained: 'She makes audiences unreasonably happy.'

The act looks easy, but isn't. On closer inspection it becomes manifest that Goldie's glossy exterior is pitted with insecurities; insecurities dating from childhood and added to, layer by layer, during the formative years. In deference to her parents, perhaps, she has always painted a picture of a gloriously sunny upbringing; but while she was infinitely better off than her own mother in those grit-laden dark Depression days, on Goldie other forces came to bear – forces which set her apart at an early age and marked her down for a unique life.

Goldie Hawn is an Oscar-winning actress whose career has defied gravity. She has been responsible for generating nearly half a billion dollars in box-office receipts and much more in ancillary earnings. She has amassed a personal fortune in excess of $100m through her acting, her work as a producer and director, and through other businesses. Along a career-path studded with pitfalls and elephant-traps, she has come through ever stronger and more focused. It is probable that we have not yet seen her best work and that the rejuvenation to her career given by appearances in the *First Wives Club, Everyone Says I Love You, Out of Towners* and *Town and Country* will continue apace. The self-questioning is over; the fun times are ahead.

She stands five-feet-seven inches high, her eyes are blue-green, she fits snugly into a size eight dress, and she has a bewitching mole at the right-hand end of an elongated upper lip. The hair is honey-coloured, no longer bottle-blonde, and is never drawn back off her face: one of her superstitions is that her forehead should never be seen in its entirety. Her body, never voluptuous, has withstood the rigours of time through the discipline of daily exercise: she spent too long in childhood dance classes to abandon the routine in later life, though it comes as a relief to learn she likes a glass of wine, sometimes more, and has never felt the urge, unlike some of her contemporaries, to lecture the rest of the world on the virtues of diet and exercise. There has been some cosmetic surgery, probably more than she will admit to, but no more than she is entitled to.

In person she is a vibrant, energetic force. Her laugh, the sagjawed cacophony which starts as a trill and ends in a shout, is what made her famous. There are other blondes, with better figures and more alluring looks, but none of them laughs like Goldie. The laugh carried her through 'Rowan and Martin's Laugh-In' when her acting could not, for it should come as no surprise to learn that there are limits to Goldie's thespian skills. Within comedy, she now reigns supreme, but during her thirty-year career the various excursions into straight drama have exposed – sometimes to everyone but her – that Goldie was put on Planet Earth to laugh and encourage others to follow suit. Perhaps at last she has come to acknowledge this for herself, but for too long an adolescent stage success led her to believe that it was not sufficient to make people laugh; that she should make them cry, too.

There was a lot of laughter in Goldie's childhood home, but the laughter was often a shield behind which other emotions were kept in check. Her father, a laid-back, unplugged musician who took the line of least resistance, laughed through more than forty years of marriage, then packed his bags and left home for good. Her mother, the intense Yiddisher momma who had seen so much grinding poverty, laughed when things went right – so laughter rewarded, as well as covered sorrow, pain, distress.

She has suffered dyslexia, anorexia, and is left-handed. She underwent psychoanalysis for seven years and according to her business partner is 'schizophrenically' ambitious. She has perpetually sought love in the arms of a good man and when the thrill has gone, has ruthlessly dumped them, for in the questing side to her romantic life there has always been a need for reassurance that she was attractive to the opposite sex. She is monogamous, but not in all senses of the word.

She appalled her publicists and management when, soon after her first marriage, she argued the merits of an 'open' marriage at a press conference. Later the remark was withdrawn, but she confesses that she has always experimented sexually within her marriages: 'If things aren't going well, you begin to open up like a flower and receive.'

Though almost prudish when it comes to her screen roles, she says she is a sexual, physical person who likes to touch, kiss and feel. She pays a certain lip-service to personal morality but in her relationship with Kurt Russell has arrived at an unjealous *arrangement* in which neither questions fleeting infidelities nor expects questions in return: 'I've been with men and I've had a great time but it doesn't mean anything,' she laughs. 'You think to yourself: well that was fun, a great time, but – *bye.*' Yet she is at the same time almost excessively maternal and obsessional about the concepts of 'family' and 'home'.

She has claimed there have been three men in her life – her two husbands and Kurt Russell – but in fact she has had five serious adult relationships as well as a number of predictable encounters with the likes of Warren Beatty. In this she is no different from any other Hollywood actress, it goes with the territory, but where Goldie stands apart from her contemporaries is that she has always publicly perpetuated the idea that 'family comes first'.

Other aspects of her personality are also hidden from view.

'Goldie's more unforgiving than I am, she's harsher,' says Kurt Russell. She herself confesses that she has 'a tendency to be too judgemental of people, to sound too righteous,' adding, 'I don't always stop to think before I act or speak.' For one who has achieved so much and stayed at the top so long, she argues that she is governed by inertia, merely waiting for life to unfold its next plans to her; and she is as capable of inconsistency as the next person. On one day she will ridicule Hollywood status symbols and on another will drop names of people she 'ran into at Dustin's'. If there is one outstanding negative feature of her otherwise joyous personality, it is a tendency to complain and, according to her second husband, feel sorry for herself: 'I'm victimised by believing in my own instincts. I was hurt in my marriages, I was a victim in them.'

As an actress she remains at the top thirty years after she won her one and only Oscar, that elusive fifteen-inch piece of bronze sculpture plated in copper, nickel, silver and twenty-four-carat gold and worth in money terms no more than a mere $250. Goldie patted her Oscar on the rump so much it had to go back for re-plating, but she has never been able to bring home a mate for it. It is not for want of trying, and in her quest for that votive second statuette, if some of her films were less than marvellous she herself has never been anything less than the complete professional. To a man, producers, directors, cinematographers and technicians vouch for her dedication to her art. On time, word-perfect, generous to fellow actors, hardworking, thoughtful and cheerful, there is nothing remotely *grande dame* about Goldie Hawn on the set.

With the inclusion of *Town and Country* Goldie has made twenty-six movies since her big-screen debut in 1969, but to many it will always be 'Laugh-In' which defined her personality and carved her a place in screen history. In terms of numbers of films made, she stands between Jane Fonda and Barbra Streisand, two contemporaries whose career-curves are often compared with her own, who made forty-five and nineteen respectively. At all events, the odds are stacked against female actors in Hollywood. If in the good old days stars like Bette Davis were able to make movies back-to-back, sometimes hundreds of them, alternating roles from comedy to drama and back again, in the present climate most actresses are lucky to get a film every other year. Careers, except for the few, are short and peter out at the age of forty: statistics show that seventy per cent of all Hollywood film roles go to men, and only nine per cent of all film and TV roles go to women aged forty and over.

Similarly there are virtually no female directors or producers. Goldie has been both: she successfully made her début with a TV movie, *Hope,* in 1997 and has produced or had a hand in the production of half-a-dozen movies, the most successful of which, by far, was *Private Benjamin.* Once, *Time* magazine described her as one of the three most powerful women in Hollywood – but if Goldie Hawn was the woman who kicked in Tinseltown's glass ceiling, the misogynistic powerbrokers and money-men have since had a chance to call in the glaziers, and Goldie is back on the landing. The deal of the decade – a seven-picture, $30 million contract with Disney – which made her the envy of every other thespian wannabe producer turned to dust within a matter of moments, and the money-men just swept the dust under the carpet.

One commodity is prized above all others in Hollywood: silence. The six or seven major studios which make up the core of Tinseltown rule with a breathtaking ruthlessness and arrogance. The money-men, the grey men in suits, ordain what should and what should not be written about themselves, their films, and their stars. Truth has only a small part to play in the equation, often none at all.

This corrupting influence spreads out, and down, until it gobbles up everyone. The press, the one counterbalance to absolute power in any society, are for the most part patsies, spoon-fed by the studios. No one with any hope of longevity in Hollywood questions whether studios are using their shareholders' money wisely or well, or whether stars have been utilised and promoted properly; there are simply loud huzzahs every time a new *Titanic* is made and not a sound when hundreds of millions are lost on madcap ideas which should never have left the drawing-board.

It is into this culture that I, a stranger in Sharktown, stepped for the first time, trying to separate the truth from the lies, hyperbole from fact, rumours and gossip from what really happened. In the end, who knows? Some people were foolish enough to help me with this story because they believed that not everyone should listen to the prattle of publicists. Some of them agreed that maybe I should step up and peep behind the façade. That doesn't mean this book was written in vengeful mood; its subject is too much fun for that.

Goldie Hawn is a joy to be celebrated. I hope her sunshine radiates from every single page that follows.

# CHAPTER ONE

# *Dear Sweet Juliet*

*'O she doth teach the torches to burn bright!'*
*– Romeo and Juliet*

In the heat of the Virginia night the cicadas creaked and the big moon rose. In serried ranks, drifting upward out of sight, thousands of eyes and ears strained to hear a clear and crystal voice intone the lines:

'Thou knowest the mask of night is on my face
Else would a maiden blush bepaint my cheek ...'

It was Goldie Hawn's defining moment, a snapshot in history she carries with her to this day. More than riches, more than her children, more than her Oscar, more than love itself – this moment sums up for her the essence of who Goldie Hawn is inside.

It was a unique performance, a one-off never to be repeated. But until that night, 16 August 1964, the eighteen-year old Goldie Hawn had been a scrawny wannabe, a backline chorus dancer and bit-part player like a million other starstruck teenagers stretched across America hoping for the big time but approaching the point of compromise. Now, cast as Juliet for a single Sunday-night performance, she turned from a girl into a woman.

Driving down from Washington to Williamsburg in her cream Pontiac convertible, the recently-unemployed dance teacher was aware that the best she could hope for was a bit-part in a new drama, *The Founders*, part of the dramatic summer season at the city's College of William and Mary. *The Founders*, an epic production on a truly

1

gargantuan scale, fitted well against the backdrop of Lake Matoaka, a vast stretch of water which spread away from the 3,000-seat amphitheatre into woodland and countryside. *The Founders* was an extravagant mix of music, special effects, pageantry and spectacle and was due to run for six weeks, with a cast drawn from professional and amateur actors living within a hundred-mile radius.

Goldie's luck was in. The previous year, her first in Williamsburg, she had been in the back of chorus-line on a similar production exploring the origins and history of the United States, *The Common Glory*. This year she had hoped that maybe, she would be offered a small speaking role. She settled into the Ludwell student apartments in the college across the road from Lake Matoaka and began the non-stop round of rehearsal, performance and partying which would last the next two months.

*The Founders* had been running for a month. Apart from helping fill the back-of-stage, Goldie had landed a small part playing Joan Flinton and she was enjoying the heat, the camaraderie, the hard work and even harder partying. The past year since leaving school had been aimless, frustrating. With few academic qualifications, she had managed to secure a job with the local authority back in Washington DC, teaching dance to young children but it soon fizzled out. Following in the footsteps of her ambitious, entrepreneurial mother, she had started a small dance school of her own. But, primed by her mother's deep desire to see her daughter become a star, she knew this was not the route to take. The future was an open book, with not a single word yet written in it.

It had become common practice for the Williamsburg cast to produce a Shakespeare play on the 'off' night, Sunday. The overall producer of *The Founders*, Howard Scammon, appointed his lead actor Donald Smith, as director of *Romeo and Juliet* and ordered that auditions take place.

The director, now Donegan Smith, a veteran of Broadway, Hollywood and a dozen TV series including 'Dallas', 'Knots Landing' and 'General Hospital', had seen Goldie onstage every night for the past month: 'I had open auditions within the dancing company and the acting company. There were around five people in contention for the part and though Goldie had a presence and was a great dancer, I was concerned: did she have a voice? Could she learn her lines? I was twenty-eight and I'd never directed in my life but I could tell this girl had a special radiance – it was intuition on my part, and I could have been wrong.' Though there were seasoned actors, professionals, in the company any doubts he may have had about his choice ebbed away as Howard Scammon – watching over his shoulder as the startlingly beautiful blonde in her hip-huggers worked her way through a soliloquy – whispered happily in his ear, 'You've got your Juliet.'

Not everyone was quite so thrilled with his choice. One actress made it clear that she was the right candidate for the part, but Scammon's policy was to allow actors and dancers at the back of the stage in *The Founders* their moment to shine in the one-off productions. Donegan Smith was never in any doubt. 'Her audition blew my socks off. As she read, I could see she had an intelligence for it, a presence, and when she was through I called her back and asked her to do it again. You couldn't take your eyes off her.' Smith gave the part of Romeo to his younger brother Lee and rehearsals took place over the next ten days between 10 a.m. and 5 p.m. Then the actors including Goldie changed and went onstage for the nightly performance of *The Founders*, sometimes in temperatures of up to 112 degrees.

Lee Smith was a reluctant Romeo. Acting at Williamsburg was a way of making money to get through college, and if he was going to star in a play, he wanted a more macho role. He and Goldie had danced together till dawn in the parties that went on till dawn – indeed Goldie was known as a party girl, a dancer with boundless energy, wanting to stay up, wanting to have fun – not a Shakespearean actress: 'Suddenly this marvellously clear, articulate, beautifully spoken Shakespeare was coming out of her mouth, I was just mesmerised.

'As we rehearsed she was a revelation, she was so focused and acted with you, to your eyes. She just learned that thing so easily, that's what amazed me because we didn't have much time. I think it was a real surprise to her that she had this talent. The words flowed easily for her, never at any stage was there a feeling of terrible effort or tremendous anxiety.'

On Saturday 15 August 1964 after the curtain came down on *The Founders*, the *Romeo and Juliet* crew and cast swarmed onstage and started their technical rehearsal for the following night's perform-ance. It went on, through a rainstorm, until dawn.

The following evening, heralded by the strains of *Fantasia on a theme by Thomas Tallis* by Vaughan Williams, Goldie's performance as Juliet of the Capulets opened to polite applause. Soon, however, the audience's mood changed as the drama unfolded. The director had discovered in his young star an actress who was both opinionated and open to persuasion, a woman of newfound maturity who could still play a convincing fifteen year old. During rehearsals she had hungrily demanded more input and more subtext from her director and when he supplied it, her next day's performance would accurately reflect that direction. And on the night, with Lake Matoaka at her back and with tier upon tier of motionless theatre-goers before her, her unamplified voice floating with clarity and emotion up in the dusk to the furthermost seats she gave what was by any standards a truly moving performance, supercharged with the agony and frustration of her own teenage years.

Lee Smith, her Romeo, recalls: 'The audience were mesmerised. It had started to rain but I can't remember a murmur or a cough or shuffling, I just didn't expect it to go down that well. We played it for sighs. Goldie was just glowing – I remember the balcony scene and it was magical. When it was finished there was a huge silence, no one wanted to break it, the tension was incredible.' At the back of the auditorium sat a group of soldiers, recruits from Fort Eustace, Virginia, bussed in specially for the evening. Hardly Shakespearean aficionados, they none the less were sucked in to the drama and captivated by the actress playing Juliet. At the play's climax, tears were flowing from their eyes and they coughed into their handkerchiefs. A suitably gratified director, Donegan Smith, witnessed their emotion at close quarters.

The review, Goldie's first, which appeared two days later in the *Newport News Daily Press,* summed it up. Under the phlegmatic headline *Romeo and Juliet Performance a Hit at Lake Matoaka Despite Rain* the reviewer Bill McLaughlin opined: 'The show was noteworthy for several reasons, among them the début of an excellent actress.

'Rain forced the interruption shortly after the play started at 8.30 p.m. and continued to fall in a light drizzle through the second act. But even during the intermission few members of the audience left their seats.

'One of the main reasons for the hardiness of the audience was found in the performance of Miss Goldie Hawn, who made her professional acting début as Juliet. An excellent dancer and better-than-average singer Miss Hawn had not done any "serious" acting until Sunday night when her work marked her out as a sure theatrical triple treat.'

Goldie's parents, Rut and Laura Hawn, had driven with their other daughter Patti from Takoma Park, Maryland, to witness this quite unexpected triumph. For the family as a whole it was a glorious moment. But for Laura Hawn, it was as if an architect was at last allowed to see the building she had created, over many long years, in her mind's eye. Fierce tears of triumph dampened her cheeks along with the hot summer rain.

The birth of Goldie Jeanne Hawn just two months after the end of the Second World War, was cause for a double celebration in the semi-detached house in a secluded and wooded cul-de-sac in Takoma Park, Maryland. An airy suburb of Washington DC, Takoma Park was just a few minutes' drive from Silver Spring where Rut and Laura Hawn had met.

A typical early American suburb, Takoma Park was part of the late nineteenth-century movement away from the cities made possible by improved transportation. The creation of these leafy places was all part of the civilising process the American nation had set itself, and residents were expected to act with decorum in Takoma Park which dubbed itself, with becoming modesty, the Azalea Capital of the World. Though by the time the Hawns came to live at Takoma Park the neighbourhood had become rather run down, Cleveland Avenue, where they lived at number nine, still had the advantage of being off the main thoroughfare and surrounded by woods. Next door on one side was Mary Gregory, on the other Harry Morningstar.

The Hawns set up in business together in Silver Spring. For though Rut's principal business was music, Laura was ambitious for her family and, in deference to the trade of a father she had barely known, founded a jewellery shop where she now employed Rut during the day as a watch-repairer. Laura enjoyed running the Flowers Gift Shop on Flower Avenue while Rut pottered about mending watches and wondering about the next gig. Playing for the vast array of dignitaries who fetched up in Washington DC in the immediate post-war years helped develop his dry sense of humour: watching King Farouk dance to your music, or the massive Eleanor Roosevelt, gave Rut and his fellow musicians much to joke about. Later he recalled sitting next to Mrs Roosevelt when she received the telegram informing her of her husband's death in Warm Springs, Georgia, in April 1945.

While Laura Hawn was enjoying the delights of a belated new baby, she was soon to intuit in the new arrival a special quality, not apparent in her first daughter. 'She told me she recognised something in me even when I was a baby,' Goldie recalled in adulthood. 'She felt there was something about me that was magnetic and she thought it should be cultivated.' With few resources, intellectual or artistic, to call upon, Laura settled for encouraging her daughter to dance, something at which she had shone in the dark days of her childhood. She had tried and failed to bring out the star quality in her elder daughter – 'Patti wouldn't buy it,' said a family member – and when Goldie was three, Laura Hawn started a regime which has lasted to this day and which is a major contribution to Goldie's lasting youth and vitality – daily dance exercises. Soon the golden-haired little girl was excelling.

Goldie was born left-handed with the added difficulties which come with that state and found herself embarrassed by her given name because of the Goldilocks jokes she was forced to endure. Laura, appalled that children should make fun of her unusual choice, took a firm line: 'Look at it this way, girl: nobody will ever forget a name like that.' And though Goldie would never meet the woman after whom she was named, Laura told her daughter all about her great aunt Goldie Hochhauser and about the harsh life of Braddock, the grimy Pennsylvania steel town where she herself had grown up, a life so very far removed from the wooded bliss of Cleveland Avenue.

Laura's restless energy, coupled with the conviction that deep inside there was a latent talent in both her girls which might be used to glorious effect one day, inspired her to start a dance class with a friend in which she enrolled her daughters. Patti later recalled, 'It was probably the only dance school in Takoma Park. She'd talked a friend into opening the studio and Goldie and I were promised as her first students. We wore little white pique dance togs Mom made for us. Goldie and I each had a natural affinity for dance, but while she was discovering pirouettes, I was discovering boys.'

The two sisters were encouraged to attend three, four, then five times a week: 'There were times when I just didn't want to go, but Mother would say "You're going!" – she saw I had potential as a dancer and she made me work,' recalled Goldie.

Laura's business life at the Flowers Gift Shop flourished in a modest sort of way and helped to provide a lifestyle those back in her home-town would have envied. In a sense she had to work for two, for Rut Hawn was a dreamer: rather than buckle down to mending the broken watches, he would wait until his wife went out, then re-arrange the shop so as to be more aesthetically pleasing. When Laura came back, she would put everything back as it was, for Rut's imagination did not stretch to wondering whether his rearrangements would have a commercial appeal to customers and window-shoppers. For a time the couple ran two stores, the other on nearby Carroll Avenue, but in 1950 they sold the second store and concentrated on Flower Avenue.

If his work as itinerant musician was poorly paid, at least Rut took great delight in bringing back more and more oddball stories from his gigs. One night he supported the pianist Artur Rubenstein and a New Year's Eve party at the White House attended by a host of high-ranking Government officials. 'Daddy had to pee real bad but he couldn't get off stage – so he went behind the curtain and peed into his glass. When the evening was coming to an end, he walked off to the toilet and people stopped to wish him Happy New Year. He must have toasted five people with his glass of pee on his way to the bathroom!' recalled his daughter. 'He was very irreverent and very cynical.'

A fellow-musician from that time, Joe Shifrin, recalls Rut Hawn's musical career. Both played for the New York-based Meyer Davis Orchestra which was always hired for major high society balls and dances in Washington DC, and also for Sidney's Orchestra. They were paid the basic rate for a jobbing musician of $17 for three hours. Rut's nephew Herbert Hawn Jr recalls: 'His value as a musician was that he could read music and he could play for any band, any performer, in their style. His mother played piano for the old silent movies and all four of her sons, at one time or another, earned their living through music.'*

Rut claimed to have played his violin for every swish affair, from debutantes' balls to presidential inaugural galas, for over twenty years. Shifrin and Hawn also played on a regular basis at the swanky Sulgrave Club on the capital's Columbia Circle, with Shifrin calling early evening at the Hawns' home, or the shop, to pick up his fellow-musician. Often when he dropped by the Flowers gift shop he would find Goldie helping out behind the counter, earning pocket money.

From the start Laura Hawn pushed her younger daughter towards the limelight. 'She was a stage mom,' says a relation. 'She was very excited but she handled it reasonably well. I believe she saw the

---

* Of Rut's brothers, Herbert briefly played guitar in a dance band, Otto moved to Nashville to become a full-time violinist, and Roland eked out a living during the Depression in the National Guard band. Blind in one eye, he had to memorise the eye-chart in order to pass the Guard's physical examination.

8

potential in Goldie from very young. There was a family reunion when Goldie was three or four and Laura said to her "Goldie, get out and sing a song or somethin'", and she got up in front of this whole group of strangers and sang a little song.'

These bursts of confidence were momentary. At five, Goldie enrolled at Silver Spring Intermediate School, a short walk from Cleveland Avenue. Stephanie Luciani, supervisor of the safety patrol Goldie would later join, recalls the arrival of a child quite different from the star she was to become: 'She was just an average girl, very unassuming, with nothing that grabbed your attention – she didn't stand out in a crowd. She was a very quiet little girl, not at all how she is now. In other children you see qualities or talents in the early days that stay with them, that they go on to use to great effect. But not little Goldie. You didn't look at her, then, and say "There goes a born entertainer."'

A slow learner, Goldie ended up in the lowest reading group in her grade, the Purple Balls: 'I thought it had to be the best group because I was the only one in it. Talk about optimism!' These learning difficulties, which persisted through high school, the kooky name, and her looks – 'my ankles were fat, my knees kinda funny and I was all angles, sticking out' – were calculated to drive a wedge between Goldie and her classmates and inculcate in her a generally low self-esteem. That was not going to deter her ambitious mother. Parents of children at Silver Spring Intermediate noted how, as their own offspring gradually dropped out of dance and ballet lessons, Goldie was still attending. 'Not because she loved it,' recalled one, 'but because her mother made her go. I used to hear the other girls talk about how her mother wouldn't let her stop.'

Wearing her uniform of khaki shirt and skirt, white socks and gloves, Goldie found some sense of value in becoming one of the safety patrols stationed at road intersections to help other children cross safely. The reward for rising earlier to position yourself at your nominated road crossing was to be invited to special outings in Washington DC like the baseball game, and the annual Christmas party thrown by the local police to encourage their young workers.

But in no other way did she stand out. Each year there was a graduation ceremony with a recital in which pupils sang or danced, but Goldie was not asked to perform. A production of *Showboat*, staged by the Parent Teacher Association, felt it could do without her as yet unsung talent.

On the one occasion when she was called upon to shine – the third-grade talent show, when she was eight – disaster struck. The night before she was due to dance solo to a recording of Sleighride, she sat on the record. Though her mother spent the next day searching out another recording, when the time came for her to dance, Goldie refused. 'But why?' asked her mother.

'Because Mrs Toomey said we had to be perfect, and I'm not perfect.'

Goldie's parents continued to push her. At ten, Rut Hawn gave his daughter piano and voice lessons. The visiting Ballet Russe de Monte Carlo found room in its chorus-line to accommodate the young dancer as they performed the Nutcracker to a largely indifferent DC audience; none the less the experience was to spur Goldie's own nascent ambitions. 'Father had the philosophy, but Mother made the demands – you are going to dancing school, you do not have a choice, I make the decisions. She thought I had a talent and she wasn't going to let it go. I had no choice,' she recalled later.

Some of her mother's determination was beginning to rub off. Aged eleven, called upon to perform at a friend's bar mitzvah, she attempted a parasol dance *en pointe*: 'I put the record on and walked out with my parasol and my point shoes, and I had to do pique turns. But they'd waxed the floor and I fell. I got up and started over, but I fell again. Now it was getting ridiculous but I went back and did it again.' Whether or not Laura Hawn was standing in the wings hissing threats at her daughter is not recorded.

She entered Montgomery Blair High School, Silver Spring, with a growing inner resolve. Though still unsure of herself as a person, she had come to rely on dance as a validation and as a consolation; for as her classmates started to blossom into young women Goldie found herself left behind: 'I remember one night in particular – I was at a school dance and I sat with all the other girls who didn't have dates,' she said. 'No one asked me to dance. I hung around in the ladies' room all night. When I came home I fell on my bed and cried. My mother came in and held me like a little baby: "Don't worry, Goldie, it'll be all right – you're just a little late, that's all."'

It did nothing to reassure her. At thirteen she made a doctor's appointment and asked him about her unfeminine form: 'I don't have any fat anywhere,' she complained. The doctor reassured her that all was required at this stage was an adequate covering of skin over bone, that the rest would come in due course, and that she would be grateful for her sylph-like form, but it did little to quell the almost pathological dislike she had by now developed for her body. 'I was never what I considered a very attractive girl,' Goldie says. 'I developed very slowly. I watched the other girls' breasts grow, and mine were just not happening.'

During the critical period when young girls spend hours gazing at their reflection in the mirror, Goldie conceived a self-dislike which would take years to eradicate: 'I wasn't a pretty child. I sort of grew into my features. I had very large eyes and a full mouth – all the things that are nice on me now, but I hated then. I really felt inadequate, you know "My breasts are too small, my ankles are too fat." I'd wear petticoats to make my hips look bigger.' She had become obsessed by the fact that boys ignored her and one day something snapped. The usually demure Goldie arrived in class with a complete makeover. 'I put on falsies and eight slips and a straight skirt so I'd look like I'd got a shape. And frosted pink lipstick and all this black stuff on my eyes, and I mixed with the bad crowd. I was a wallflower, guys didn't like me, I was underdeveloped. I wanted to be recognised for doing something bad, but the teachers knew I wasn't like that and so did I. I knew I was play-acting.' None the less she was sent home by the biology teacher Stuart Marder, who told her her dress was 'not appropriate' for the classroom. A classmate recalls she just blinked her eyelashes and simpered 'Yes, Mr Marder' before disappearing home, to return freshly scrubbed and demurely dressed.

The Silver Spring winter uniform – saddle shoes, nylons with seams, button-down shirts, crew-neck sweaters and straight skirts – did nothing for Goldie. Even in the summer the bobby-sox look – smart coiffed hair and perfectly applied pink lipstick to complement the full cotton skirts, thick cotton sweat socks, ballerina flatties and sleeveless blouses with Peter Pan collars – did little to broaden her appeal.

At twelve she developed a passion for Elvis Presley. In 1957 the King was at the height of his powers. Already a household name after his appearance on the Ed Sullivan Show, and a promising film star with the release of *Jailhouse Rock*, Presley was now touring the country wearing a $10,000 gold-and-rhinestone tuxedo, horrifying parents and sending teenage girls into paroxysms of hysteria: 'He made me feel sexy when I was twelve,' recalled Goldie. 'I remember going fishing with Daddy and he had his classical music on the radio and I said "I'll never like that rock'n'roll – I love classical music," and he said "Good for you, kid." A year later I discovered Elvis – 'Don't Be Cruel', 'Hound Dog' – and, my God, I suddenly felt like a real woman. Something happened to me – I *got* it. Daddy was completely out of his mind – his little girl began doing exactly what she said she'd never do. It was "Take that lipstick off", "That skirt's too tight", "Turn that radio down."'

If this truly was a sexual awakening, then the long years ahead would prove, as in many a teenager's life, to be full of frustration, longing, unfulfilled dreams and disappointment. Goldie's mental processes were way ahead of her physical development. Panic set in.

The desperate search for the adulation so easily achieved by her classmates drove her to become a cheerleader, but even this had little effect on the opposite sex: Goldie would have to wait until she was seventeen for her first kiss. Eventually, though, full adolescence arrived and with it the longed-for figure: 'One day I was lying in bed and I felt these little bumps and I thought I had *tumours* because I was also a hypochondriac. I ran downstairs and said "Mommy, feel these! What is this? I'm scared."' Her mother turned to Rut and smiled, 'Goldie's budding.' None the less, in an age and culture when an abundant bosom equated with sexual allure, Goldie remained modestly proportioned, an accident of nature which would serve her well in later life but in her teens was simply another blow to her esteem.

At school, what helped Goldie through this exhausting period of self-doubt and loathing was the dancing. As she matured she complained less and less about being dragooned into dance class by her mother: 'Ultimately it was the dancing that helped me grow out of the awkwardness – dance made me feel strong, it gave me a sense of perseverance, made me feel straight and pulled-up.' And while other girls made their first dates on a Saturday night, Goldie stayed home in her room, put on the LP record of *West Side Story* and danced and acted out all the parts till late into the night. Her dreams, if they weren't of the boys who had callously rejected her, were of the years ahead when she could be in the chorus of a Broadway musical. She had no wish to be a star; her low self-worth would not allow her to even think such a thing. At that stage she had no role-models and if people asked her what she wanted to be in life, she would merely reply, 'Happy!'

How much this is a reflection on her parents' bumpy relationship is anyone's guess. The couple slept in separate bedrooms and led semi-detached lives: music was all and everything to Rut, while it was the chain-smoking Laura's determination to move on and up through her own efforts. Goldie describes her parents' marriage as a 'fair' one – 'it wasn't blissful by any means' – but the couple were running at different speeds and with different agendas. In adulthood Goldie summed it up thus: 'My father played the saxophone, violin, clarinet. By day he was a watch repairer. He'd close the store, come home at six o'clock, lie down for half an hour, get dressed, and go play a job. Daddy was different from Mommy. She was the business-woman, he was the dreamer, very creative. He liked to be alone, liked to play golf, fish, do singular sports like that. He wasn't competitive.'

Driven by the memory of the parched, polluted steel-town of her youth, Laura Hawn *was* competitive. But if there were deep-seated differences between Mr and Mrs Hawn there was a determination to hide them as much as possible from the children.

Rather than face an empty house after the day's lessons – for if

Laura wasn't working in the gift shop she was running her dance class and Rut would be on his way to a gig – Goldie found a home-from-home with her friend Sylvia Colen. Sylvia lived round the corner on Boston Avenue, having moved from Silver Spring where she had been the next-door neighbour of a teenage Sylvester Stallone. The Colen family readily adopted Goldie and she often spent the night sharing Sylvia's twin-size bed. Goldie developed a special fondness for Richard, one of Sylvia's four brothers, who suffered Downs Syndrome; and to those who observed her it seemed as though the Colens provided a family atmosphere which somehow was lacking in her own home.

At the weekends the Colens would drive out to the sea at Bay Ridge Beach where Goldie's stick-thin body would be all the more apparent: one day while swimming in a bikini the falsies she wore in her bra popped out and floated away. However privately mortifying this moment may have been she responded to the incident with her customary piping laugh. And with Sylvia Colen, there were many laughs. Together with their friend Babs Cospin, they worked out an act in which Goldie and Babs, a bleach-blonde, pretended they were from Sweden. Putting on an exaggerated accent Goldie would pretend to be the smart one while Babs, now a top radiologist, pretended to be the dumb one.

'She would out-eat us all,' recalls Sylvia. 'My mother was a wonderful cook and she would come over every Friday night and have dinner with us. She was this skinny little thing and she would eat more than all of us; we would say "Why aren't you gaining any weight?" But she burned it off because she was so active.'

Goldie and Sylvia would go to Friday-night dances organised by the local church and, in the absence of any invitations from the boys, would dance together, Sylvia taking the lead. Later Goldie found a male dance-partner in Joey Renaudo and their jitterbugging would cause the other couples to stop and admire. 'She was always laughing and smiling when she was dancing, you could tell she was enjoying herself,' recalled Sylvia.

The Colens' hospitality was repaid one Christmas when Sylvia went over to the Hawns' house on Cleveland Avenue, picking up a cut-price Christmas tree on the way, and sledding down the back slopes in the woods behind.

The usual sibling rivalry existed between Goldie and Patti. 'She would play with my make-up, my shoes, my jewellery, my diary,' recalled Patti. 'My dates usually began awkwardly, mostly because of Goldie. She's a born mimic. I could always count on her to ruin my entrances, especially when I first started wearing high heels. My date would be waiting at the bottom of the stairs. Down I'd come, trying to keep my balance, and my cool. Goldie would follow, imitating my wobble. My date would double up with laughter, but, at that age, her humour escaped me completely.

'There was the Greek statue book. As an adolescent I was embarrassed by the figleaf photographs. Knowing this, Goldie would wait for the opportunity to spring the book on one of my dates and eventually I had to hide it. But in spite of the little-sister pranks she pulled on me when we were growing up I could never stay too angry at her. And no matter what went on between us during the day she would always break me up at the dinner table with her imitations of friends, relatives – almost anyone. Nobody made me laugh like my sister.'

If Goldie nurtured any ambitions to become an actress as well as a dancer, they were thwarted by the regime at Montgomery Blair High School. Taking part in the school's dramatic productions was seen as a privilege which had to be earned by an acceptable academic performance. Goldie was denied several leading roles she might otherwise have captured with minimum effort, had it not been for the fact she was scoring C grades or worse in her major subjects. She had to be content with minor roles in *Bye Bye Birdie, Carousel* and *L'il Abner* before – as a result of extra summer classes – bringing up her biology grade sufficiently she was allowed the starring role of Blanche Dubois in Tennessee Williams's *A Streetcar Named Desire*.

This inability, or unwillingness, to rise to the academic threshold which would allow her starring roles frustrated her drama teacher Richard Pioli. Though he was able to discern an acting talent, Goldie was unavailable to him – not merely through the school system which disbarred her, but because dance classes still took up so much of her spare time. In addition to classical ballet she had started jazz and modern dance, and now helped out as a part-time teacher in her mother's dance class. Mr Pioli told the school's newspaper *The Silver Chip* he didn't think Goldie would ever act professionally. 'She didn't take full advantage of her talent,' he recalled. 'She didn't pursue it as she could have – she couldn't try out for leads because she had so many dance extra-curricular activities.'

But with *Streetcar* Goldie finally emerged as an accomplished performer, at ease with herself and, at seventeen, at last beginning to feel a confidence which had eluded her all her teenage years. Mr Pioli observed, 'Most other girls were frightened, self-conscious and looked awkward, but she was in character from top to toe. She projected, looked like she knew what she was doing, and was enjoying herself.'

In the February before graduation Goldie got her first car, a cream Pontiac convertible, bought on George Washington's Birthday, a public holiday when the custom is for used car-dealers to sell off one car for a dollar. Goldie was not the lucky winner that day and had to pay full price, but it gave her a freedom which added to her burgeoning self-confidence. The only thing she lacked was a steady boyfriend: she cast her eyes in the direction of handsome Bobby Gray, a classmate, but his affections lay elsewhere.

Goldie had now tasted success onstage, but academic attainment remained beyond her. With the approach of her graduation from high school the question of what she was to do next became a pressing issue. 'I remember having long talks with my parents about Goldie's occupational prospects,' said Patti. 'She couldn't type. She was far more interested in being a cheerleader, dancing class, school plays and her bubble hairdo. Marketable office skills just weren't on her agenda.'

The summer of '63, and graduation approached at an alarming pace. Goldie, with no clear plan as to what to do, turned to Richard Pioli and asked about the possibility of a career on the stage. 'I didn't think she would make it because she hadn't been serious about her acting,' he said. 'We all knew she had the talent but we didn't think she'd go through with it.'

Goldie left Montgomery Blair four months short of her eighteenth birthday, her graduation year book entry adorned with a photograph of her wearing the customary black crew-neck sweater and single string of pearls, but the accompanying text demonstrating how little she had participated in the life of the school. While other girls listed their careers as pom-pom girls and majorettes, or noted their involvement in the myriad activities Montgomery High offered, from philosophy to butterfly-collecting, from the Civil War to astronomy, Goldie was notable by her absence from all these activities. She was, however, a member of the Powder Puff Club, a small and inward-looking organisation run by Richard Pioli and devoted to uncovering the secrets of stage makeup. But though in the year she graduated, nineteen pupils were awarded the Thespians Honour for 'devotion to the advancement of the dramatic arts ... Thespian points awarded for work on school productions ... honouring outstanding contributions to Blair's theatrical productions', Goldie's name was conspicuously absent from the list.

Goldie said goodbye to Montgomery Blair without a backward glance and clearly with little regret. Though she had finally found a role and identity late in her school career, there had been too many snubs, too many disappointments, too many embarrassments, for her ever to feel warmly about the place. Her ambition to star in the school plays had been thwarted, as she saw it, by the intransigence of the school authorities. They had held back her natural development, at the same time reminding her painfully of her academic short-comings. And, years later, despite repeated entreaties for her to come and deliver the school's yearly Commencement Speech she never responded. 'We don't hold her in very high esteem. We don't even get the courtesy of a reply,' remarked the current principal's secretary, Christine Grasso. 'It appears she is too good for us. She needs to put something back into the school and the community she comes from.'

An understandable position for a school which feels snubbed by its most famous alumnus, but one which ignores the fact that the desire to get away is often part of the impetus which makes life's achievers achieve.

None the less Montgomery Blair continued to remind their former pupil of her obligations and in 1989, during the preparation of an article for the school journal on Blair's Rich and Famous Alumni – they include Carl Bernstein of Watergate fame and leading US TV personality Connie Chung – they sent a young reporter, Shira Robinson, to track down Goldie. Ms Robinson never achieved her goal, but instead wrote about her frustrated pursuit of the actress, highlighting the obnoxious behaviour of the Creative Artists Agency who handled Goldie's affairs. This had the required effect, stinging Goldie into agreeing to a written question-and-answer 'interview' for the school magazine. Though much of the content is predictable enough, there are occasional flashes of insight into the tortured life she led as a schoolgirl: how she hated going to the dance classes which, in the end, separated her from her peers, but that her mother gave her no choice; how she did not like school; and how boys of her own age found her unattractive but older boys liked her, which created problems.

She also spoke at some length about why she had snubbed her class's twenty-fifth anniversary reunion: 'A twenty-fifth reunion would not be easy for me. It has nothing to do with my not wanting to reunite with people I once knew. It has to do with my philosophy, and that is for twenty-five years I have not seen, spoken to, or invested in any of these people.'

She went on, 'My life has taken a very different turn. I cherish my schooldays for what they were. I cherished their friendship at the time but living so far away and having so little time .. even for my very close loved ones ... I find that my priorities do not permit me to enjoy these get-togethers. I'm not a great person for looking back.'

Taken all in all, this was a gesture calculated to silence once and for all those who had implored her return to Montgomery Blair. Blunt to the point of rudeness, it demonstrated how painful her schoolgirl memories remained a quarter of a century later.

While her classmates went on to university and higher education, Goldie was left with no clear plan as to what to do with her life. There was a moment of reflection over her almost complete academic failure – 'I wasn't a great student, I was forgetful, flighty, sort of light on my feet' – but then came the realisation that with no mundane qualifications to bind her to a second-rate office-based career, her childhood dreams could become reality. After two weeks of agonising she called her old drama teacher. 'She said "I've decided I'm really interested in theatre and I'm going to make it my career",' he said. 'I told her I was thrilled but that I wished she had said so before because she had a lot of work ahead of her. She asked me where to start and I told her to take some acting classes at the American University.'

But before that Goldie was to experience for the first time the thrill of appearing before an audience – not of tens or hundreds, but of thousands. One performance as Juliet would, quite completely, change her life.

# CHAPTER TWO

## *Out of This Furnace*

*'At my poor house look to behold this night*
*Earth-treading stars that make dark heaven light'*
*– ibid.*

Oscar-winning film star, producer, director, deal-broker, business-woman, mother and lover, Goldie Hawn is today, despite the ever-present giggle, a driven woman. Kurt Russell, her partner of seventeen years is continually amazed at the work-hard ethic which drives her ever onward, even at the age of fifty-four. Her career has spanned more than three decades, during which time most of her contemporaries have left the stage, she sits atop a $100 million fortune, yet gets restless if there is no new project on her desk to trouble-shoot. So what is it that makes Goldie run?

To understand the deep and abiding thirst she has to accomplish new goals it is necessary to look back at her family's 300–year history. From the tales of her ancestors she derives strength, yet the dark shadows of the past keep her precariously *en garde* for the future.

Goldie's ancestry is in essence the story of America, of immigrants who came to a new land to make good. The popular myth is that Goldie's father, Edward Rutledge Hawn, was a direct descendant of Edward Rutledge, the youngest co-signatory of the 1776 Declaration of Independence. In the mid–eighteenth century many Rutledges – recent immigrants from Ireland where they had settled after Cromwell's conquest in the 1650s – made their home in the Carolinas and Virginia. Goldie's earliest recorded Rutledge ancestor, however, was a mere contemporary of Edward and his more famous brother John* not even a close relation.

* The statesman, Chief US Justice and co-signatory of the 1787 Constitution.

At the time that the future statesman Edward Rutledge was growing up in the Georgian splendour of Charleston, Joseph Rutledge, Goldie's true ancestor, was being raised further north in Amelia County, Virginia, on a 150-acre ranch in the fork of the Bush and Sandy Rivers where his parents had lived since 1743.

Life here was altogether rougher, with all the dangers that frontiersmen had to face in a country still suffering raids at the hands of the native American Indians. In early adulthood Joseph moved to the more tranquil climes of South Carolina, where he met and married Mary Paschal, raising eleven children, of whom the seventh was christened with his wife's maiden name. The young Paschal Rutledge followed the family's fertile tradition, producing nine children; the eighth of which was a daughter, Mary, born in Greenville, South Carolina in 1827.

This is where the famous Rutledge name leaves Goldie's family tree for the best part of a century, for Mary Rutledge married Henry Johnson; their son, also Henry, fathered a daughter, Claire, whose son Edward – Goldie's father – was given Rutledge as his second name, by now the belief being that the family, all those years ago, had connections with the famous law-maker.

Goldie's grandmother Claire Johnson was born in 1881 in Newport, Arkansas. At the comparatively late age of twenty-three she married Otto Hawn in a ceremony at the Presbyterian Church in Newport on a sunny midsummer day in 1904. Otto had arrived in town on the Iron Mountain Railroad from Bollinger County, Missouri, where his family, immigrants from Germany, had lived for three generations as farmers.

The Hawns had changed their name from Hahn some time in the early years of the nineteenth century, having emigrated from Bavaria in southern Germany a century before. Goldie's earliest traceable ancestor on this side is Jacob Hahn, born about 1682 in the town of Freckenfeld, in wine-growing Pfalz country. Jacob's son Johannes, born when Jacob was thirty, was a prudent man, not marrying until he was forty-five and then only when he had successfully made the trip to America.

The Hahns quit Germany of necessity. In 1689 the countryside around was overrun by the marauding armies of Louis XIV, who then built Europe's strongest fortress at Landau only to have it continually assailed by Habsburg armies. Finally Freckenfeld became part of Louis XIV's empire, and advertising campaigns invited the war-weary natives to get out and start again in *die neue Welt*. Starving and homeless, they left in their hundreds for a country of which they knew precisely nothing.

Johannes, a bricklayer and still unmarried in his forties, left with his brother Conrad and a Freckenfeld couple called Dierwachte. In the company of the five Dierwachte children they started their lengthy journey by foot and horse across Holland to Rotterdam. The Dierwachtes never made it, but Johannes and Conrad did: arriving at Rotterdam in the late summer of 1751 they boarded the ship *Janet* together with 218 other bewildered and lost souls, exiled from their native country by the marauding French. For four weeks they endured the perils of the Atlantic, their crossing broken only briefly by a landfall at Cowes, Isle of Wight. They arrived in the New World on 7 October 1751, to be greeted on the steps of the Court House in Philadelphia by one Joshua Maddox, where they declared an oath of allegiance to their new motherland in a tongue none of them could master.

Johannes Hahn was fifty-three, and finally settled at Clarks Creek, Tryon County, North Carolina, before his wife gave birth on 27 October 1765 to their son, Christian. The family stayed in North Carolina, moving to Lincoln County, and by 1800 Christian was married and father of a newly-born son, Sampson. Twenty-four years later, Sampson was married and fathered a son, Alfred, who took the decision to change his name to Hawn. This was less a conscious attempt at Americanisation than a rationalisation of the way the name was now pronounced. Alfred moved on to farm in Bollinger County, Missouri, where his son Aaron and grandson Otto were born.

Otto Hawn, Goldie's grandfather, had possibly the least pioneering spirit of any of his line. Having made the momentous step of moving from Missouri to Arkansas, he then settled for a less exacting life. At nineteen, he established himself in a railroad workers' boarding house in Union township, Jackson County, rising early to labour first on the Iron Mountain Railroad which had carried him south then on its successor on the Rock Island railroad. A decade later he was married to his wife Claire, whom he called Clara, and eased his way into the less energetic career that would see him out – as telegraph operator on the railways. By now the family had moved to Little Rock, into a household which included his mother-in-law Mary Johnson, and the couple's first two children, Otto Jr and Edward Rutledge – Goldie's father – were born. Later they moved on to El Dorado, a small oil town fifteen miles away.

'It was true frontier, the real American West, where cowboys would walk down Main Street with pistols on their hips,' recalls a member of the family. 'There were oil claims and land fights, but the Hawns never owned any land.'

Two more boys were born to the Hawns – Herbert, known as Deg, and Roland known as Dooley – who with Otto Jr, known as O.D., and Rutledge, arrived at roughly two-year intervals. (Later Rut, already keen on his apparent lineage back to Edward Rutledge, was to adopt another piece of *faux* ancestry by claiming that he descended from Abraham Lincoln's first and only true love Ann Rutledge, an innkeeper's daughter from New Salem, Illinois – but in all likelihood he was ignorant of the family history beyond his grandfather's generation.)

The Hawn brothers were all musical, and after quitting school Rut, following in O.D.'s footsteps, decided to make a living as a dance-band musician. Arkansas was suffering the Depression as much as anywhere and the only place where a guaranteed living could be had was New York, and there Rut headed, only to be steered south to the calmer waters of Washington DC in due course. Nearing his twenty-third birthday, he heard of his father's death at the age of fifty-one; he had been killed in a railroad accident. But, by now working hard as a musician, he did not attend the funeral.

While the rest of America shivered in the Depression, Washington

DC was ablaze with light and awash with parties. Rut worked non-stop and was barely out of his tuxedo. Rooming in a boarding house in nearby Silver Spring, he soon caught the eye of a fellow-inmate, a lively Jewish girl with a melodious voice and a loud laugh.

The girl thought Rut was a butler or waiter. Finally a conversation sprang up and she learned his story. In turn she told him hers and very soon it became clear to Rut that where this girl, Laura Steinhoff, came from was a harder place than any he had experienced in his travels from Arkansas to New York. She told him about a novel by Thomas Bell called *Out of This Furnace*. For all its apparent fiction-alisation, it was in effect a brutal snapshot of life in Braddock, Pennsylvania, a steel town on the edge of Pittsburgh.

Set in a bend of the Monongahela River, Braddock had been Indian country: they surrounded and annihilated General Edward Braddock, British general and commander-in-chief, in 1775 while commanding an expedition against the French-held Fort Duquesne. His lasting memorial is the famous last words uttered as he took his fatal bullet, 'Who'd have thought it?' The same might be said of an elegant, glorious Grenadier whose name would be forever attached to one of the ugliest habitations that industrial man ever saw fit to create.

In *Out of This Furnace*, Bell wrote, 'After the soldiers came the settlers – more and more of them all the time. They cut down the trees and built houses and laid out their dreary, unimaginative pattern of streets and alleys, beginning at the river's edge and working back toward the hills: River Street, Willow Way, Washington Street, Cherry Alley.'

This was the preparation for a new world, dominated by the vast steel mills built by the Scots-born industrialist Andrew Carnegie. Thomas Bell described with anger and passion the arrival of the mills in Braddock, stripping the hills bare of vegetation, blackening the sky, the earth, and the lungs of the workers.

Immigrants continued to pour into the valley and, to house them, real estate speculators threw up houses which became a charac-teristic of the towns around Pittsburgh, with long ugly cell block-like terraces. They were filled as soon as they were finished, and made no apparent impression on the housing shortage or the rent level. In the old country the Slovaks had been an oppressed minority, a peace-loving ethnic group of peasants and shepherds whom the centuries had taught patience and humility; the very sort of uncomplaining workers who would step forward into the blast furnaces and rolling mills, often to their deaths, as they now did. What ever hell Braddock offered, this was a better life than they had known.

Though the town had made strides to civilise itself from the early days described by Bell, those who had any vision of the future got out.

Laura's family, the Steinhofs, were Slovakian Jews from Hungary who joined the exodus of that poverty-stricken and war-torn region in the days prior to the establishment of the Austro-Hungarian state in the mid–nineteenth century. Their escape was to walk hundreds of miles though Austria, Czechoslovakia and Germany to the docks at Bremen to find a ship which would allow them to flee to a new life half a world away. That they should have to walk from New York, where their ship docked, to Pittsburgh, came as no extra hardship. Those who survived were toughened for the generations ahead, generations who came bitterly to accept the casual waste of human life in the steel towns.

Laura Steinhof, born in the coal city of Uniontown on 27 November 1913, came to Braddock from nearby Connellsville, another steel town much in the mould of Braddock. Her mother, born Fanny Weiss, died when she was small and her father, Max, a jeweller, felt unequal to the task of bringing up a small girl alone in the Depression. So the child was put on a bus and sent the few miles to stay with her mother's sister, Goldie Hochhauser.

Though Thomas Bell was describing the late–nineteenth century Braddock, little had changed by the time Laura's maternal grand-parents Jacob and Esther Weiss established their pharmacy on the corner of Talbot Avenue and Eighth Street soon after the turn of the century. The whole town was dominated by the looming presence of the Edgar Thompson Works, one of the largest steel rolling mills in the world. Not only did it command the skyline but its stench filled the air, adding to the coal dust from the fires burning in every one of the cramped one-up-one-down terraced houses which people called home. At the Edgar Thompson, men worked seven days a week, twelve hours a day; but poverty still ruled the streets.

By the time Laura was sixteen, Braddock was at the peak of its pitiful population of 25,000, yet it was more densely populated than New York City. Squalid and cramped, the houses around Talbot Avenue and Eighth Street had outside toilets set around a court; water came from a well or street-pump. It was common to see children walking shoeless even in winter and suffering the effects of malnutrition.

Jacob and Esther Weiss's daughter Goldie married a huckster – or street trader – Joe Hochhauser, and was forced to make a home in the cramped store-rooms over her parents' shop. With four boys of her own (though one died in infancy) Goldie still readily welcomed her niece Laura, and though the family, as well as the whole town, endured years of grinding poverty, their home life in the store-rooms was happy enough. Laura would run up and downstairs and play hopscotch in the street called Cherry Alley which ran behind the building.

Joe, like others who could not afford shop premises but who followed the entrepreneurial ambitions of their forefathers, would take a whole day to travel to downtown Pittsburgh to get fruit and vegetables at the produce yards. Then he would sell them the next day from his horse and wagon, running the wheels of the wagon on the streetcar rails because it was easier for the horse to pull. Goldie's mother Esther used to help and sometimes Laura was allowed to come too.

During Prohibition in the 1920s, recalls a resident, Joe Hochhauser and his father-in-law used to make moonshine *slivovic* to keep the Braddock blues at bay: it was impossible to keep the steel-workers' morale up without the occasional help of raw alcohol. Later Joe worked in Blumenfeld's Grocery Store and later still he became a butcher: each new job was an infinitesimal step forward in the family's prosperity. But prosperity was a relative word in Braddock.

The Jewish presence in town was a significant one, with families from Hungary, Austria, Poland and Lithuania making perhaps a tenth of the populace; with two synagogues, a community centre and a common voice which articulated against the appalling conditions, they were a force to be reckoned with. The Jews established many of the shops around Braddock Avenue during Laura Hawn's childhood, though the town, dirt poor as it was, felt the chill of the Great Depression almost as badly as anywhere in the United States. In the post-First World War years it had more than its fair share of breadlines of unemployed, mounting mortgage foreclosures, and closed banks. Here, as much as anywhere, there prevailed that grey despair that the country's complex paralysing economic forces could never be fathomed or overcome. It was a bewildering time for a young child to grow up in.

The weak and ineffectual in Braddock succumbed to these economic forces, but the Jewish community, so recently forced from their own countries by similar recession, bravely rode out the storm and, as the *Living East* section of the *Pittsburgh Post-Gazette* pointed out in 1984, many of these people were to become living examples of the 'success of the American dream – these hardworking, Yiddish-speaking shopkeepers and others [who] did well enough to move away'. No one stayed in Braddock if they could get out, particularly after the mill shut down and the main street was shuttered up.

Jacob and Esther's other daughter Sarah was one of these, marrying up and moving away to the leafier climes of Laurel, Maryland. Goldie and Joe with their sons and adopted daughter went to live at 3 Mills Avenue in Braddock. Later, during Laura's early teens, they moved again to more spacious premises at 317 Holland Avenue.

Laura had dark hair and big, dark eyes, and those who remain in Braddock remember her in childhood for the way she continually laughed: 'a very popular and pretty girl with a lot of friends,' recalls her contemporary Eugene Litman. A lively figure first at Hayter then at Braddock High School, she was clearly destined for a brighter future than the steel town could provide. As soon as she graduated,

Laura said goodbye to her best friend Phyllis Blumenfeld and was sent to stay in Laurel, Maryland with Goldie's son Alan and his wife.

Laura Steinhof met, and married, Rut Hawn very quickly. At first glance they were not an obvious match, with Rut's laid-back Arkansas charm and Laura's fiery intensity. But long engagements were not a feature of those post-Depression days and the ceremony was set to take place at Rockville, Maryland, on 30 April 1936. Laura was twenty, Rut twenty-seven. Almost immediately Laura became pregnant.

Luxuriating in the dappled shadows of Maryland, she learned one day with horror that back in Braddock, the Monongahela river had burst its banks. Street upon street back from the river were flooded and residents were forced to abandon the ground floors of their homes, taking refuge in the already cramped bedrooms until the water subsided. The sanitation, already stretched to breaking point, now failed and the disease which followed swiftly in its wake claimed many lives. Others, particularly the old, died from starvation because no-one could reach them.

If there was a Hell on earth, thought Laura Hawn, it must surely be Braddock. As she awaited her confinement she resolved there and then to do everything in her power to put as much distance between her past life and her future.

Edward Rutledge Hawn Jr was born on 10 February 1937, almost exactly nine months after the wedding. Within a month he was dead. The cause was Sudden Infant Death syndrome, or, in common parlance, cot-death; one of the most shocking ways for a baby to die because a parent can never quite believe that an apparently completely healthy child can cease to live without the appearance of the slightest struggle. A family member recalls, 'Laura went away after that. When she came back nobody ever mentioned it again. Since they didn't know anything about SID back then, I assume there was guilt and stuff, but I never heard Laura dwell on it.'

Soon after, she conceived and gave birth to a daughter, Patti, a consolation for the loss of little Edward. But it was nearly eight years before, at thirty-one, she conceived a third time and on 21 November

1945 Goldie Jeanne Hawn was brought into the world.

Goldie was a Thanksgiving baby, and named for the woman who had taken Laura in to her own family and loved as if she were her own. As she cuddled the little blonde bundle to her, Laura whispered to her baby, 'I want you to put Aunt Goldie's name up in lights.'

# CHAPTER THREE

# *Biting the Apple*

*'Night's candles are burnt out'*
*– ibid.*

After a fruitless year spent since graduating from High School, Goldie was encouraged by her drama teacher Richard Pioli to apply for a place on the drama course at the American University in Washington DC. On the back of her recent triumph as Juliet, she was cast for a part in the University Players's production of André Gide and Jean-Louis Barrault's adaptation of *The Trial*, by Franz Kafka.

The local newspaper, *The Eagle*, in a preview piece hinted that working under the director, Professor F. Cowles Strickland, was no picnic. Certainly the atmosphere in the darkening days of late autumn lacked the heady, carefree ways of Williamsburg. But after six weeks' rehearsal, on Thursday 29 October 1964, *The Trial* opened at the American University Theatre. It ran for two weeks and the playbill announced that Miss Goldie Hawne [sic] would be playing Miss Burstner. Though once again the Hawn family turned out to see their fledgling star, on this occasion she failed to catch the attention of the critics.

Soon after, Goldie quit her studies. 'I never intended to finish college,' she said, not entirely convincingly, some time later. 'I just wanted to get a little background before turning professional.' What is more likely, however, is that the learning difficulties she had suffered at school, and the continued regimentation of formal education combined to convince her there was no point in staying somewhere where she would not shine.

There was nothing left for Goldie in Takoma Park, or in Washington DC. The alternatives hardly bore contemplating: a drab career as a child's dance teacher or, if that failed, unskilled labour in an office or bar. That glorious moment in the rain at Williamsburg which rarely left her waking thoughts had permanently set her aside from her contemporaries. But with no special skills outside dance and her still-limited experience as an actress, she was virtually unemployable. Even the lowest achievers at Montgomery Blair had managed better than she.

By now Laura Hawn's deep-seated ambition had taken hold in her daughter. Goldie started travelling to New York each weekend to take dance classes at a studio on East 50th St, the pre-pubescent dream of becoming a chorus girl in a Broadway show now taking flesh.

New York in the mid-sixties was a city struggling to achieve world acceptance, though 'Peace Through Understanding', the theme of the 1964/5 World's Fair, had a hollow ring when contrasted with the political undercurrents of the time. Despite Governor Nelson Rockfeller's efforts to prove that New York was a city of its time, the metropolis could be more accurately summed up as a decaying collection of racial ghettos plagued by slums, crime, drugs, welfare corruption and heavy-handed landlords.

But the lure of the city proved too great and Goldie took the plunge to move there. Collecting together what little money she'd saved from her local government job she hitched a ride into Manhattan: 'I had a little money saved and I put it towards trying to break into showbusiness. After all, I'd been training all those years and I wanted to make something of my dancing skills.'

She gave herself a deadline of two years to become self-supporting. 'Either I was going to make it or I'd find something else to do with my life – I wasn't going to waste myself on a dream,' she later remembered, though in truth the range of options open to her was narrow. The prospect of an untravelled, inexperienced, gamine, ingénue arriving in one of the most sophisticated, dirty, frightening, yet exhilarating cities in the world is a daunting one, yet Goldie committed without a second thought. 'It wasn't at all terrifying. I just went into that town *head first*: I hitched a ride from Washington. I didn't even have a place to stay.'

After a week she found an apartment on West 70th Street between West End and Columbus, not the most fashionable part of town but somewhere where a few dollars was able to buy a space in an apartment already occupied by three other girl dancers: 'I just loved that city – I was eighteen and anything was good. It was wonderful to be in New York, auditioning for parts, talking to people, riding taxis.'

Soon she was to discover the bleak reality of auditions: there were many dancers and few parts. She tried for Broadway shows, then for off-Broadway shows. At the famous Copacabana Club she was told she wasn't sexy enough, and quite soon the gloss was beginning to wear thin: 'Those dance auditions were awful. You'd find these guys hanging round trying to pick up women for other things.'

If this sounds disingenuous it has to be remembered that Goldie was still inexperienced with the opposite sex, unsure, and *en garde* in a city which seemed to be peopled with men wanting just one thing. 'I'm a dancer, a legitimate dancer!' she protested, but the men seemed not to listen.

One who looked more kindly on her was the choreographer Phil Black, whose famous studio she would walk to, down Broadway to 50th Street, each morning. Black had a reputation for being a perfectionist and hard taskmaster, pushing his dancers for hours, demanding that they put their lives in his hands, turning a commercial enterprise into a family. Sizing up what he saw before him, Black came to an unusual conclusion: 'She was different from the average girl, she didn't have the looks, she didn't have the figure, but she did have all the drive and attitude she wanted to go places. Wally, a dance teacher in Baltimore, used to send his students to me and she came up with eight or ten others. She had energy and personality. She was a sweetheart. She'd do anything and never complain.' He offered her a place in the troupe which would dance in his show at the World's Fair, the forthcoming three-month jamboree in the Queens district designed to boost the dingy city's worldwide importance. The Fair, sited on newly-reclaimed swamp and wasteland, boasted something for everyone, from the very first computers to video-phones, from entertainment to architecture; a prototype Disneyworld.

Today Phil Black recalls the New York stage début of the gamine from Maryland: 'She wasn't very pretty, she's prettier now than she was then. One thing she doesn't know is that when I bought her up for the job, I thought I had control but the producers said, "She's too skinny." I told them to forget it, I'd already given her the job. But I had to fight to keep her because she really was skinny and some of the girls were very buxom. I forced the issue and she stayed. I was right – she had such energy. There were five shows during the day, five at night, and she was doing them all.'

Goldie Hawn's first professional job, then, was in a tent called The Old Texas Pavilion, little more than a vast western-style bar on the sprawling World's Fair campus. She and three other girls danced a routine called the CanCan-A-GoGo to the general indifference of tired and thirsty customers who were more concerned with the activities of the barmen than the dancers onstage: 'It was the hardest work I've ever done. We were the whole show, we had to do cartwheels, we had to do kicks, we didn't know where the hell we were going. I thought I was going to fall into the bar what with the CanCan, the kicking, the riding-down, the coming up, the jumping, the screaming – then running off, twenty seconds to change our clothes while the band vamped; now we're on as go-go girls, it was ridiculous!'

The show started with a fifteen-minute Can-Can number, followed by a medley of dances of the moment – things that were being danced in the fashionable Peppermint Lounge – like the Twist, the Monkey and the Jerk. Phil Black recalls, 'There were twelve dancers altogether, dancing in groups, very choreographed. There were two stages and the show had to come down from the top stage to the bottom stage and keep dancing, it was pure dancing all the time.'

One of the barmen, a twenty-one-year old Greek American called Spiro Venduras – a would-be singer with his own trio – paid rather more attention to Goldie than the thirsty audience, and eventually his interest bore fruit. He took her on a date, and they fell in love. He became Goldie Hawn's first real boyfriend, the affair lasting a year.

Spiro lived round the corner from Goldie with his mother and grandmother, but during the course of the affair, Goldie moved to another apartment at 888 Eighth Avenue. This was a favourite haunt of young dancers with some of the apartments in the high-rise block featuring a bath in the kitchen and a toilet in the yard. Not all the girls were destined for the same starry future and one inmate of 888, a talented dancer, developed diabetes and went blind.

The World's Fair job lasted three months, and at the end Goldie found herself as unemployed as before. During the time she had been dating Spiro, the couple had taken to going to a bar around the corner from her apartment called Jilly's where Spiro's friend Sal Conti was a barman. With money running out, Goldie abandoned her pride and the sure knowledge that, if she was not to be a classical dancer, then she would be a jazz dancer of repute. In the meantime, she signed on with a go-go agent called Ron.

The mid-sixties was the period when 'dolly birds' ruled – or, more correctly, were ruled. It was the age of the Playboy Club, and with the coming of sexual liberation, it was deemed acceptable for men's magazines to have nude centrefolds (though not *vice versa*) and for there to be jokes about nipple-counts. Skirts grew shorter, men grew more patronising; and into this arena stepped a new phenomenon, the go-go dancer. Little was required from these women except to wear a lot of makeup but few clothes, and be prepared to stand on table-tops and shake and shudder to the latest pop music hits.

Certainly, this was not dancing as Goldie understood it, but she described herself as a dancer to Ron, which meant only one thing: dollars. 'I'd go down to his office on Sixth Avenue and say "Do you have anything for me today, Ron?" and he'd send me to these really bad places. Sometimes I wouldn't even get paid. During that period was when I auditioned for the Copacabana and I didn't make it. But I left the audition saying, "What the hell, I'll go out on weekend and do my gigs."'

She danced on pedestals and in cages, and on tables that wobbled in seedy low dives. Mostly she wore tiny mini-skirts and sequin pasties on her breasts – innate modesty, an anger at what she was doing, and the ever-present feeling that her breasts were too small combined to stop her from dancing topless, always a lucrative option for other girls to increase the standard $20 fee. She had no idea that across town, a rather better-endowed girl of a similar age named Bette Midler was making her début in showbiz in very much the same demeaning way.

One night Ron, always keen to make his $5 fee, sent Goldie to a club in New Jersey called the Peppermint Box: 'I went in and met the boss, who was drunk, and he told me where to dance. I got up on to this table that had three legs – a man was sitting at the bar looking at me and I thought he was sympathising with me. I turned around and he had pulled out his cock. He was jerking off. Well, my knees buckled and I thought I was going to faint, but I climbed off the table and went to find the boss, but the boss had passed out. So I couldn't get my money and I had no ride home. I said, "I just gotta get outta here!"

'I'd been dancing to Dean Martin's 'Everybody Loves Somebody Sometime' – can you imagine! And this guy kept on looking at me and saying "Put the record on again and make 'er dance, make 'er dance."'

With no money in her purse, she asked some friendly truckers to drive her home and arrived back on Eighth Avenue in a huge Mack truck.

Soon after she was dancing in a cage at a club called Entre Nous run by 'deze-and doze' kind of guys when one of the managers came over and shouted, 'Hey, Goldie, there's a guy at the bar who wants to meet you'. She recalls, 'I said, "Hey, I'm not here for that! I just want to dance." He said, "You're fired" – just like that. And I'd been so happy making $97.50 a week.'

The culture which went with go-go dancing was never likely to offer more comfortable experiences, no matter where she went, but Phil Black sees this dogged progress as evidence of her commitment as a dancer: 'She was ambitious and she knew she had to put herself out on the line. She knew you didn't wait for people to come to you. You've got to expose yourself out there and be seen, which is why she wasn't afraid to do go-go dancing. A lot of dancers wouldn't have done that.

'You had to be a smart cookie, though. The element that owned those clubs were always hitting on the girls, they were easy targets. The girls were struggling, and a lot take the offer and they get in trouble too, but Goldie wasn't like that. She was her own person, you could see how smart she was.

'She liked her men. She used to like to go out all the time, she wanted to keep going, even I couldn't keep up with her. But she was enjoying New York, she just loved the city and what it stood for and the sleazy joints didn't get her down.' When work failed to materialise Phil Black would take pity on her and take Goldie out to dinner, only to discover her handbag full of carrots and celery. 'She was a health addict, though she looks healthier now than when I knew her – she was skinny with hardly any breasts and though she had the talent, she didn't have the looks. The Latin Quarter used big busty girls for dancers, and the Copacabana used beautiful girls, they were all like models – but she just didn't have the looks.'

For a while Goldie found some relief and quasi-respectability in working a Connecticut supper club where the bow-tied patrons would watch her dance then try to emulate her gyrations themselves. That way she would earn $75 in a weekend, enough to pay her rent and to spend the rest of the week going to Broadway shows, attending auditions, reading the trade papers and hanging out with Spiro.

Goldie and Spiro's grandmother Mrs Venduras developed an affection for each other. Separated from her own folks she became part of the Greek extended family which lived on 70th and Columbus. Mrs Venduras would go to church and light candles for her grandson's girlfriend, and such was the gratitude Goldie felt for those who provided this home-from-home, she made a special journey back down memory lane when she won her Oscar so that the old lady could see and touch it for herself.

'She was my first love, it was an affair,' says Spiro now. 'She was very naïve – we're talking a sweet girl from Takoma Park, Maryland, moving to New York. You're in a position where you're trying to get ahead in a craft which you really don't know yet but you're anxious to see what you can do. You get put in situations, because everyone's a trickster more or less, getting you to do things you don't want to do just to get on in the world.'

Manhattan in the mid-sixties had a chic which was only matched by Paris and Rome: swinging London had yet to find its identity. In Manhattan, unlike later in London, everyone tried very hard to be grown-up: for women the look was Jackie Kennedy; for men it had to be very sharp, very Brooks Brothers. Soon Goldie found herself knocking on the door of a discotheque in Manhattan called Dudes'n'Dolls, on Fiftieth Street and Third Avenue, and for the first time she discovered an inside-track venue where the stars hung out. By midnight at Dudes'n'Dolls the crowd might include Frank Sinatra, then courting Mia Farrow, the TV show host Johnny Carson, athlete Joe Namath and ball players from both the Giants and the Jets. Sammy Davis's mother was the hat-check girl. Comfortingly nearby for the peripatetic night-owls were the Stork Club, Nanny Wolfe's, PJ Clark's and a stand-up comedy bar called the Ratfink Room. But along with Danny's Hide-a-Way, Jilly's and the Copacabana, Dudes'n'Dolls was 'happening', the place to be.

The proprietor, Bobby Van, opened the club in November 1965, modelling it along the lines of the very first discotheque, the Crazy Horse in Paris. Here as at the Crazy Horse the theme (if theme it be) was the Wild West, with teepees, war-drums, dancers in head-dresses. By contrast the décor was op-art black-and-white. Four dancers would perform at night, two at the cocktail hour, and a couple at lunchtime; some achieving more fame or notoriety than others. The Copa's lead dancer Darryl Shayne came on to do the nightly top-spot, while Goldie was relegated to days with occasional night relief work. Another exotic creature who turned patron's heads was a girl called Lisa Hepler, who drew nationwide headlines when she was hauled offstage in mid-act by FBI agents investigating the theft of a mink coat in California. When taken down to the precinct it emerged that Lisa was, in fact, a man.

Goldie performed her act – in Indian headdress, leather mini-skirt, halter top – to a mixture of latest hits by The Monkees, The Supremes, The Rascals, and Britain's Tom Jones, who was the latest sensation in New York with his sell-out show at the Copa. Jones and friends would retire to Dudes'n'Dolls once the show was over and catch the occasional glimpse of the girl from Takoma Park strutting her stuff; but however hard she tried, Goldie could not make it to the place where Jones himself was performing, a fact which continues to amaze Darryl Shayne. 'I don't know why, that was a real no-talent job. There were only two girls that required talent and those were the two ponies* – the rest were just showgirls that just stood around and looked pretty. Their only job was to follow the girls up front.'

In the end, it was probably a vital lack of self-confidence which robbed Goldie of her opportunity to dance at the Copa: 'I got right down to the end [of the audition] and they wanted to see me with my bangs off my forehead. The minute I took my bangs off, that's it. I am not ever going to show my forehead again. That was my security, my bangs.'

The situation was doubly ironic, for Goldie found herself auditioning for the director Herb Ross who was staging a show there; ironic because Ross's sister had lived with Goldie's mother during the Second World War and they had all known each other; ironic also because later, when Goldie became master of her own medium, she employed the man who turned her down as her director in the ill-starred film *Protocol*. Laura, ever-purposeful, telephoned Goldie when she heard of the audition with Ross: 'Goldie, you call him up and tell him who you are.' But Goldie, for reasons of her own, chose not to. The still, small voice within told her maybe she wasn't good enough, maybe she didn't have the look, maybe she was way too skinny. Outwardly, 'I don't want to impose' was her line.

So Dudes'n'Dolls remained her focal point. This, even at $15 a shift, plus tips, was a step up from the Peppermint Box in New Jersey. But it was not what Goldie wanted for herself. She had the daily discipline of dance lessons at Phil Black's studio, where another culture prevailed and where the *maestro* was putting together for her a song-and-dance act. 'I heard her singing voice, it was a cool jazz

* Lead dancers.

sound,' he recalls. So it came as no great surprise to her flatmates when one day she walked into her Eighth Avenue apartment and announced she had quit Dudes'n'Dolls. Bobby Van remembers, 'We had a tiny little platform in the middle of the bar and during the lunch-hour we would have a girl get up there and dance so that people could see through the window from the street. We had a Puerto Rican day manager who asked her to get up there one lunchtime and she refused – she took it as an insult. So he fired her, or she quit.' Bobby refrained from pointing out that, although the purpose of the exercise may officially have been to draw attention to passers-by that the club had go-go dancers during the day, it had the added attraction for male patrons that they were able to look up the dancer's skirt at close quarters. Goldie's boyfriend Spiro sympathised: 'All of a sudden they want you to get up on top of a bar – what happens after that? That's enough to scare anybody.'

What happened after that was that Goldie got to meet Al Capp. Capp was a national institution, whose Li'l Abner cartoon character had charmed the nation for generations. Beginning syndication in 1934, by the post-war years Li'l Abner was the most popular comic strip of all time, with its characters Daisy Mae, Fearless Fosdick and Joe Btfsplk appearing in hundreds of newspapers, and eventually in animated cartoons, on stage, in a movie, in comic books and in soft-toy form.

Her encounter with this much-loved figure demonstrated how naïve Goldie remained, even after her months-long immersion in metropolitan life. Making her way from the Candy Jones modelling agency, where she had signed on in the hope of making a secondary income through photography, she was stopped on the street by a man who told her how unusual her face was: 'If he had told me I was beautiful I would have known he was full of shit and walked away. But he said the right thing and gave me a whole load of bull. He told me Al Capp was casting parts for a television version of Li'l Abner which has a wonderful character called Tenderlief Ericsson and I seemed like the right girl for the part. Had I ever acted before?

'And I said, yes, I have done *Romeo and Juliet*. So I got in his Cadillac thinking, this is great! I'm driving down Amsterdam Avenue in a brand-new Cadillac convertible, my mother and father will never believe this! And he said to me, "You must be very nice to Mr Capp, because he can do a lot for you." I was really excited.'

Capp's gofer continued to prime Goldie for the next fortnight, painting a rosy picture of how much money she was going to make – the figure of $800 a week was wafted temptingly under her nose – and how she would become a big star: 'My initial thought was, God! I'll be able to put wall-to-wall carpeting in my mother's house! So I learned my lines and I went to this apartment, very nervous. The butler came in and said, "Mr Capp would like you to pour the tea, he always likes his ladies to pour the tea."

'I sat there waiting for Mr Capp and finally he thundered in with his wooden leg. He had great presence, a very deep voice, "Goldie I heard so much about you. I understand that you are a very nice girl. You are going to work very, very hard for this part."

'He was in his bathrobe. I said, "Mr Capp, I'm a dancer and I know what it is to work very hard." He said, "Good, now would you stand up and start reading." So I read very loud. He said, "Goldie, speak softly for the cameras, because they can hear you."

'I was sucked in. I believed this man really wanted to help me. Then he told me to go across the room and pretend his eyes were the camera, and take the beads I had hanging from my neck and put them in my mouth and act like an imbecile. So, like a jackass, I took the beads and put them in my mouth and acted like an imbecile.

'Then I started to get very nervous. I smelled something coming. He said, "Would you walk to the mirror and lift up your skirt, because I think you can play Daisy Mae." I was very proud of my legs; it wasn't something I was shy of. So I lifted up my skirt. He said, "Higher." I went up an inch, he said, "Higher." I went up another inch. It finally got to the point of no return and I said to myself, "That's it, it's not going any higher" and he told me to come and sit next to him – at which point he completely exposed himself. And this *thing* was staring at me!

'I looked at it and started to shake. Then I threw the script down and did what any nice Jewish girl would do. I said, "Mr Capp, I would never get a job this way." He replied, "Oh, I had all of them, all the movie stars. You'll never make it in this business. Why don't you go back and marry a Jewish dentist because you're never going to make anything of your career." "You don't have anything. You're nothing," I cried, running out of the apartment.'

Such rejection had little effect on the old goat. Almost a year later Goldie was walking down Eighth Avenue when a young man stopped her in the street, told her she looked special and wondered whether she had ever heard of Al Capp? 'I said, "You're nothing but pimps for this man! Get away from me!" He said, "No, please, I'm not! I want to send you a script!" I said "Send me a script and send me a *contract*!" He said, "Please let me buy you a hamburger", so I said OK. I got a lunch out of it, so that's pragmatism.'

It was not an isolated incident. Though the Candy Jones model agency doubted they would be able to advance her career they sent her off for test shots: 'I went to this photographer and he took some pictures and then said, "Come on, I'll show you how I develop in the darkroom" – and I believed him! And he attacked me. I looked down at his hand and it had a wedding band on. I yelled, "Don't do this! You're married!" so he took me outside the darkroom and said, "Look, you'll never be a model. You don't have the face for it." And he said to come back into the darkroom and he'd show me why, and I went back into the room like an idiot, and he attacked me again. I had things like that happen to me all the time.'

Across town, Bette Midler was undergoing the same baptism of fire. A former pupil of Radford High School, Hawaii, Midler arrived with similar dreams and ambitions as Goldie, only to have them crushed among the whores and junkies who shared the Broadway Central hotel with her. While Goldie was dancing in the smart end of town, Bette made do with gigs in Union City, across the bridge in New Jersey. Like Goldie, she refused to dance topless or to take customers home, and spent her days on the endless dispiriting round of auditions and dance classes before getting her first paid job as a back-up singer for Johnny Barracuda, an unlikely Caribbean performer, in the African Room on West 44th Street.

The toughening process was far from over. With job prospects looking bleak, Goldie accepted a three-month contract to dance in a nightclub chorus-line in Puerto Rico: 'I danced with Viosa Costello on the back of the line. Her big asset was her big brown ass. She'd always show it. That was her thing. So I danced with her for a while.' But the management at the Condado Beach Hotel, where the faithful, admiring Spiro came to watch his gorgeous Goldie, were less than happy with her attitude. There was a row when she discovered the male dancers were being paid more than the females and she was fired. As at Dudes'n'Dolls, she was not prepared to curb her tongue. 'She was always kinda light,' opined Bobby Van. 'Not flaky, but she didn't take her responsibilities too seriously.'

There were patches of happiness along the way. The great American tradition of summer stock theatre – often open-air productions taken on tour – gave her an opportunity to get away from the vulgarising culture which was hemming her in. She drove up to New England with a theatre company which was putting on musicals including *Guys and Dolls* and *Kiss Me Kate* and was allowed occasional one-liners, though it was difficult to put the same motivation into 'Has anybody seen an earring round here?' as she had into Juliet's 'O happy dagger, this is thy sheath; There rust, and let me die ...'

But there were some consolations. *Guys and Dolls* came around to Washington DC and Rut Hawn played in the orchestra for the first, but far from the last time, his daughter was up onstage. Sy Green, a fellow-musician, recalled, 'Rut was a big, big supporter of Goldie's ambition. Later in her career he would rush out to the nearest news-stand to buy magazines and look up all the articles on Goldie – anything that had Goldie's name on it he would buy.'

In the chorus-line of *Kiss Me Kate* her eye fell on the wiry, dark form of a dancer eight years older than her, Gus Trikonis. Like her boyfriend Spiro Venduras, he was of Greek extraction – dark, mean and moody: 'I was very green then, a real baby. He was a father figure to me.' As her relationship with Spiro drew to its natural conclusion, she found herself falling in love with Trikonis. Unlike Spiro, Gus's life appeared to be taking the same route as Goldie's.

Finding, for the first time, a fraternity among fellow artistes Goldie began to relax into the theatrical life. There were moments of comradeship, hilarity and occasional embarrassment: 'Like when I peed onstage. I was in the chorus of *Kiss Me Kate*, we were in Springfield, Massachusetts, and one of the actors was playing a strong-man. I was in a tutu, but the strong-man couldn't find his loincloth at the last moment, so he showed up in a girl's leotard! I laughed so hard I peed down my legs. It was visible from the light-booth, so you know everyone had to be going, "God, what's *happening* to this girl?" I didn't run offstage, though – I stuck it through.'

But the season came to an end and her new-found friends drifted off, back to the insecurity of unemployment and the onset of a particularly vicious New York winter. It was time to get serious. A choreographer friend called and said there was work waiting in California if she was prepared to take the plunge. 'I left my four room-mates, said goodbye to my boyfriend, packed up my dog, went to California and never came back.'

Her first job was dancing in the chorus at the Melodyland Theatre in Anaheim, south of Los Angeles, in the chorus of *Pal Joey*, starring the crooner and former teen idol Frankie Avalon. The stage version of Frank Sinatra's 1957 movie about the rise of a flaky nightclub entertainer was a sell-out hit, co-starring Yvonne de Carlo and Barbara Nichols. Goldie hoofed it in the back of the chorus and managed a single one-liner alone onstage with the star:

Girl: Joey, Joey – where you going?
Joey: Me? I'm going to Broadway. To the Copacabana!
Girl: (sardonic): Oh yeah. I HUYD!

Frankie Avalon says now that, every night, Goldie stopped the show with the delivery of that line. 'I told her, "You've got it!"' But when the season ended there was no more theatre work, and when Avalon moved on to Las Vegas he found that the girl he had spent time encouraging back at Melodyland, listening to her hopes and aspirations, was there ahead of him – right back in the chorus line.

Goldie had landed a job at the Desert Inn, then the biggest gambling joint in the United States and one which prided itself on the lavishness of its floor-shows. Already Elvis Presley had played Vegas, paving the way for virtually every other known showbiz figure to follow suit. Dancing girls were all-important to the city's tinselled image and whole platoons of them would bus in from Los Angeles and work until they could work no more. The Desert Inn's producer Frank Sennes Jr would turn out monthly shows based on some topical theme, and the format would usually include a comedian, a singer and dancers. The closed-in lounge was next to the casino and the purpose was to draw crowds into an ersatz feeling of high-rolling luxury.

Backstage it could not have been more different. The same threats to Goldie's peace of mind were here, as in New York: drugs, drink, predatory men, violence. But when you were dancing in such shows as *Once Upon a Mattress*, from ten at night until five in the morning, four shows a night, sleep was the safest escape from all of that. 'It was really rough,' she later remembered. 'All I wanted to do was get a steady job on something like the "Jerry Lewis Show" as a dancer. That would have been Utopia – find a guy, get married, finish. Instead I was up all night, sleeping all day, and I turned into a thing.' She glimpsed herself in a TV commercial she'd made: 'I was in a red wig looking like somebody's pet monkey. It was a crappy life.'

Avalon bumped into her as she came offstage from a scantily-clad girly revue called *Les Crazy Girls*: 'I was surprised to see her in a girly show. She poured out her heart to me, she said things weren't going the way she wanted them to go, but the talent was there for all to see. I told her, "God's delay is not God's denial".' Avalon's kind words, in Anaheim and in Vegas, were rewarded five years later when he had a call asking him to visit Goldie in her Hollywood home. 'She popped open a bottle of Champagne and raised a toast. She told me, "I want to share something with you. I just signed for my first film."'

But in the desertland of Vegas in 1965 there was no hint yet of the stardom to come. Goldie worked and worked until finally, like every other chorus dancer before and since, she snapped: 'I did that town until I couldn't take it any more. It was too much. I took my car and my dog and I left town at six in the morning. I fled that place, and it was a great feeling.' Lurking in her mind was the possibility that she could create her own stage show and take it on the road, but after telephone calls to Rut Hawn, whose life had been spent in buses and trucks, she realised this was one dream that would never come true. 'It's a lousy life,' her father counselled. 'Think real hard about it.'

Curiously, among the hundreds and thousands of faceless glamour-girls in fishnet tights and paste-on smiles, Goldie was remembered with affection by the stage crews who worked with her. 'She had something which set her apart even then,' recalled the Desert Inn's stage manager Fred Aaron; but the warmth she generated outwardly was matched by a chill she felt inside.

She called her mentor Phil Black in New York at five in the morning to tell him she'd walked. 'Her mother told her to ring me for advice. I said if someone gives you a job and pays for you to go there, you can't just walk away. They'd paid a lot to take her out there and I said you just don't do that – I didn't want her to get a bad name with the choreographers because if word spread, she'd never get another job. The next thing I know she's standing in the doorway with her dog.'

Despairing, but with one last spurt of determination, she returned to Los Angeles where Gus Trikonis was already established and set about another round of auditions, promising herself that if she had not found work within a fortnight, she would accept defeat and return home to Takoma Park. One day before her self-imposed deadline, she landed a bit part in an Andy Griffith TV show.

Though virtually unknown outside the United States, Griffith had become a cult figure with his eponymous show, a domestic sitcom, networked across America. By the time Goldie appeared, it had been running for seven years in black and white and had been in the top ten slot for every year of its existence. In celebration of this achievement a showcase programme, *The Andy Griffith Looking Back Special*, was created for him, featuring the country singer Tennessee Ernie Ford and a co-star from the weekly show, actress Maggie Peterson.

Among the many millions who tuned in that night to watch Griffith was a young talent agent working for the William Morris organisation's Los Angeles office called Art Simon. As the show's end-credits rolled and the commercial break began, Simon walked across the room and picked up the telephone.

After years of wishing and hoping and thinking and praying, Goldie Hawn was finally about to become famous.

# CHAPTER FOUR

# *Sock It To Me*

*'O Fortune, Fortune, all men call thee fickle'*
*– ibid.*

'Rowan and Martin's Laugh-In' was conceived out of a combination of fear, loathing, and ambition by the US network chiefs, in general a backward-looking group of hardline rightists who were impervious to the changing ethical and behavioural climate in America.

In January 1967 CBS commissioned 'The Smothers Brothers Comedy Hour' for their all-important Sunday night prime-time slot. The commission came more out of desperation than any great sense of inspiration and almost immediately was regretted, for the Brothers, only seen once before on network TV in their own show, and that an abject failure, floated in from left-field with an alternative menu of youth culture. Within weeks they had become the standard-bearers of anti-establishment TV. CBS chiefs were appalled at the dangerous-looking guests booked by Tommy Smothers for the show – Buffalo Springfield, Electric Prune, The Grateful Dead, all of whom used the show as a platform to air their anti-war views through their music.

None the less the show was making the ratings and the rival NBC network, fearful for their advertising revenue, slowly came to realise that the world had moved on. It was no longer acceptable to foist Frank Sinatra, Dean Martin, Andy Williams and their ilk on to a young audience who found these showbiz legends ultimately resistible.

A young producer, George Schlatter, had come up with what appeared, on paper at least, to be a new variant on the comedy-variety theme. To be called 'Straighten Up and Turn Left', it was conceived as an updated TV version of the Broadway revue of the 1930s,

'Hellzapoppin', which had critics reaching deep into their store of expletives, but which charmed the audiences with a mixture of blackouts, slapstick, and other timeworn devices.

Schlatter decided to front the show with two relatively unknown nightclub comedians, Dan Rowan and Dick Martin, and NBC hurried a pilot into production, with the possibility of a series commitment if the audiences responded. As a production team was assembled someone thought up a more conventional title, 'Rowan and Martin's Laugh-In', but one which nevertheless tipped its hat towards the Smothers Brothers' audience who, when they weren't watching TV, were engaged in the sit-ins and love-ins which were the hallmark of the times.

Viewed at thirty years' distance, 'Laugh-In' seems weak by comparison with the Smothers Brothers' show or 'That Was The Week That Was'. In the more liberal climate of Britain, it was permissible, if shocking, to hang pictures of politicians in the studio then walk past punching them full in the face in payment for some alleged misdemeanour. In Britain, should David Frost and his team choose to have Harry Belafonte sing 'Lord, Lord, Don't Stop the Carnival' over a seven-and-a-half minute clip of the mindless police violence of the Chicago riots, the BBC's Director General Hugh Carleton Greene would have silently nodded his approval. In the States, when the Smothers Brothers tried it, they found the clip missing from the show when it was transmitted. Censorship – worse, self-censorship – was endemic; and even before he started George Schlatter faced the distinct possibility that in trying to woo a young, hip audience, he could find his show closed down for trying too hard.

Schlatter had been heavily influenced by 'That Was The Week That Was' and its successor, 'Not So Much A Programme More A Way Of Life', which ran in Britain from 1962 to 1965. On both sides of the Atlantic a new post-war generation was growing up to find itself confronted by a set of attitudes and values which seemed out of tune with the times. In Britain the old school tie reigned supreme; in America the moral majority held levity and freedom of expression in check. It was suffocating.

Schlatter, with his piercing eyes, thick eyebrows, pencil moustache and goatee beard seemed an almost sinister figure to those, Goldie Hawn included, who were auditioned by him. One of the 'Laugh-In' regulars, the British actress Judy Carne, recalls Schlatter saying, 'Dick Martin is … well, he's a little weird. He insists on making whoopee with all the women in the cast.' Miss Carne, recognising this for the sexual challenge it was, instantly offered her body to the entirely innocent Martin; but Schlatter had merely been establishing whether his future employee lived by the 'old' values or whether she was part of the new, hip generation.

Rehearsals for the pilot show took place during July 1967 against the backdrop of the Monterey Pop Festival, along with Woodstock one of the defining moments of rock music history: onstage came Janis Joplin, Jimi Hendrix, Otis Redding, Simon and Garfunkel, Hugh Masekela, The Who, Ravi Shankar. The music was helping to shape the political, cultural, and behavioural attitudes of a new generation in a way that music had never done before, and in so doing helped pave the way for the astonishing success of 'Laugh-In'.

But it was not 'Laugh-In' yet. The pilot show was called 'The Rowan & Martin Special' and during its painstaking development the seeds were sown for what was to follow. Though a cast including Arte Johnson, Henry Gibson, Ruth Buzzi, Jo Anne Worley, Pam Austin and Judy Carne was assembled, it did not include Goldie Hawn; and though the gimmick of body-painting slogans is later remembered as being one of Goldie's more lasting contributions to the show, it was Judy Carne who was the guinea-pig, spending three hours in make-up having her bikini-ed body daubed by a pink-faced artist only to be ogled by a grim-looking group of men who turned out to be NBC's Broadcast Standards Committee – the self-censors. They ordained that the American viewing public was not yet ready to view a bare female navel on their TV screens, so Miss Carne had a doorbell painted on her midriff below the words 'Postman Ring Here'. The effect on that viewing public when the pilot was aired on 9 September 1967, was electric: a hip and zany comedy show relying on old vaudeville favourites – slapstick, innuendo, blackouts, song and dance – yet seeming young, fresh, original, spontaneous.

But spontaneous it was not. On the first day of rehearsals George Schlatter dropped a script, twelve inches thick, on to the table. Each 'spontaneous' idea had been worked out in advance, and though at the outset Schlatter called on his actors to ad-lib their way to a better performance, he kept an iron grip on the finished product, spending hours in the cutting-room achieving the effects he was after.

Within forty-eight hours of the pilot's transmission NBC had commissioned a series from Schlatter, to start early in January 1968. He had still never heard of Goldie Hawn, nor she of him, but still on the lookout for extra background talent he trawled the NBC studios in Burbank. On the set of the soon-to-be-forgotten sitcom, 'Good Morning, World', he discovered the star who was to become more famous and more rich than he would ever be. Goldie was still only twenty-one, and trying hard to adjust to the modest fame accruing to her via the sitcom.

Art Simon, the William Morris agent, had succeeded in tracking her down, though at first she refused to return his calls, reckoning him to be another of those 'deze'n'doze' guys who had dogged her footsteps from New York to Las Vegas. Finally, and with some force, Simon established his credentials and hauled her over to the studios presided over by Sam Denoff and Bill Persky, creators of the fabulously successful 'Dick Van Dyke Show'.

'Good Morning, World', their latest creation, was about two disc-jockeys, one single and one married, and they were looking for an actress to play Sandy, the next door neighbour and friend of the married DJ's wife. All in all, a standard US sitcom format.

Denoff recalls they had seen a lot of contenders for the part but, as William Morris were packaging the show, they listened to Art Simon's recommendation that they should see his new discovery. 'We gave her a scene to audition where the wife and Sandy are having a cup of coffee and are discussing a problem. We sent her the pages and she came in quite marvellous-looking with this wonderfully expressive face. And she brought her own cup and pot. We said, you don't have to do that, but she told us "No, no, I practised with these at home."

'She was not a trained actress at all and she had no experience. But, as happens so often, you spot something that is original, and marvellous, and sweet, and although she wasn't exactly the way we imagined the character would be, that's the fun of doing it when you find someone who makes it come alive. So we hired her.'

Though ambition pushed her forward, other aspects of Goldie's complex personality struggled to keep up with the changes which seemed to be happening at a bewildering pace. She made a brief return to New York, as if to contrast her old life with the new: 'So much had happened to me, and it was something that I'd feared. I didn't want it to affect my life, I didn't want it to change my personality. I just didn't want to be any different from the way I was, but after getting this part and being promoted in this TV series – which nobody had yet seen – I was starting to feel strange. There I was at the Hilton, which was not a place I could ever have afforded to stay, a bottle of Champagne on my table and autograph-hounds who didn't know me from Adam calling me up. I started to lose my sense of balance – I was in a new world.'

She revisited her old haunts – the apartment on Eighth Avenue, the Dudes'n'Dolls discotheque, Phil Black's dance studio, Central Park. She called on Spiro Venduras's family and told them her good news, and went looking for her former flatmates: 'I was feeling different already, and trying very hard to hold on to who I was.' She was discovering, slowly, the distancing process which comes from arriving in a bigger world and returning to the smaller one. She went home to Takoma Park and found that even her family's attitude had subtly shifted – here was no longer the girl who would find it hard to hold down a typing job, here was a star: 'It was a dark area for me, a time of confusion, the most frightening thing that had happened to me.'

On her return to Los Angeles she began to suffer the classic symptoms so many young and successful people had suffered before her – a sense of isolation, a greatly reduced sense of self-worth, the haunting fear of failure even before success had properly arrived. She found it impossible to walk into public places without feeling nauseous: 'What was so scary was I had no walls to touch, I was all on my own.' A form of anorexia nervosa set in and, unable to eat, her weight plummeted to 90lb. She entered analysis, a process of psychological propping which she continued for the next seven years. With no mentors, no advisors, and no rule-book to consult, having a psychiatrist's couch to lie upon had its comforts.

Persky and Denoff, unaware of their protégée's inner turmoil, were so delighted with her dedication and guileless charm that on her return, after the first series of thirteen shows, they decided to reward her. 'We said to each other we are paying this child peanuts, just nothing, so we decided to give her a rise,' recalls Denoff. 'Shock waves went through the industry! They said, you are going to give an actor a raise without them even asking for it? And Goldie herself said, "Why are you doing that?" She couldn't believe it.'

With Art Simon still employed full-time at William Morris, Goldie grasped early that she needed proper advice and representation if she was to break through to the next level. She approached Persky and Denoff to ask whether they might handle her affairs, but they pointed out that they were writers and producers, not managers: 'Sweetheart, you'll be all right! We'll watch over you!' And they did, taking her through many of the twenty-six episodes of 'Good Morning, World' until she came to George Schlatter's attention.

'One day when we were filming, George came on the set. He was planning a new-style free-form comedy show. He thought I was funny in some way he couldn't explain, so he signed me up as one of a dozen girls that were going to dance in the background,' Goldie recalled later. 'I mean, honestly, no one had any idea of what I could do.'

Schlatter's attitude was 'videotape's cheap' and it was his policy to keep the cameras rolling through take after take, hoping to pick up on ad-libs and fluffs. Though this led to headaches in the cutting room, he found something he was looking for as he asked Goldie – one of many of the background cast – to read a one-liner caption off an 'idiot' board.

Schlatter later recalled that Goldie had been picked out for her goofy, gamine face, but that once she arrived at rehearsals no one was quite sure what to do with her: 'So we just let her dance to start with and she looked kinda cute. Then we decided to give her an introductory line to a sketch. Well, she blew it. Not once, but three times. And each time she broke into this embarrassed giggle.

'The third time the director gave her the cut sign, but something hit me at that moment. "Never stop her again," I told him. "Never. That is absolutely adorable."'

For a one-time Juliet who had held spellbound a rain-soaked auditorium of 3,000, an actress and dancer who prided herself on perfection, it was a perplexing and not wholly wonderful moment. There was in Schlatter's moment of genius an unpleasant truth to be faced: that though she had come a long way from Takoma Park, there was still a long way to go. Despite her experience on 'Good Morning, World' she was uneasy in a studio full of polished professionals, all of them with vastly more experience than her. She had been given the dunce's cap and told to wear it with a smile.

Later she rationalised it: 'They gave me these straight things to read, like "News of the Future" and I'd get it all mixed up and people would just laugh, and I'd crack up at my own stupidity and they just kept the cameras going. I'd say, "No, wait a minute," and it would be like someone was tickling me, I'd laugh so hard.'

Whether or not the laugh was truly genuine, with 'Laugh-In' Goldie's appointment with destiny had arrived.

Within eight weeks of the opening programme on 22 January 1968, and now with Goldie included in the team, 'Laugh-In' became America's highest-rated TV show. Schlatter had assembled an inspired cast, and as their faces became familiar to US and British audiences so too did their catch-phrases: Judy Carne's 'Sock It To Me', followed by a bucket of water, a boxing-glove or a trapdoor exit; Arte Johnson's German soldier peering from behind a potted palm and muttering '*Vairy* interesting ...'; Rowan and Martin's incessant references to 'beautiful downtown Burbank', where the new NBC studios were housed, and such all-purpose rejoinders as 'you bet your sweet bippy'. As much as anything, it was the *look* of the show which grabbed peoples' attention. The schoolroom imagery and childlike daubings contrasted with the often risqué script content provided a satisfactory child/adult counterpoint. For those with colour TV sets the use of nursery-school primaries jumped out of the screen.

And, of course, there were Goldie's fluffed lines. Within weeks *Look* magazine had singled her out for special attention, describing her as 'TV's dumbest and most delectable bonbon.'

The cameras loved her face, and the viewers loved her persona. 'People never reacted to my giggle until "Laugh-In",' Goldie recalled later. 'And to start with, people in the business treated me like the Giggly Girl – they thought I was *stoned* because I was laughing all the time. They'd say, "What's she on?"'

Goldie fluffed her way through her lines – 'I forgot the *question*!' she would expostulate – and subjected herself to the weekly body-painting. The idea was so new that at the outset no one bothered to check whether the paint came off; only after complaints from Goldie and Judy Carne that it sometimes took three or four days to get their bodies clean did someone look into more easily removable make-up.

In a bikini, as at all times, Goldie looked gorgeous; but her hesitant performance was not all artifice – Schlatter saw the potential in his discovery, but during her 'Laugh In' days it was far from realised. Placed against seasoned showbiz veterans, her act seems now tinsel-thin by comparison, but the sheer joy she emanated more than compensated for her lack of experience.

The show was meticulously scripted by a group of writers holed up in the Toluca Capri Motel in nearby Toluca Lake, where they cranked out sketches which sometimes would not be aired for weeks. Outrageous material which was never going to see the light of day was commissioned by Schlatter specifically for the censors: the idea was to desensitise the grey men so that the less risqué sketches would seem tame by comparison. One writer described Schlatter's scripting technique as 'a cat-and-mouse game with the censors: the point was to see what he could get away with'.

'I agree with you guys,' Schlatter would say to them. 'Some of these things *are* pretty wild. But the problem is, you've snipped out nearly twelve minutes that I've got to make up.' And he would usually end up successfully bartering. 'All right, if you won't let me have the gay joke, you *gotta* let me keep the nun joke.'

'My fiancée just found out she's been taking aspirins instead of the pill,' went a one-liner. 'She doesn't have a headache, but I do.' All delivered without the slightest hint of *double-entendre*.

Nothing was left to chance by the men from NBC's head office. At Monday script conferences they would sit in the shadows with their faces buried in the script, searching out, but not always detecting, the subversive message. Sex, the Vietnam war, soft drugs; they were all there, sometimes too hidden for even the streetwise audience to get the joke.

Schlatter was a Democrat, his head writer, Paul Keyes, was a Republican, a combination which allowed for broadsides to be directed at all targets in the political spectrum. It was an attitude which worried and confused the censors no end.

Unconnected with the rapidly developing youth culture, they innocently allowed through a scene where two hippies greet each other in a park. One says, 'Hi.' The other replies, 'You too?' The next day the censors were back, apoplectic with rage. 'You must think we're a bunch of schmucks,' one yelled at Schlatter. 'How do you think I felt when my kid turned to me this morning over breakfast and said, "That dope joke last night was really *cool*, dad!"'

Goldie's innocent looks, her dizzy personality and childlike persona removed her from some of the sharper barbs. It was given to Judy Carne to have a wig whipped from her head by an invisible wire to reveal an apparently hairless scalp before she delivers her one-liner to camera: 'Oh! I've never been *bald* before!' – 'balling' then being America's favourite euphemism for sex. Once again the censors were incandescent with rage when it was pointed out that the wool had been pulled over their eyes.

The humour of 'Laugh-In' travels badly across time. The world now feels itself to be wiser, hipper, more informed, less uptight than in the sixties, whose legendary age of liberation must be set against what had gone before. Watching re-runs of those early, ground-breaking programmes would tend to leave most contemporary viewers with a single question: What was all the fuss about? But at the time, the cocktail of humour imbibed by 'Rowan and Martin's Laugh-In' viewers seemed as potent as a brutally dry Martini.

Taking, as an example, a show from November 1969, seeing an uncomfortable Michael Caine declaiming pompously to camera: 'You should get out of Vietnam', it is hard now to see the humour. The caption-cards and flash-frame messages quip: 'Refrigerators are frigid', 'Worms are for the birds', 'Premier Kosygin, iron your curtain', and, predictably given the show's overall ethos, 'War is good business'. The Fickle Finger of Fate Award, doled out each week to a public figure who had earned the show's obloquy, went on this occasion to a racist judge. A few weeks' earlier Dan Rowan had presented another Fickle Finger of Fate Award to Senator John Pastore of Rhode Island, who was trying to establish a review board to screen television for sex and violence. But Rowan had been guesting on the rival Smothers Brothers show, where writers and artists trod a very much more dangerous tightrope. Perhaps unsurprisingly in that dark and unenlightened age, it proved to be the Brothers' last show.

According to the US Nielsen ratings, one out of every four Americans watched 'Laugh-In' during the 1968–9 season. One statistic to prove its popularity was that the show was watched each week by more people than had ever seen *Gone With the Wind;* but a more telling indicator was that bars across the country, not yet equipped with TVs, habitually emptied just before 8 p.m. on Monday nights, 'Laugh-In's slot. Soon the merchandisers stepped in and lunch-boxes, 'Sock It To Me' T-shirts, raincoats, jigsaw puzzles, neckties, chewing gum, school supplies, beachwear and sleeping bags appeared in stores all over America. But while this made NBC rich, the stars of the show continued to receive their basic wage with no extras.

Before long the stars of the day who arrived at NBC to appear on more conventional shows found themselves being led down a corridor by an enthusiastic Schlatter, offering them '$210 and a lot of love' if they would make a guest appearance on 'Laugh-In'. Among the more unlikely recruits – given that the giants of the big screen still looked down on television as cheapjack entertainment – were Douglas Fairbanks Jr and John Wayne. As time progressed Schlatter cast his net wider, successfully attracting increasingly unlikely characters before arriving at the evangelist Billy Graham and, finally, Richard Nixon.

The show's head writer, Paul Keyes, had written jokes for Nixon's speeches over the years and, as the presidential elections loomed, he suggested to the campaign staff that an appearance on 'Laugh-In' might show the lighter side, if that there be, of his friend.

Surrounded by secret service agents, Nixon looked incongruous as he walked on to the brightly-painted set. His eyes darted round the studio nervously as George Schlatter asked him, 'We'd like to have you repeat some of the phrases from the show. For example, would you say, "You bet your sweet bippy"?'

'You bet your *what?*' Nixon asked.

'You bet your sweet bippy.'

Nixon surrounded himself with aides. One emerged to ask Schlatter, 'Mr Nixon would like to know – what's a bippy?'

'Never mind,' soothed Schlatter, 'we'll try another one. How about saying, "Goodnight, Dick"?'

Further deliberation ensued before the spokesman announced the verdict. 'No, no, I'm afraid Mr Nixon couldn't possibly say "Goodnight, Dick". It carries the wrong connotation altogether.'

Schlatter had to suffice with the politician uttering 'Sock it to me.' With predictable lack of insight, Nixon turned the excitable exclamation – by now on the lips of millions – into a question. Nevertheless when he was elected President six weeks later in January 1969 political observers opined that his fleeting appearance on 'Laugh-In', uttering 'Sock it to *me?*' may have contributed to the defeat of his opponent, the liberal vice-president Hubert Humphrey.

George Schlatter labelled 'Laugh-In's time-slot 'the kamikaze hour'. The opposition networks were running 'Gunsmoke' and 'The Lucy Show'; there was no more audience to go around. Yet within weeks Lucille Ball had been knocked off the top slot and the 'Laugh-In' team watched with awe as their ratings continued to soar upwards while the tried-and-tested shows started to stumble and fall.

Wielding this sort of power made Schlatter a hard taskmaster. Driven by his creation and the public acclaim, he demanded more from his cast, his crew, and his writers. Judy Carne recalls being summoned by a production assistant from her dressing-room on to the studio floor where she found Goldie in tears. Schlatter had ordered her to make a drop through a trapdoor, but to Judy it looked more as if he had asked Goldie to set foot on the gallows.

'Listen,' said the producer. 'We're trying to get her to go through the damned trapdoor. She's having a *breakdown* about the whole thing and I don't know what to say to her. Why don't you give her a pep talk or something ... I don't have *time* for this.'

Judy took the view that Schlatter was being excessively cruel in insisting on something that clearly terrified his young star. 'It was humiliating for her to be standing there, scared to death, in front of everybody,' she recalled. She encouraged Goldie by pointing out the mattresses to break her fall, and instructing her on how to execute a trapdoor fall without hurting herself: 'I know it looks silly,' sniffled Goldie, 'you do it all the time. But I'm *petrified* ...'

'Just do it this once,' responded the older actress. 'I'll be down there. I'll catch you if necessary. Don't you dare give him a chance to make you look like an asshole. He'll never let you live it down.' And with that, Goldie's tears dried, her jaw set, and she allowed the trapdoor to swallow her up.

Schlatter seemed to thrive on the idea of creative tension between his artistes, and at the beginning of each 'Laugh-In' working week he would set actor against actress as they read through the script. 'There was a lot of joking around at these script meetings,' recalled Judy Carne, 'but beneath the laughter was a layer of tension. If you didn't read a line convincingly the first time, it would be assigned to some-one else.'

Soon the set displayed advertisements for such non-existent entities as CFG Airlines or CFG Automat. The initials stood for Crazy Fucking George, as he was now known by the entire production team. Those who worked with him recall his maniacal hunger for new material, and how he would drive everyone crazy with his quest to find and secure it. Big enough to take the joke in good part, he had the initials inscribed on his attaché case.

Schlatter seemed to take a diabolical delight in keeping his cast on edge. 'Week after week we kept on dreaming up fiendish new ways to distract Goldie,' he recalled. 'We had meetings on the subject. "OK, what are we going to do to Goldie that's really awful tomorrow night?" She knew something strange would happen – it always did – but she never knew what. Often we would switch the cue cards on purpose, or else the crew behind the camera would do things to distract her like make faces or hold up dirty words.'

And every week there was the body-painting. While Judy Carne jauntily took it in her stride – she once ordered a male make-up artist painting her legs, 'While you're down there, do a favour for a friend' – Goldie found it time-consuming and irritating. The two women would lie on boards and swap recipes and details of their love-lives. Judy noticed that Goldie was a voracious reader, always carrying a book, – 'usually something Freudian'. This memory is underlined by Billy Barnes, who wrote all of the 'Laugh-In' music: 'She was a very bright, determined girl. We used to go to lunch in a place called the Smoke House and there'd be this gang of comedians and we'd say, "Come on, Goldie", and she'd somewhat reluctantly agree, carrying her book with her. When they all started telling their funny stories she'd open her book and she'd start reading at the table. I'd say, "What are you reading, Goldie?" And she'd have her nose in *War and Peace* while everyone else was letting off steam.'

The Smoke House was where the cast and crew would unwind after the show 'and be naughty' according to Barnes: 'Every major star wanted to be on "Laugh-In" and these young kids were thrown into sketches with these famous people, but Goldie wasn't at all fazed by them, she had that charisma immediately, she had star quality right from the start.' So much so, he recalls, that when she first set foot on the set all the girls looked at her, disgusted, as if to say 'Oh, who is *this*?'

On one bizarre occasion Goldie and Judy were told that Salvador

Dali, the surrealist painter, had become so bewitched by 'Laugh-In' that he wanted to come on the show and personally paint their bodies. It never happened, but the attention on these innocently-enough daubed bodies became so intense that the censors sent down a memo ordaining that make-up artists were not allowed to paint the inside of the actresses' thighs. Calves, knees, and outsides of the thighs were fine – but no inner thighs. 'To establish this demilitarised zone,' recalled Judy, 'we were actually *measured*. Goldie and I just wanted to get the bloody thing over with. What we didn't want was lengthy discussions on whether a paintbrush was allowed two or three inches from our groins!'

As she points out, these taboos were ridiculous, since in 1968 the Americans were bombarding Vietnam and the resultant footage was being pumped out on TV each night; far, far more shocking than the worst possible sketch the 'Laugh-In' team could think up.

The constant need to be funny took its toll on many of the cast: Goldie counselled Judy Carne after she developed a mental block about her face; she became unable to see its features when she looked in the mirror. With her own experience of psychotherapy now several years old, Goldie recommended Judy to a therapist. 'I was so grateful to Goldie for being there at a time when I desperately needed someone to point me in the right direction,' she says.

Billy Barnes recalled the constant anxiety too: 'At that time I used to drink and it drove me to sobriety.'

This downward pressure from Schlatter produced a special camaraderie between the women on set – Goldie, Judy, Ruth Buzzi and Jo Anne Worley. On one occasion the producer arranged with Hugh Hefner, boss of the Playboy organisation, to have the den mother from the Bunny Hutch at the Playboy Club come over to beautiful downtown Burbank and turn the women into Bunny girls. Goldie, conscious of her sparsely-furnished figure, was not encouraged at the thought. 'This isn't going to work very well with *my* body,' she said as she eyed the various costumes hanging on a rack. But, as Judy Carne recalls, the inside of a Playboy outfit is architect-designed. With built-in foam rubber shelves and excruciatingly tight corseted waists, she and Goldie were transformed – sufficiently so for them to devise a plan to take the outfits home to 'entertain' their menfolk that evening.

It was about this time that the universally positive press coverage Goldie had been given – unprecedented for such a junior arrival in TV – started to turn sour. As the show's popularity grew with its audience, critics started to snipe at Goldie's baby-doll appeal, arguing that it pandered to the lowest common denominator. But the actress wasn't complaining and nor were her colleagues taken in by her act. Judy Carne recalled, '"Yeah, Goldie's dumb," we used to say. "Dumb as a *fox*."'

Since the rule in popular journalism is always to take the opposite tack to the general view, showbiz writers started a whispering campaign suggesting there was all-out war between Goldie and Judy Carne for pole position in the show. One story proclaimed: 'The "feud" rumours are only whispers now, but they're getting louder – and it looks like a certain blonde and an English lass are heading for a showdown.'

'Nothing could be further from the truth,' Judy Carne wrote later. 'Goldie and I were good friends and we loved working together. I'd been able to ignore this kind of journalism in the past, but after a while insecurity set in and the stories started to eat me up. I began to wonder if perhaps something *was* going on that I knew nothing about. When I approached Goldie with my worries, she admitted having gone through the same trauma over the stories. It was a tremendous relief to talk it out with her, to realise that this conflict had been the fabrication of gossip columnists. We made a pact, agreeing that we would never take the word of a disturbing news story without discussing it face-to-face. That way, we thought, no outside forces could ever jeopardise our friendship.'

Hardly the first such agreement to be made between two actresses, it nevertheless held little meaning for either one. Judy Carne, six years older and an actress since childhood, with a star-studded past behind her, a marriage to Burt Reynolds, an allure capable of bedding Steve McQueen, a hippy who took drugs and hung out with rock stars, was all the things Goldie was not. They could never be close friends, and though Goldie must have continued to worry about the influence Judy had with George Schlatter, this was a situation from which no one derived any satisfaction. Judy confessed, 'The more I had to tell myself these stories were meaningless, the more my insecurity grew.'

The newfound truce held sufficiently long for Judy to discuss with Goldie the growing pressure she felt. Goldie recommended a visit to her analyst in Century City, near where she and Gus Trikonis now happily lived. It provided a temporary respite for Judy, but elsewhere the pressure was being felt with equal horror. The writers, holed up in the Toluca Capri Motel, were going stir-crazy: the manager complained that they were scrawling graffiti on the walls of their rooms. Fearing eviction, George Schlatter's co-producer Ed Friendly dispatched a crew armed with paint brushes and ladders.

That night, after the other writers left, the most brilliant of their number, David Panich, stayed behind. Next morning he was discovered asleep on the floor, the walls around him covered with the bitter slogan 'I must not write on the walls' repeated, thousands of times.

Goldie took refuge in needlepoint, a skill she acquired from her mother Laura, and encouraged another co-star, Arte Johnson, to follow suit. There were still moments of pleasure: on a flying visit to the 'Laugh-In' set as a *quid pro quo* for the Christmas special NBC was staging to herald his TV comeback after nearly a decade in the wilderness, Elvis Presley, a great hero of Goldie's, made a point of coming over, patting her on the head, and telling her that she reminded him of a newly-hatched chick. To be touched by someone she so deeply idolised was to stay with her long after Presley's death, but it was a passing moment. The pressure on set and in the dressing rooms at 'Laugh-In' continued to increase daily: the informality, the ad-libbing, the extempore joking was replaced with a heavily formulaic policy, entirely understandable from Schlatter's point of view since the pressure to remain top of the ratings only grew with time.

Eileen Brennan, later to co-star with Goldie in *Private Benjamin,* was also on the show at the time and recalled her friend receiving letters from her father. One read, 'You are laughing, laughing, laughing in 'Laugh-In' but don't forget to cry sometimes too.' Given the circumstances, Rut Hawn's well-meant advice was superfluous. After thirteen shows Brennan had had enough and bailed out: 'I hated it. I had to get my ass out of there, it was not something I felt comfortable doing and no fun for me.'

Soon Judy Carne could stand it no longer and quit too, and it would not be long before, under Art Simon's guidance, Goldie Hawn followed suit: 'If I had any problems at all, it was after two-and-a-half years of doing the same thing over and over again. There were just no surprises left for me. I had to empty my head of everything I knew – never looked at a script – and wait till the red light went on. And when it did, I just had to *go* for it. And that became very, very difficult.'

That was just part of the story. A rather more crucial factor was that 'Laugh-In' was fast becoming a vortex, a downward spiral of repeated jokes and situations into which the artistes' integrity was disappearing at a giddying rate. George Schlatter's grip on the programme grew tighter by the week, leaving the more ambitious actors in the company in despair, for once they were allotted a signature-piece there was no room to grow beyond it. Judy Carne's departure was in large measure due to her disappointment that Schlatter could not admit that her 'Sock It To Me' joke – where the utterance of this phrase, or similar, brought down an increasingly bizarre physical retribution on the actress – was tired, and was beginning to upset her. Schlatter, they said, had become a megalomaniac.

Despite the fact that she was receiving all the fan-mail, sacks of it each week, Goldie, and more particularly her agent, saw little return on walking it round the block for another season. By now she dominated the headlines wherever she went; clear blue water had appeared between her and the rest of the 'Laugh-In' team. At Akron, Ohio, over 100,000 people turned out to see her open the annual Soap Box Derby. When the show was taken on the road during the summer, with Dan and Dick, Ruth Buzzi, Jo Anne Worley and Henry Gibson, the photographers wanted pictures only of her.

Art Simon knew enough to proceed with caution. Coca-Cola offered Goldie $100,000 to appear in their latest commercial. She was nonplussed: 'Fantastic, Art … that's great!'

'Goldie,' he said, looking her in the eye, 'I want you to think about something. What do you want to *be*? Do you want to be known as the Coca-Cola Girl – or do you want a long-range career in films?'

Goldie could not see that one might preclude the other. 'Art, you don't understand. I have no clothes, I have no car …'

'You'll be all right, Goldie,' he said, coolly. 'You'll get them soon enough. I don't think we should accept the offer.'

Realising this was not a joke, Goldie began to cry. 'But *why?*'

'Look, I know it sounds like a lucrative offer right now, but if you want to save yourself for movies, you've got to turn it down,' he explained.

'It was the most brilliant managerial advice I'd ever heard,' recalled Judy Carne, who took part in the conversation. 'It took a lot of faith on both their parts. If I'd been advised by people with half Art's foresight, I would have been spared a lot of blunders in the years to come.'

Goldie Hawn's involvement with 'Laugh-In' barely lasted two years, yet of all the actors employed on the show in its lengthy run, her name alone is remembered with any familiarity. These days little is heard of Rowan, or Martin, or Billy Barnes and Alan Sues, Barbara Feldon, Ken Berry and Larry Hovis, and far less of the mainstay stars, Henry Gibson, Arte Johnson, Ruth Buzzi, Judy Carne and Jo Anne Worley. Lily Tomlin's contribution was short, her departure acrimonious.

Of them all, Goldie's appeal was unique, and instantaneous. From the first appearance, her eyes bulging with innocence, her hair teased to the sky, the superincarnation of the dumb blonde, nations either side of the Atlantic fell in love with her. Audiences adored her giggly warmth, her ridiculous absent-mindedness, her mala-propisms, her elusive sex-appeal. As George Schlatter had said after her initial audition, 'I didn't know whether to fuck her or take her home to Mom.'

*Life* magazine was quick to pick up on Goldie's magnetic appearance – 'the sex appeal of Lolita and the innocence of Charlie Brown' – and, at a moment in a young actress's career when the speculators can move in and wreck a promising future by over-emphasis on the sexual appeal of their property, Goldie resisted. Through endless press calls and photo sessions her act remained giggly, naïve, non-threatening; whether by the guidance of Art Simon or, more likely, her own instincts forged in the classroom at Silver Springs where the other girls had sex-appeal and she didn't.

While Lily Tomlin had to sue to get out of her 'Laugh-In' contract, with the aid of Art Simon Goldie managed a nimble, if not entirely painless, exit – even though she had signed for three years. Laura Hawn revealed later that her daughter had been under intense pressure to stay: 'My greatest fear for her was when she left "Laugh-In". She was offered the moon but she left, she said she wanted to grow.'

More likely, it was Art Simon who wanted her bank-balance to grow. Negotiations had been going on for some months between Simon and a number of Hollywood studio bosses, all of whom wanted to sign the Dingaling, as she became known. The Hawn entrepreneurial skills, learned in that little jewelry shop in Flowers Avenue and which were to demonstrate themselves to such dazzling effect later in her career, were kept well-hidden during these meetings. All most producers could see was a lively, lovely, blonde, a sizzling hot property with which the whole of United States, and apparently half the population of the civilised world, were in love. Comparisons were earnestly made around boardroom tables: one studio likened her to Marilyn Monroe, another to Lucille Ball. In truth, her appeal was unique and trailed in no one's footsteps, but studio bosses are not sensitive men and the sight of Goldie incurred in them all an uncontrollable lust; a lust for the money they were convinced she could generate.

In the end Art Simon focused on one studio and one producer: Columbia, and Mike Frankovich. For one who was born in Arizona, Frankovich's career had made a curious start, in British films – in

1952 he had produced *Decameron Nights,* starring a very young Joan Collins. He had just finished *Bob and Carol and Ted and Alice,* a well-received spoof on 1960s free love among the middle classes and was delighted to have a new, fresh talent to mould. In all, he was to make four pictures with Goldie.

Frankovich's first attempt to launch the gamine television star on to a box-office audience was a vehicle imported from France in one of Columbia's buying sprees, a farce by Pierre Barillet and Jean Pierre Gredy retitled *Cactus Flower.* The play, adapted by Abe Barrows, had transferred to Broadway with great success, with Lauren Bacall as the leading lady. Frankovich chose Walter Matthau as his leading man and employed Gene Saks, who had just finished working with Matthau and Jack Lemmon in the Neil Simon comedy *The Odd Couple,* to direct.

The story centres on prosperous, middle-aged dentist Julian Winston, a bachelor who is determined to stay that way. His professional life is organised by a starchy secretary, Stephanie, and his private life by his much younger mistress, Toni. Toni believes that Julian is married with a family and, in despair, attempts suicide. A horrified Julian tries to make amends by proposing marriage but Toni does not want to be a home-breaker, so Julian is forced to invent an unfaithful wife. A delighted Stephanie is only too happy to play this part, since it is one she has coveted for real, and seizing the moment, blossoms forth as a lovely, funny woman to whom Julian then proposes marriage.

On Broadway Lauren Bacall had triumphed as the long-neglected, frumpy secretary Stephanie but when it came to casting, Frankovich chose instead Ingrid Bergman, an actress ten years her senior. From a box-office perspective there was much cachet to be had in luring back the exiled Miss Bergman from her eighteen-year sojourn in Europe, even though by now the actress was fifty-four and fairly implausible as a thirty-five-year old dental secretary. But America was waiting with bated breath for Bergman's return, for she was as controversial a character as Hollywood had produced in half-a-century of moving pictures. Running away with director Roberto

Rossellini and abandoning her five-year old daughter Pia was one thing; getting pregnant by her lover while still married to her husband was quite another. In the early 1950s, film stars had to be squeaky-clean in public whatever they did in private, and a vicious American Press turned on Bergman with unprecedented venom. She received thousands of letters from fans condemning her behaviour and her once-great movie career was effectively terminated. So though Lauren Bacall was ideal for the part, Frankovich wanted it to go to Bergman. And while Goldie played her part for $50,000, Bergman received a staggering $800,000.

Both Goldie and Matthau, booked into the Beverly Hills Hotel, were extremely nervous of meeting their co-star. The face of *Casablanca* was legendary; the reputation from all those years of exile by now awesome. Frankovich recalled, 'Walter Matthau is notoriously unimpressionable. But just before Ingrid arrived, he looked very worried and kept nagging me "How do you think we will get on? Will she like me?"'

She did. The same question was voiced by a terrified Goldie, but later she reported, 'I thought I'd be intimidated by her, so intimidated I wouldn't be able to function. It wasn't that way at all, I didn't feel I had to compete. I just felt privileged to be in the same picture with her.'

Relations with her other co-star were what might be politely termed professional: 'Walter called me "Goldala". To him, I was like a child. He was amazingly clean. I had a cold, and he came on the set with a Lysol can and sprayed everything, including himself. God *forbid* that he should get sick.'

Though Hollywood, and by extension America, was willing an outstanding performance from Bergman, in the end it was no more than a charming interpretation of Bacall's stage role. But then Goldie's own performance could at best be described as charming also. As is so often the case with the Academy Awards, Goldie was *not* the Best Supporting Actress that year; but the sympathies of the Academy and the whole nation were with this unique, bubbling, giggling ray of sunshine that had entered the national consciousness three years before and had remained there ever since. Goldie won her Oscar as much for who she was as for what she'd done.

But that was in the future. For now Goldie's relationship with Gus Trikonis which had turned serious with her arrival in California, was ready to move to the next stage. After finishing filming *Cactus Flower,* Goldie and Gus flew to Honolulu and were married on 16 May 1969 in the District Court. The unshruggable Art Simon came too and acted as witness, signing his name Arthur I. Simon. The other witness, Shizue Teshima, was dragged in by Judge John Chinen from her secretarial work elsewhere in the court offices, a duty she performed cheerily enough as she had on many occasions before when couples turned up for marriage with not enough people to make the quorum. There was no photographer, recalls the judge now, no fuss, and the licence was arranged speedily: 'I just made sure they understood what they were entering into and made each of them promise to be true and faithful to each other. I was very surprised and very happy to marry them.' Though Goldie had always proclaimed herself a traditionalist when it came to family matters this, the most important day of her young life was arranged in haste and executed without finesse.

But being married was fine. The father-daughter relationship which Goldie had found so comforting in the bewildering world she was now inhabiting was reciprocated. 'There was something vulnerable about Goldie that made me want to watch out for her,' said her husband later. She was 'bananas', and if their relationship was not initially a love-match then it was at least 'amusement at first sight'.

Goldie had originally found a small apartment in Studio City across the street from Disneyland and when they first got together Goldie and Gus enjoyed a romantic, starving-in-a-garret existence. 'Those were marvellous days,' Gus recalled. 'We were flat broke but we were never lonely. Friends dropped by all the time and most of all, we had each other. We shared everything, that's what made our relationship so special.'

Very soon, though, the balance started to shift in the relationship. From being the caring, protective, more experienced figure, Gus found himself washed aside by the tide of public attention which engulfed his wife after her début in 'Laugh-In'. During this period, his career had progressed no further than dancing a routine with Debbie Reynolds in *The Unsinkable Molly Brown*: 'Things changed so quickly. Within a year we had moved from our little apartment to a home in Bel Air, and Goldie was earning an absolute fortune. Besides, she was getting all the phone calls and all the attention, and I found that very difficult to live with. No matter how much she tried to reassure me, I just couldn't see what she needed me for; I felt that I was in the way and a hindrance to her new-found fortune. Also she wanted to have children very badly and I wouldn't let her. I just didn't feel we were ready to start a family. I couldn't have supported them properly, and it was very important for me to do my fair share financially.'

Adding to the increasingly unsettled nature of the relationship were Goldie's continuing psychological problems, which had plagued her since her 'Good Morning, World' days. As the adulation and the publicity increased throughout her tenure at 'Laugh-In' she became increasingly traumatised by her stardom. In a rare interview Laura Hawn confided, 'It was the toughest period of my daughter's life. She couldn't come to terms with the world of success. You see, Goldie has always needed a nest, security. Sudden stardom offered her nothing to hold on to. It frightened her so much'.

The pressures continued to grow in the marriage: 'While everything was zooming for me, nothing was happening for him. For that whole period, after I was a hit in 'Laugh-In' and the movies started happening, all I was doing was working very hard to keep a hold on myself. I was in the marriage, and keeping that together was much more important to me than my work. I kept thinking of myself as a working girl, not as a star. I'd come home from the studio, make dinner, and be with Gus. We didn't go to parties because people treated me as The Object and ignored Gus. I wasn't flaunting my accomplishments in front of him. They didn't really have that much meaning to me anyway. I really held myself back a lot so my success wouldn't cause him pain.'

Later, as the relationship deteriorated her tone grew less sympathetic: 'Gus couldn't cope with my success. And my money. And the house. And all the pretty things he couldn't afford and I bought. I was made to feel guilty. It isn't in my nature to feel guilty for something I worked for, it never has been.'

# CHAPTER FIVE

# *Galatea*

*'It is the lark that sings so out of tune*
*Straining harsh discords and unpleasing sharps*
*Some say the lark makes sweet division'*
*– ibid.*

Having demonstrated the ease with which she could make the transition from television to movies, Goldie was ready for the next challenge. Her career was moving in exactly the way Art Simon had ordained it – away from high-demand, middle-income TV series to low-demand, high-income movies. Goldie's price was rising, though she only earned $50,000 from *Cactus Flower*, it was enough to buy the wall-to-wall carpets it had long been her desire to provide for her parents back in Takoma Park, something Laura Hawn had never been able to afford. Under Art Simon's guidance she made herself into a corporation and started to invest her growing income.

But having optioned her for three movies, Columbia Pictures were unsure about where to point their latest star next. Frankovich inconclusively trawled through possible vehicles for Goldie, but none of the scripts in development seemed right. In desperation he recalled a project he had bought several years before, an English comedy which had had a successful West End run called *There's A Girl In My Soup*. It was just another of those foreign projects bought off the shelf by the studio with the vague hope that a visionary writer might turn it into a halfway commercial property.

Essentially a parody of mid-sixties sexual manners, the theme was as English as roast beef: ageing Lothario with automated love-nest and bulging address-book falls for the gamine charms of a young girl he picks up off the street. But though he ends up bedding her, she's smart enough to ensure him wedding her too. Attempts to Americanise it, setting it first in New York, then Los Angeles, had failed and the project was put on ice. Now Frankovich returned to the people he had outbid for the rights, Britain's Boulting Brothers, and asked whether they might think about making it for Columbia Pictures. The Boultings' answer was yes, but with a proviso: they wanted their contracted star Peter Sellers to play Danvers, the roué TV personality.

Frankovich was appalled. Sellers's name, in the movie industry, was dirt. Despite a brilliant career embracing a dozen highly-crafted and exquisitely-executed portrayals including the cranky union leader Fred Kite in *I'm All Right Jack,* and despite being embraced by Hollywood, where he became a superstar with films including *Lolita, Dr Strangelove, A Shot In the Dark* and *I Love You, Alice B. Toklas,* no one now wanted to touch him. The reason lay in the filming a year or so before of Ian Fleming's last James Bond novel, *Casino Royale.* The film had proved to be one of the worst box-office flops in post-war movie history, despite a cast including David Niven, Orson Welles, Ursula Andress, Woody Allen, George Raft, Peter O'Toole and others. Though misconceived on an epic scale, with half-a-dozen directors including John Huston, Val Guest and Robert Parrish each filming segments which then had to be dovetailed together, and with an utterly hopeless script, millions were poured into the production in the hope that money, if nothing else, would save it.

Relatively speaking, all went well until after five weeks' filming, Sellers walked off the set never to return. 'He left them absolutely in the lurch,' one film veteran recalled later. 'He chose his own director and at the end of the five weeks when he disappeared, so did the director. It was disgraceful – the most unprofessional thing any actor could ever do.'

*Casino Royale* failed in the most spectacular fashion, with critics seeking out new depths of obloquy with which to lambaste it. It became a by-word in the industry for misconception, and for pinning one's hopes on a temperamental, some said mad, star. 'Hollywood had changed him,' one director said. 'There, they allowed him anything he wanted.'

And so the discarded and unused stage-sets for *Casino Royale* still

Cherry Alley.

*Above:* Musicians all – the Hawn brothers with their mother. Goldie's father, Rut, is on the right.

*Below:* Goldie at thirteen enjoys a picnic at a friend's house.

*Right:* Ocean City days: Goldie aged sixteen with schoolfriend Richard Harfield.

*Below:* The Powder Puff Club, Montgomery Blair High School, 1963. Goldie stands centre, front row.

*Above:* Family party time at Bay Ridge Beach – Goldie (right) with her adoptive family, the Colens.

*Left:* Happy at home – someone else's home. Goldie with the Colen family.

*Right:* Just another dancer with stardom on her mind: Goldie (top left) aged seventeen.

Party time in Ocean City: aged eighteen with schoolfriend Lesley Derow.

High School graduation – a smile, but no job prospects.

*Left:* Aged eighteen, and a new sultry look for a publicity photograph.

*Below:* Before stardom's embrace – a bit-part in the historical costume drama, *The Founders.*

*Above:* The defining moment – Goldie as Juliet, Williamsburg, Virginia, 1964

*Left:* The first step to stardom – playbill, summer 1964.

WILLIAMSBURG SHAKESPEAREAN PLAYERS

*Present*

# Romeo and Juliet

*Right:* A cute look for TV's 'Rowan and Martin's Laugh-In', but the body painting worried the censors.

*Left:* Goldie and husband number one, Gus Trikonis.

*Below:* Takoma Park's most famous daughter returns on a visit, 1969. Goldie is pictured with her childhood friend Sylvia Colen.

*Left:* There was always room for Dad in her shows: promotion material for Goldie Hawn TV Special *circa* 1970. Rut Hawn had a guest spot.

littered the British film studios at Shepperton and Pinewood, a living reminder of what it was to put one's faith in Peter Sellers. He was, to all intents, a washed-up star, a has-been. Yet the Boultings clung to the belief that if Sellers were to work for them, as he had in the pre-Hollywood days, they could control him. Frankovich, according to Roy Boulting, was terrified at the thought: 'Christ, you want me to go back to Columbia and say you want to use *Sellers*? I can't do that.'

The Boultings dug in their heels, saying they would not make the film without their star; and eventually Frankovich persuaded the Columbia paymasters that, if they wanted an instant comedy for Goldie, then *Soup* was it; that *Soup* could only be made by the Boulting Brothers; and that the price for making *Soup* was taking on the deranged Sellers. Finally, an agreement was reached that Goldie and Sellers would make the film together, after the Boultings had politely watched a screening of *Cactus Flower* and expressed their satisfaction at the potential of their new female lead. It went without saying that neither had seen 'Laugh-In' on television: there was then, as now, an intense snobbery in the motion picture industry about the small screen. If important directors and producers ever watched the box, they never let on. And though 'Laugh-In' had conquered Britain in just the way it conquered America, the Boultings genuinely remained in ignorance of Goldie's enormous pull.

Sellers was allowed no say in his choice of co-star. Though he may not have seen it that way, he was on probation, and this film was his last chance for retribution. The Boultings were prepared to play hardball and were more concerned with pleasing their paymasters at Columbia than deferring to the cranky behaviour of the man who, after all, they themselves had made a star. Sellers's opinion of Goldie was not sought and, for once, he kept his thoughts to himself.

Goldie arrived in Britain, her first protracted trip to a foreign country, in the spring of 1970. The flight was particularly arduous and she went straight to bed at the Dorchester Hotel in Mayfair. That evening, she was due to meet her director Roy Boulting and co-star Sellers, together with Boulting's wife Hayley Mills, for dinner at Le Français, a small restaurant in the Fulham Road.

'The car brought Goldie from the Dorchester and I met for the first time this woman who was charming, with a lively sense of fun. I felt an immediate rapport,' recalls Boulting. 'But this was not an easy meeting. Peter was late, decidedly late, and I thought, "You rude bastard. Here's this girl arriving in this country for the first time to play in a film and you can't be bothered to show up." When he finally did I was very angry, because he was very high on something or another. And because he was a man who resisted with a certain anger the advance of years, he was desperately trying to show Goldie he was cool. He kept clicking his fingers in the way people did at that time to show they were "swinging". This went on stupidly and quite spoiled the conversation – this was the opportunity for two stars to meet each other, to look at each other, and to talk. They were, after all, going to be spending the next eight weeks together in close proximity and it was incumbent on them both to create a good impression. I didn't know what to say to Goldie – I wanted to tell her, "Look, this man is a brilliant artist but a damn nuisance." I felt so sorry for her.'

By 11.30, when jet-lag was beginning to kick in, Boulting rounded off the dinner and went out to order a car for Goldie. But Sellers, still manically clicking his fingers, insisted on taking her himself in his Rolls Royce convertible. When they arrived at the Dorchester, Sellers, by now almost hysterical with passion, tried to talk his way up to Goldie's suite. At the time, she had been married less than a year and Sellers had only recently announced his engagement to Miranda Quarry, stepdaughter of the wealthy Lord Mancroft. For the best part of an hour they sat, Goldie dropping with jet-lag and trying to be polite to her rapacious and urgent co-star, while determined to keep his hands off her. Sellers's ham-fisted and lengthy seduction, under the bemused gaze of the night doorman, was a failure, and it put a distance between the two stars.

But whatever the tensions created on that first night, Goldie was determined not to allow a permanent rift to develop between her and her leading man. 'Once we started filming she was as professional in her approach, and a delight to work with, as he was unprofessional and an absolute shit,' recalls John Boulting.

On the first day of shooting, in the middle of the afternoon, Sellers halted a scene between him and Goldie and came over to speak to Boulting.

'That continuity girl,' he said.

'Yes?' said Boulting, startled.

'Get rid of her.'

'Whaaaat?' exclaimed Boulting.

'Get rid of her. Now.'

Boulting asked what the matter was.

'She doesn't like me. She's got a very evil look. And I don't like that look of hers at all. Get *rid* of her!'

Boulting later explained to friends that the continuity girl, an extremely pleasant and efficient employee, had suffered a bad accident which left a large dent in her forehead. She was very conscious of it and consequently very quiet. Sellers had picked the most vulnerable person on the set to humiliate. Boulting, determined to avoid a row on the floor, thought quickly.

'I'm sorry you feel that way, Peter,' he said smoothly. 'She would never have done the film had you not been in it. She had other offers, but when she heard you were making this film she said, "That's the film for me."'

'Oh. Oh, all right.'

All this was played out before Goldie's eyes but the selfish bastard, as Boulting calls Sellers, did not win the day. Whatever fears she had of her vindictive and predatory co-star soon she was able to share them with Gus Trikonis, who was flown in by Columbia to make a documentary about the making of *Soup*, whether as a sop to their star as a protective measure is not explained: certainly there were plenty of directors in Britain available to do the not particularly demanding work, and certainly it quashed what Boulting described as Sellers's 'big ambition' – to bed his co-star offset as well as on.

Shooting progressed bumpily, Sellers taking a grim delight in basing his character on the Earl of Lichfield, a photographer cousin of the Queen whose speciality was girly calendars. The actor Graham Stark, Sellers's long-time friend and associate, recalls driving down to

Shepperton on Sellers's invitation to take pictures of Goldie. A gifted photographer, Stark had occasionally taken portraits of Sellers's leading ladies to general satisfaction, but on this occasion when he arrived on set after lunch the first person he saw was Roy Boulting, white-faced and agitated. Boulting pulled him behind a piece of scenery and whispered hoarsely, 'What do you do? What do you do with him?'

'What are you talking about?' stuttered Stark.

'Oh, Christ,' moaned Boulting, 'we're having such a day with him.' And as Stark's eyes accustomed themselves to the lights he could see a motionless set with a cameraman standing still, looking intently at the ceiling. Sitting in a pool of light was Goldie, 'looking a bit crushed, a bit dejected, gazing into space' recalls Stark, while further off into the distance he could see his friend having yet another terrible tantrum. Mentally Stark consigned his much anticipated photo-shoot to the waste-bin and turned back to Boulting who was whispering, 'What can we say? What can we do? What's the angle?'

Stark picked up his camera case, shook his head sadly, muttered, 'Nothing to do with me, mate' and trudged back to the car park. It made a mockery of Boulting's boast to Mike Frankovich that he and his brother could control the wayward star.

The actor Nicky Henson, who played Jimmy, recalls that it would often take sixteen or seventeen takes to get Sellers up to concert-pitch, by which time his fellow-actors were exhausted from the repetition. Henson describes the atmosphere on set as 'tricky' and between takes he sat with Goldie on the edge of the set while she crocheted: 'I remember Goldie finding Peter's behaviour very strange. She had just got married and I think she wanted to be anywhere but stuck in Shepperton making a movie. She was terribly homesick and I used to sit and talk to her as she crocheted. She was doing a wonderful job, very professional, they were very lucky to have got her – they obviously got a bargain.'

Boulting himself blithely brushes off the question of the nude scene he asked Goldie to shoot, claiming it was in the script and that, when asked, she did it without demur: 'She had to do this scene and no one had told her about it. But she was very game.' Boulting told her he would clear the set and explained that the scene would be in long-shot and merely show her getting out of bed and walking around it into the bathroom: 'It came as a bit of a shock to her, but she did it.'

That is not Goldie's recollection. Given her still-potent feelings about – as she saw it – her bodily inadequacies, it is unlikely that she would have agreed in advance of signing her contract to the nude scene. Almost certainly that arrived with one of the daily rewrites, cleverly providing Boulting with newspaper headlines around the world – 'Goldie Strips In New Movie!' – but running against the wholesome image she was intent on creating around her name. Later she tried to have the footage, innocuous though it was, removed from the final cut, but without success. 'I don't think I'll ever do another,' was her curt comment when asked how she felt about the scene.

'We were well into the filming schedule when I learned I was expected to strip. Well, that wasn't in *my* book. Like I said, I'm real middle class, and there was nothing abut nudity in the contract, so I refused to play a love-making scene in the nude. Nobody ever suggested Peter remove any of *his* clothes, so why should I?'

The filming of *There's A Girl In My Soup* was a testing experience for both its stars. For the first time, Goldie had come up against one of the motion picture industry's monsters, yet since she was so new she could not complain about a well-established and much-loved co-star. This was the moment where she had to learn to bite her tongue when asked about working with Sellers, and it was only much later that she allowed herself the luxury of offering a hint of what it was really like. Even then her answer was a masterpiece of understatement: 'I loved Peter very much. He was such a fine and delicate and, at times, neurotic spirit. It was like balancing a friend on the fine point of a needle, because he was thrown off-balance by anything and everything. He also had one of the great comedy senses of all time, understanding what was funny. On this film we had terrible problems, I just crossed it off as a bad day at work, but the tensions revved Peter up to the point where he was unable to function. To me, a movie is a movie and, Christ, I'm just thankful that I get to make my living this way. To him, it was more than that. It crossed into his work. He was a great master. Unfortunately, it mastered him.'

As for Sellers, apart from the unfortunate continuity girl, the director and the various other targets of his poisonous temper, he had major difficulty with his willing, compliant, ever-smiling co-star. In the middle of shooting came the news that Goldie had won an Oscar for her part in *Cactus Flower*.

A shudder went round cast and crew when the announcement was made, for Sellers by now could not bear the mention of his fellow actors. The idea that a girl, still new to the business and young enough to be his daughter, could walk away with the greatest prize the movie industry could bestow, a prize that had so far eluded him, was unbearable. Sellers had been nominated for his 1964 performance in *Dr Strangelove* and with the benefit of hindsight it can be seen to be clearly an Oscar-winning performance; while Goldie's part as Toni in *Cactus Flower*, while delightful enough, was barely worthy of the Best Supporting Actress Oscar and was probably won on a 'sympathy' vote – she was by now headline news in US newspapers virtually every day – and Sellers's bitterness went deep. Roy Boulting judiciously confined on-set celebrations to a glass of Champagne, Sellers was given a bunch of flowers to hand to his co-star, a photograph was taken, and the problem was got over as quickly as possible.

Still concerned to make a good impression, Goldie took Boulting's lead and made light of her Academy Award, something she was to rue more and more in later years as a second Oscar continued to elude her: 'My greatest regret is I won it too early. It came too soon, too easily. I wasn't even there to accept it, I was in London doing a film and when I got back, nobody cared. I didn't even like myself in that film.'

The night she won the Oscar, she forgot she had been nominated: 'I just went to sleep that night and somebody called me the next morning with the news – "Whaaat?"'

Filming shifted to the South of France, Goldie staying at the

Carlton in Cannes, her co-star at Cap Ferrat. By June, largely thanks to a completely professional and uncomplaining performance from Goldie, *There's A Girl In My Soup* wrapped, on time and on budget.

Goldie had been away for three months, her first protracted visit abroad, and could not wait to get home. Gus had remained by her side for the whole three-month shoot and by now the couple were getting on each others' nerves. Though desperate to make his own way in the movies, he had made little impression on anyone concerned with the production and was seen by most as a mere 'Mr Goldie' figure, keeping her happy while the buffets of Sellers's incandescent temper fell elsewhere. Few newspapers took the trouble to notice him, though one wrote, 'Her husband, a hand-some ex-dancer who is the same age as Goldie [sic] but smokes a meerschaum pipe as if to underline the fact that he has grown up rather more responsibly, tries to sober up the conversation. He is potentially a serious-minded young man inclined to talk about socio-economics and political matters as if to reassure himself that the world is not entirely nutty. He has invited himself on a day out with Goldie as she is ferried around in a Rolls Royce … and is clearly *de trop*.' In other words, this man is boring. Such references, few though they were, served only to drive a wedge further between husband and wife.

Three months before, on her arrival in London, Goldie had told a newspaper, 'I'm determined our careers won't keep us apart. We won't allow it. I personally don't want to go on location again for as long as this. Distance doesn't always make the heart grow fonder. We are all human and we all have certain needs that must sooner or later be satisfied. So unless you hold together physically and work at that, you're not going to have a marriage. And a happy marriage is more important to me and more fulfilling than any kind of possible fame.'

Three months later, maybe, she would have liked to retract some of those thoughts, for in her absence Art Simon had been working hard on the next steps she must take up the career ladder. 'He's the brains of the outfit,' conceded Goldie. 'All these fabulous things in my life are thanks to him. Myself, I've always just let things happen. If

I had stayed on my own I'd probably still be dancing in the chorus at the Desert Inn.'

The fabulous things continued to present themselves on an almost daily basis. When trouble loomed – as it did when a potato-chip company issued without permission 10,000 posters bearing her giggling face – Art Simon rode to the rescue. He slapped a $1.5 million lawsuit on the errant company, saying his blissfully unaware client was 'embarrassed and humiliated' by this invasion of her privacy and the trouble went away. Yet on the domestic front things remained uncomfortable between her and Gus. The return to Los Angeles and their apartment in Studio City only served to remind husband and wife of the ever-growing gulf between their two careers. Only five years before, Gus Trikonis had been the voice of experience who could guide Goldie's first tentative steps on the road to stardom; now he was unable to keep up as those steps turned from a stroll to a mad gallop.

For Sellers and Goldie there was a permanent parting of the ways. Bitterly, Sellers learned that a love-struck Billy Wilder, creator of some of Hollywood's greatest classics including *Some Like It Hot*, *Sunset Boulevard*, *Double Indemnity*, *Ninotchka*, *The Seven-Year Itch* and *The Apartment*, was writing an original screen story for Goldie, while all he had to look forward to was a string of unmemorable flops over the next five years until *The Return of the Pink Panther* restored his fortunes in 1975. And yet who was the winner in this sorry cinematic encounter? Sellers walked away with a $350,000 fee for *Soup*; Goldie received just $50,000.

Flying back to the States, Goldie finished off a glorious year by collecting a clutch of awards to accompany her Oscar, including the National Association of Theatre Owners' award for female star, the Hollywood Women's Press Club award for most co-operative new-comer of the year, and the *Los Angeles Times* Woman of the Year award. But the greatest thing that happened to Goldie in 1970, according to the young star herself, was a return to TV with a special, 'Pure Goldie': 'It was the best thing of everything in that year. And you know what the best part of that was? Me dancing. Like I was back in the chorus again.' This desire to return to basics was understandable, given the buffets she had recently faced. The scenario recalled her days as a chorus girl, allowed her to sing a medley of Beatles hits, and made much of a comedy sketch about an aeroplane that is so vast it has its own swimming pool and barbecue pit. Guests included chat-show host Johnny Carson and former 'Laugh-In' team-mate Ruth Buzzi. But the London *Times* critic, Leonard Buckley summed up the general mood: 'She blinks. She bubbles. She giggles. And we are at once enslaved. But a girl needs material to keep us that way, and that was what our Goldie just did not have. Of course the show was mildly entertaining. But there were long tracts of it in which you had to keep reminding yourself of the real ability of its star. The wide-eyed mocking verve that makes her so special never got a chance.' The show was a disappointment for all concerned and an experiment Goldie was not likely to repeat in the near future.

If the material was thin, it in no way detracted from the way in which Goldie was able to enslave journalists and writers assigned to cover her story. The US *TV Guide*'s Rowland Barber watched a routine in preparation for the show and gave his first-hand account of what it was like to witness Goldie the dancer. 'It is a perpetual astonishment to see Miss Hawn at work,' he wrote. 'She has, in person, the pale translucence of bone china held up to the light. Caught in mid-flight she is all saucer-eyes, goldilocks, dimples, and twinkle-toes – a breathless creature, not quite real, who somehow followed the wrong Yellow Brick Road and wound up in a television studio. Yet, as a performer, she is just plain strong. She possesses an inexhaustible fount of kinetic energy and grace.'

'Laugh-In' left Goldie with few fond memories of TV: 'I left that series because I refuse to be a slave to anyone or anything. That's all behind me now. No more funny faces. I think my future's in movies since making *Cactus Flower* and *There's A Girl In My Soup* but I don't intend closing the door on TV – it's been too good for me.'

Of Art Simon, she added, 'He saved me from staying in a line of chorus dancers for the rest of my days. He saw me dancing in a television show with twelve other girls. He said he couldn't take his eyes off me, because I had potential, or something. At first I was suspicious: I'd been dancing in Vegas where some of the biggest cowboys in Texas used to date the girls from the show, used to pay $100 for their company. But I was never interested.'

Simon remembered, 'I went backstage after the programme and I gave her my card. I asked her if she did anything else besides dance. She thought I was propositioning her, giving her the same routine she'd heard hundreds of times before in Vegas; she refused to phone me, so I phoned her. I told her I was a legitimate agent, that my intentions were strictly honourable and all I wanted to do for her was get her work. Finally I convinced her, and I had her working on "Good Morning, World".'

By this time Simon considered that Goldie had put enough clear blue water between Goldie and 'Laugh-In' to allow her a brief return to the show. It was not a success. Schlatter's continued downward pressure, changes of personnel and a bunker attitude towards Goldie made for a very bumpy ride through rehearsals: 'It was a strange experience. The writers didn't recognise that I'd grown since I left the show – it was almost like when they first hired me and didn't know what to do with me. Now, I go back as a guest and they have me reading lines as if nothing had happened in my life since I left.'

In truth there was a mutual suspicion fostered by the age-old TV-versus-Hollywood prejudice, and everyone felt uncomfortable: 'It wasn't quite the same old gang. There were all these new people standing off to the side, watching me, staring at me – oh, did I get anxious vibrations from them!'

In an echo of her stand-off with her old school, Goldie added, 'They say you can't go home again. Well, you can but it's awfully hard. Like the people I knew before – before all this – girls I danced with in the chorus, or my old teachers. It's so hard to make them understand – I've grown, sure, but I'm still Goldie.'

Another small cloud on the horizon presented itself when Mr Blackwell, the Hollywood designer notorious for issuing his Worst Dressed Awards, chose to include Goldie in his New Year's list. Accompanying her were Sophia Loren, Carrie Snodgrass and Faye

Dunaway, but for Goldie he coined the sharp reprimand, 'A shaggy dog on stilts.'

Meanwhile negotiations continued for the crucial follow-up to her Oscar-winning performance in *Cactus Flower*. Art Simon, Frankovich and Goldie herself all had high hopes of the promises made by Billy Wilder that he would write an original screenplay for Goldie. Speaking to the veteran Hollywood writer Roderick Mann she enthused, 'It's exciting working with him, isn't it? He's promised to tell me all about his experiences with Marilyn Monroe when they filmed *Some Like It Hot*. He was the first person to spot me, actually. He saw me in 'Laugh-In' and told Mike Frankovich that I'd be right for *Cactus Flower*. So far I'm just a personality, but I'm working on my acting – I know Billy wants me to tackle a part where I'll have to act. Though I have done some big roles in the past,' she assured the writer. 'I played Juliet when I was eighteen …'

Things might have gone decidedly differently if Wilder, by now sixty-four, had kept his promise. Behind him, apart from the quintessential Hollywood comedy *Some Like It Hot*, his credits included *Witness for the Prosecution*, and *Irma La Douce* as well as half a dozen Oscars for writing and directing *Lost Weekend*, *Sunset Boulevard* and *The Apartment*. But by now his powers were waning. His most recent film, *The Private Life of Sherlock Holmes*, had opened to mixed reviews, and whether he had Goldie in mind for the part in his next offering, *Avanti* – which finally went to another blonde, Juliet Mills – history does not record. If he had, it would have done Goldie no favours since the film, which starred Jack Lemmon, became another also-ran. Thereafter Wilder only made one more movie, *Fedora*, and the chance to turn Goldie into a second Monroe – a vain dream at any event since she was funnier but with nowhere near the sexual allure – was lost.

Whatever disappointment was felt over this failed project, it soon disappeared when the prospect of a film with Warren Beatty presented itself. By the early 1970s Beatty was established as Hollywood's number one heart-throb, having made his début a decade earlier in Elia Kazan's *Splendor in the Grass*. His leading ladies had included

Vivien Leigh, Elizabeth Taylor, Natalie Wood, Jean Seberg, Leslie Caron and, most famously, Faye Dunawaye in *Bonnie and Clyde* and Julie Christie in *McCabe and Mrs Miller*. The Christie/Beatty romance had dominated Tinseltown's gossip columns for the past five years but the affair climaxed with *McCabe* and was virtually over by the time Mike Frankovich introduced Goldie and Beatty.

The attraction was instantaneous and reciprocal. Both were suffering in their relationships and as production of *$*, or *Dollars*, or *The Heist*, as the film was variously known, got under way they only had eyes for each other. The twinning of their talents seemed like a surefire thing, but as Hollywood has proved again and again, there is no such thing as a guaranteed box-office success.

Directed by the veteran Richard Brooks, who had *In Cold Blood* and *Cat On a Hot Tin Roof* among his credits, the story centred around Beatty playing a security expert who decides to crack the foolproof burglar-alarm system he has just installed in a German bank. Goldie played Dawn Divine, a callgirl who becomes his partner in the heist by telling him of the illegal deposits of money her clients have put in the bank. None of the men, the couple reason, would dare complain to police when their ill-gotten gains were stolen.

Brooks, born Ruben Sax, was an obsessive who believed in keeping a tight grip on his actors, his crew and his script. After spending six weeks touring Norway and other European countries he settled on Hamburg, Munich, and the surrounding mountains for locations and ordered that principal filming should commence in Munich in November 1970. *Dollars* was shot almost entirely on location, with the bank scenes filmed in a converted Munich art gallery.

Goldie and her co-star soon learned from Tom Shaw II, the assistant director, that Brooks's style was to keep actors and technicians completely in the dark. They would not be allowed to see the daily rushes because the director believed it would ruin their performance. At best he could be expected to hand out a couple of scenes at a time, and there was a strong suspicion that he was writing the script as he went along. The veteran cameraman Petrus Schloemp recalls, 'Brooks used the script only as a starting point and liked to improvise. He was a control freak, very firm with the actors. And though he was a smoker himself he banned smoking on the set because he claimed it stopped people concentrating and meant they only had one hand to work with.'

Goldie's reaction to Brooks's oddity was to play it straight. As always, she turned up on time, word-perfect, make-up complete, and with a smile on her face. Beatty, on the other hand, found it more difficult to cope. One evening he confronted the director: 'Jesus, Richard, how do I act without a script?' but the inscrutable Brooks dismissed his star, saying the next scene would be with him the following day. Beatty's reaction was, 'How the hell am I supposed to work out the character's motivation if I don't know what's happening to him ten minutes ahead?' But suggestions for his character's motivation and development went unheeded by Brooks and on one occasion when the director asked Beatty to go to a window and look down Beatty responded, 'Ah. I have to look down. What is out there? What am I looking at? Why am I looking out?'

'*Just look out, Warren*,' bellowed Brooks.

By comparison, Goldie had found a way to charm the nightmarish director. She would tease him and continually play up to him, and Brooks, pretending to be exasperated, melted. Even so, there were moments of acute discomfort as she laboured under his heavy-handed ordinance. Years later she singled out *Dollars* as the one film she would like to erase from the archives: 'I just didn't like my character or what I did with her. It was just a totally unthought-out, unconscious performance. I remember one scene in which I felt very manipulated. That was when I had to look at the money for the first time in the safe-deposit box. The director said, "When you look at this money I want it to be an *orgasmic* experience for you. You've never seen this amount of money before and I want it to be just like you're having an orgasm." I felt I wanted to dig a hole as deep as I could, crawl in it and out the other side, because it was as if I had all those people on the set out there suddenly watching me have a private moment. If I were asked to do the scene today I'd say, "Sorry." Then, I just didn't have the guts.'

`The tension was rising on-set and off. Petrus Schloemp recalls that the lack of a script also made the technical side of movie-making much harder. This was coupled with an unusually warm winter in Bavaria, so there was nowhere to film the dénouement, a crucial stunt sequence where, during a car chase, a car slides on an ice-covered lake, cracks the ice, and slowly sinks into the water. Eventually a suitable lake was discovered at Lillehammer in Norway and cast and crew were shipped out.

Even then there were problems. Officials in Lillehammer declared that they could not dump a car in the lake because of the likely effects of pollution and, in the end, an agreement was brokered that the car's engine would be taken out so there could be no fuel leakage, and that the car would be winched back out again next spring (the water was more than 100 metres deep and when the thaw came it was virtually impossible to find). The stunt took ten days to film, one reason being that because the engine had been taken out the car could not get up to speed to perform the stunt. Then again, because the engine had been removed the car was no longer heavy enough to crack the ice and sink.

Beatty became disenchanted, recalled Petrus Schloemp: 'Julie Christie was on set for two or three weeks and while she was visiting he couldn't concentrate. Very often the next morning he wouldn't come to work even though the crew, Goldie, everybody was ready to shoot.' Richard Brooks was furious. He talked about replacing Beatty with another actor and grew increasingly unhinged as Beatty became more and more nonchalant about punctuality. The director sent a car for him one day to the Four Seasons Hotel in Hamburg, but the driver was unable to locate him. Finally at 11 o'clock Beatty turned up on the set complaining he was hung over, and was sent home. 'Warren, did you read your contract? This is *not* the way I like to work!'

Cast and crew stayed at a hotel outside Hamburg called Belle Oue and in the evenings would sit and drink in the piano bar with their director. Beatty, bored, would go out on the prowl with a couple of males from the crew, while Goldie would read her lines and go early to bed to do her 'beauty regime'.

Wives and partners are deemed a liability when films are made on location and the fleeting visits of both Julie Christie, now at the very end of her relationship with Beatty, and Gus Trikonis, were viewed with barely-veiled hostility. Trikonis had been wheeled out to direct a documentary on the making of the film, as he had for *Soup*. 'Separations are just no way to run a marriage,' Goldie had commented on her arrival in Germany. But where with *Soup* there was an anxious Roy Boulting keen to keep his leading man out of his leading lady's boudoir, there was no such paternal interest from Richard Brooks. As far as he was concerned, his stars could fall in love and all it would do would increase the onscreen tension. By the time the production reached Norway, he had got his wish.

Though for Goldie and Beatty there was some pleasure to be got from their special closeness, there was little to be gained from making the film. 'It is hard to understand why Beatty would turn down several movies which became major hits then turn up in one that barely challenged his ability,' wrote his biographer John Parker. 'Caper movies were fashionable, and this one had the benefit of an ingenious plot to rob a bank, but it was frivolous and lightweight. The critics poured scorn on him for wasting their time, not to mention his own. He too seemed to have coasted in it, treating it as nothing more than a paid vacation.'

'I thought it was going to be a big picture,' Goldie later remarked ruefully. 'It smelled like a hit but it was a total bust. I can't look at the picture now. I've seen it one-and-a-half times and the second time, I had to turn it off.'

The critics hated *Dollars*; nor were the Columbia studio bosses exactly ecstatic, since it made very little of the folding stuff at the box-office.

The only consolation during the whole débâcle was the quixotic determination of the students of Dundee University that Goldie should become the ancient institution's new Rector. This post, ceremonial insofar as it existed at all, required very little of its incumbent apart from a ritual visit to the Scottish city in order to be cheered by the admiring undergraduates. The ensuing campaign, launched in part to rid themselves of the present incumbent, the actor Peter Ustinov, included the distribution of 15,000 pasta models of Goldie in bowls of soup, in honour of her last movie. For the unlettered actress, it was a charming gesture warmly to be welcomed but sadly, due to a postal strike in Britain, her nomination acceptance form was never received. One student sold his car and tape-recorder so that he could fly to Hamburg to deliver a second form, but the mission was doomed to failure: the world had moved on and Goldie had returned to America.

There she nearly caused her publicist heart failure when, during the course of a press conference, she advocated the idea of an open marriage. The assembled journalists, mouths agape, took notes but in general forbore from writing them up: the story fitted neither their nor their editors' preconceptions of *what* Goldie Hawn was. Goldie was taken outside and given a sharp dressing-down by the publicist: 'Are you crazy? Whatever you may do in your private life, keep it away from the press. They build you up, then they destroy you. Don't *ever* give them that chance.' It was advice that Goldie was to follow with only the occasional exception.

To keep his star fresh before the public gaze, Art Simon signed with Dave Victorson, entertainments director of the Las Vegas Hilton, for Goldie to star in her own live show. It was not so very long ago in her short life that Goldie had been in the world's gambling capital as a hoofer, treated as the lowest of the low until she could take no more. Now there was the prospect of a triumphant return to the place where she had experienced her lowest ebb.

She took along Gus as her dance director, her father as a jobbing musician and various other friends. 'She seemed to be surrounded by a whole bunch of people, all being supported by her,' says Sy Green, who bumped into his fellow musician Rut Hawn at the Hilton. 'Rut invited us up to Goldie's penthouse and when she saw me she gave me a great big hug and a kiss. But there was a little dog messing on those expensive carpets. My wife asked Goldie: "Doesn't that bother you? Aren't you worried about this?"' But it seemed not to.

Goldie's great hero Elvis Presley had made his famous comeback in Las Vegas in 1969, blowing away the dreary years of a sterile film career with his electrifying reappearance in top-to-toe leather. In an instant, Presley's decision to play Vegas turned the city into a hipper place: until then it had been the exclusive territory of such oldsters as Frank Sinatra, Tony Bennett, Dean Martin and Sammy Davis Jr. Barbra Streisand had done a show, unsuccessfully, and now it was Goldie's turn. She was given Presley's penthouse suite – 'It was quite something – he'd shot just about every chandelier in that place. There were bullet-holes in the ceiling they'd patched up as well' – and set about rehearsing.

Dee Dee Wood, later to choreograph *Mary Poppins* and *The Sound of Music* was hired to create the dance routines and Billy Barnes from 'Laugh-In' was brought in as musical director. The show was road-tested in Colorado before being brought into town and the Hilton audiences loved it. Equally, the experience so shook Goldie she never attempted a show outside a TV studio ever again. Joe Delaney, the entertainments editor of the *Las Vegas Sun* for more than thirty years, says she overstretched herself: 'Gladys Knight and the Pips opened her act. Their closing number before Goldie came on was 'Help Me Make It Through the Night'. Now Gladys is a power-house singer and Goldie made the mistake of coming on and following Gladys's dramatic ballad with a dramatic ballad of her own; she came out a very poor second and never really recovered.

'She would have been better off giving the audience the Goldie they knew from films and from "Laugh-In", the little sexpot wise-cracker. Instead she tried to be a serious singer and it just didn't work. She is not basically a singer, she was a dancer, but again it was a throwaway. I don't know what they were trying to prove in that show but whoever she was portraying, it wasn't her.

'Had she opted to come on as Goldie Hawn, and not as Ann-Margret or Shirley Maclaine or Juliet Prouse, it would have been fine. But she was in the mode of other types of performer when she was quite a unique performer in her own right. That uniqueness was not exploited and not used, it was a big mistake.'

Billy Barnes concurs. 'It was not a big hit, I hate to say.'

The Hilton's entertainments manager Dave Victorson, cocka-hoop when he signed Goldie, was more subdued when he saw the show. He confided to friends that he hoped if Goldie came back that she would get it right next time. But she never did, and a dozen years later in an interview with *Playboy* she said, 'It's one of the things I'd like to forget about.'

Returning to Los Angeles was no escape from this career-low and it was around this time that she started to rely heavily upon the assistance, comfort and support of a number of psychics, among them Virginia-based Patricia Maclaine. Today Maclaine says, 'I don't know how many others she goes to. She's been a client for twenty-seven or twenty-eight years.' Sadly, being a psychic she can remember little of what she has told her client after a consultation, but Goldie increasingly turned to such people as she began to rely less and less on her analyst: the crutch she needed to help support her was getting lighter.

Now came Goldie's fourth movie. Whatever the merits of *Butterflies Are Free* as a stage-play there was no denying it was the wrong vehicle for Goldie: too low-key, too static and lacking in real drama or humour. The audiences who flocked to the cinemas to see their 'Laugh-In' girl came away disappointed and even the critics, Goldie devotees to a man, sounded deflated in their praise. It was time to think again and now that the Universal contract had been completed it was time to look elsewhere.

Somewhere along the way Goldie found time, with Art Simon's encouragement, to extend her appeal into the recording field. Other Hollywood stars had successfully combined a singing career with films and, as the daughter of a professional musician, it seemed a perfect fit. Later the producer Andrew Wickham, an English-born protégé of the Rolling Stones's manager Andrew Loog Oldham, was to describe the LP album *Goldie* as being ahead of its time, but this was probably said with tongue firmly in cheek. Recorded in no less than six separate studios in Nashville and Los Angeles, *Goldie* had hands-on help from Buck Owens, Dolly Parton, Porter Wagoner, the Buckaroos and other country luminaries; and the album contained songs by Bob Dylan, Van Morrison, Joni Mitchell and Donovan. In theory the piece should have worked well but with the possible exception of Jerry Ragovoy and George David Weiss's 'Ring Bell', Wickham and his fledgling recording star could not find the magic. Though 'Ring Bell' might have made a breakthrough single, for at this time Goldie's appeal was at an all-time high and her looks were at their peak, the decision was taken to release Joni Mitchell's 'Carey'. Sadly the disparity between the two women's vocal quality – as with Gladys Knight – was all too apparent; as an experiment it was deemed a failure not to be repeated, nor spoken of again.

But once more Goldie found some consolation in this unhappy foray into pastures new: she got to employ Rut Hawn as a session-musician, the first recording he had ever made, and she found further comfort in the arms of her handsome producer. Marianne Faithfull in her autobiography *Faithfull* drily observes, 'Andy Wickham had a fixation about blondes. He finally found his Galatea in Goldie Hawn.'*

No further attempts were made to record Goldie's voice for another twenty-five years, until George Martin bravely included her in his curious tribute album to the Beatles: along with such figures as Jim Carrey grunting *I Am the Walrus* and Sean Connery intoning *In My Life,* Goldie gave an enthusiastic rendition of *A Hard Day's Night.* As with nearly all novelty records it failed to capture the public imagination.

'Laugh-In' had given Goldie her identity, *Cactus Flower* had given her an Oscar, *There's A Girl In My Soup* and *Dollars* had maintained the public's lively anticipation of her next surprise; but *Butterflies Are Free* signalled an end to all that. In the space of four movies the Columbia boss, Mike Frankovich, had virtually reduced America's most glamorous new star to the status of an also-ran. Goldie's profile was still high in Hollywood – an Oscar is an Oscar is an Oscar – but the Columbia studios were unequal to the task of finding her proper platforms

* Virgil's Galatea seduced Acis with her song. '*Galatea … lascivia puella'* wrote the drooling poet.

to exhibit her undeniable talent and charm. But the contract at Columbia was now complete, and it was time to look elsewhere.

Even in the business, however, there were worries. The Oscar had hiked her fee dramatically but, asked the money-men, will we be getting value for money if we take her on? Or will whatever film we put her in look like a watered-down version of *Butterflies*? Of her Oscar-winning contemporaries, Barbra Streisand, who won Best Actress with *Funny Girl* and Jane Fonda, who also won Best Actress for *Klute*, no such anxieties were being expressed. In the year that Goldie made *Butterflies*, Streisand had made *What's Up, Doc?* and was about to shoot *The Way We Were* with Robert Redford; Fonda was moving on to *Steelyard Blues* with Donald Sutherland. There was no contest. Goldie, with her special appeal and a massive reservoir of goodwill for having made the nation laugh could, inexplicably, boast no such future.

Long and anguished talks with Art Simon failed to produce a single script worthy of her attention. Goldie felt frustrated by the constraints placed around her. She viewed herself as a serious person – certainly, those who knew her agreed she took herself terribly seriously – and would have welcomed a wider critical acclaim. Playing the ditsy blonde, though it paid the bills, was getting boring. And it was just a shade demeaning.

Over at the Universal studios Richard Zanuck and David Brown had just arrived on a contract to produce feature films. First up was *The Sting*, which was to earn them four Oscars by trading on the double appeal of Paul Newman and Robert Redford. But on the list of other projects Zanuck and Brown were keen to develop was a story called *The Sugarland Express*; and a director who had yet to make a full-length cinema feature, Steven Spielberg.

At the same time the efforts of Art Simon had finally secured Goldie, in October 1972, a three-film contract with Universal. It was not the smartest deal going, since by allying herself to a single studio for her four previous films Goldie had seen her stock fall with each successive production; who knew that the same might not happen again to the point where she was unemployable? But it was the best Art Simon could come up with, and she took it.

*The Sugarland Express* was not as it sounded: far from a jolly caper aboard a train it was a stark tale of poor white trash on the run, with death as its inevitable conclusion. Quite unlike anything Goldie had ever tackled before, it came as a relief to her – and, as it happened, to Zanuck and Brown: by the time she committed to the film in December, half-a-dozen front-rank actresses had already turned it down. These actresses, maybe, smelled something that Zanuck and Brown could not. Nor were the producers inclined to listen when they went to the head of Universal, Lew Wasserman, to tell him that Spielberg and *The Sugarland Express* were a surefire pairing. 'We think Steve has a great future,' Wasserman told them. 'But I have to tell you we do not have faith in this project.'

But Goldie was not privy to this: she was simply delighted that someone, anyone, wanted to explore her potential as a serious actress. 'I always thought she was a dramatic actress, for she took her comedy very seriously,' Spielberg said later. 'So I met with her – we had a great afternoon – and you could tell she was thousands of kilowatts smarter than the people of "Laugh-In" had ever allowed her to demonstrate.' This summed up Goldie's dilemma – that even the smartest young man in Hollywood found it difficult to walk past the indelible character she had created for herself.

The story-line of *Sugarland* was based on a real-life incident from 1969 when Ila Faye Dent, a shoplifter newly released from prison, sprang her husband Bobby from a remand centre and set off to 'rescue' their baby son, being held in care at a foster home in Wheelock, Texas, taking with them as hostage a member of the Texas Department of Public Safety. The resultant car-chase involving over 100 vehicles captured the public's attention, and the story had stayed with Spielberg as he worked his way up as a director from television series like *Colombo* to Hollywood. Spielberg's biographer Joseph McBride comments, 'The young mother's desperation over being separated from her baby provided fertile ground for a working-out of Spielberg's complex feelings about his own family. Spielberg conceived Lou Jean [as Ila Faye had become] as behaving like a spoiled child, sexually manipulating her husband to go along with her whims and finally throwing an infantile tantrum that causes him to walk into the fatal ambush.'

It was a crucial film for both Goldie and Spielberg, presenting a challenge to which the actress rose with complete confidence. From those critics who could tear themselves away from their preference for the ditsy-blonde stereotype there was lavish praise: her performance was raw, gutsy, deeply felt and compulsively watchable. Art Simon had swung her a $300,000 fee on a total budget of just under $3 million and she realised that all eyes would be on her for the duration.

Filming was entirely on location in Texas and started on 15 January 1973. Spielberg was only twenty-six, Goldie just a year older, and rumours of a relationship between the director and star soon sprang up on set. Later Goldie batted off the gossip-mongers by saying blithely, 'I've heard that one too. But there's no truth in it. Steve is just one of the many men I've met in showbusiness.'

Another Spielberg biographer, John Baxter, observes that the director recoiled from relationships which might have forced him to assume responsibility for another's emotional well-being, but since Goldie was still married to Gus, this was not an issue. Whatever the degree of their intimacy, it did not last: later, when filming in San Antonio, Spielberg was introduced to a pretty young waitress by his cameraman, Vilmos Zsigmond, and for a time she became his close companion.

Spielberg made a creditable, some say outstanding, movie; both technically innovative and dramatically powerful, it was to win the Best Screenplay award at the Cannes Film Festival, yet to this day it is repudiated by both the director and his star, for the public rejected it so forcefully it was pulled from cinemas shortly after its release.

In part, the fault lay with Universal's marketing division, who could not make up their minds how to sell the goods to the public. The film's title and the promotional posters allowed the public to imagine that with a sweet title like *Sugarland* and the adored Goldie Hawn starring, they were in for an amusing, escapist treat. As Andrew Yule, another of Spielberg's biographers, comments, 'The commercial canker at the movie's heart lay in the two petty criminals with whom audiences were expected to empathise. Quite simply, they declined the invitation *en masse.*'

*Sugarland* did Goldie no favours: analysts said the film's commercial fate was sealed once the decision was taken to cast her. Richard Zanuck concurred, 'It wasn't a happy picture and people didn't want to see her in a serious role – they wanted to see her as a goofy gal.'

Spielberg differed. The film's failure, he said, 'was not due to the presentation of Goldie as an anti "Laugh-In" character, but to the promotional campaign, timing, release pattern and appreciation of the film by the studio. It had nothing to do with Goldie being rejected by the audiences.' But Goldie could not be blamed for feeling that she *had* been rejected, that the decision to sign with Universal was a mistake, and that she had the prospect of two more films with them before she could escape.

The film wrapped in March. Two months later Goldie announced that her marriage to Gus Trikonis was over, but in truth the couple had last lived together as man and wife in Las Vegas the previous year: 'I honestly thought the marriage would last. He's eight years older, and I know about the age differential, but I relied on him as a man of fortitude, as a man who would not let success – my success and his striving for success – break us up. We tried so hard to make the marriage last, but people don't change, the trunk of your tree remains basically the same. Gus is Greek, he was the father of his family for many years, he couldn't play second fiddle. I had married an older man whom I proceeded to fashion into a father figure, I was his little girl. I didn't know then about real love. But then one day the little girl grew up and that's when the fireworks started to fly.'

The newly-fashioned California property laws designed to give modern, liberated women a half-share in their husband's fortune had also been designed to work the other way round, and Gus Trikonis walked away from the marriage with $75,000. 'I would rather pick up dog-shit in the street than take money from a marriage partner,' Goldie reacted angrily. It was a blow she was to agonise over, and refer back to, many times in the following years.

There were other regrets. The publicity from that press conference where she advocated open marriage, still billowing like mustard gas around her, caused her pain and she tried to make amends: 'I would rather have said anything then that would have rationalised my staying in the marriage. But in truth I don't believe in open marriage or in no-fault/no-guilt, do-your-own-thing type of relationship. I do believe in fidelity.' A confusing standpoint, but one which seemed to satisfy her critics.

Still she felt it necessary to set the record straight. Talking to the veteran writer Rex Reed, she explained, 'I got married in 1968 right after *Cactus Flower*. I had a lot of success all at once and my husband worked too hard to equal it. He never made it. He's Greek, and it's very important to Greek men to bring home the bread and butter. He wouldn't let me give him anything: we had no luxuries. He was always talking about his pride, about his pride was too big to allow his wife to pay for anything – now he's demanding $75,000 of my money. I figure it's worth it to buy a new life, but what happened to the pride?'

To another writer, Lloyd Shearer, she returned compulsively to the money which, in truth, she could well afford: 'He took $75,000 from me – $75,000 I don't feel he deserved. And I still resent it.'

# CHAPTER SIX

# *Turning-Out Years*

*'One fire burns out another's burning'*
*– ibid.*

Rich, beautiful, famous – and free – Goldie need hardly worry about shortage of male company. The sexual experimentation to which she obliquely referred during her marriage to Gus left her with a number of close male friends, happy to be called if she felt like lifting the phone. But work came first, and the next film she was due to shoot, *The Girl From Petrovka*, was already casting and in pre-production.

The story of a Russian girl who falls in love with a Moscow-based American journalist, *Petrovka* was Goldie's second outing for Universal, again produced by Zanuck and Brown, but from the outset looked no more promising than *Sugarland*. Having had leading men of the calibre of Matthau, Sellers and Beatty among her more memorable films, she was now cast against the much lesser-known Hal Holbrook, not exactly a dream-team pairing, and there was confusion over whether the film was to be shot in Russia or Yugoslavia.

The start date kept being put back as the production, jinxed from beginning to end, stumbled to establish a firm location. The director Robert Ellis Miller flew to Moscow in a bid to persuade the authorities that, though the Cold War was far from over, there was no reason why East and West should not warm to this story of cross-Curtain love. Three weeks later he returned to report, in a fever of frustration, 'After that trip I wouldn't even attempt to try to convince them to let me make the picture in Russia. I mean, put the political attitude of the piece aside, the details of getting it together would drive you up the wall. Nobody's willing to make a decision in a totalitarian set-up, it's much safer to pass the question on to a higher level – which would obviously slow down the filming schedule.'

Following the post-Vietnam war thaw in East-West relations, new peace initiatives by Leonid Brezhnev and Richard Nixon, and the start of the Strategic Arms Limitation Talks, Hollywood bamboozled itself into believing that a new order prevailed at the Kremlin, and that at last a chink of light might be shone on the old enemy. Hollywood was also ready to kid itself that any film shot east of the Iron Curtain could be made for a fraction of the price of its Western equivalent. Robert Ellis Miller was not the first to fall victim to this misapprehension, nor would he be the last. He bitterly recounted, on his return to the US, that although his planned production of *Petrovka* would bring much needed foreign currency to the cash-starved Russians, he had been prevented from visiting various parts of Moscow and the film in his camera was confiscated after he took photographs of possible locations. He was advised that where the script showed people walking because they had no car, that would not be allowed. If it wanted to show buildings with paint peeling off, that would not be allowed. A girl with too much make-up – '*Nyet*. We do not have girls who wear too much make-up.'

While Goldie sat impatiently in Los Angeles, desperate to start work on the new film as a means of distraction from the break-up of her marriage, Miller tried again. This time it was Yugoslavia, a sufficiently bleak eastern-bloc country to pass, cinematically, for Russia, but with a more enlightened regime. They would start filming *The Girl From Petrovka* there in April. Rehearsals started in London, at a time when the capital was gripped with IRA bomb threats; a canny Richard Zanuck, the film's producer, reasoned that the IRA were unlikely to bomb the Irish Club and so rented space there, ordering the actors to drink Guinness and prepare for their trip behind the Iron Curtain.

But three months later Miller was no further forward and once again shooting was postponed, until early autumn. In late September, nine months after the proposed start, the Yugoslavian authorities changed their minds and refused permission for the film to go ahead. The script had been translated into Yugoslavian, and the *apparatchiks* did not like it – scriptwriter Alan Scott put their last-minute change of mind down to the untimely arrival in Belgrade of Soviet premier Alexei Kosygin and the fact that the Yugoslavs, mindful of the military invasion of Czechoslovakia five years before, wanted to do nothing that might upset him. 'This film presents a black picture of Soviet life,' trumpeted the official party newspaper in Belgrade, 'and profanes the sacred October Revolution.'

Once again Miller relocated his production, this time to the less contentious city of Vienna. Already $300,000 had been spent on the production without a frame having been shot, and tempers were riding high – not least Goldie's: 'I went to Russia to research my part, got all the way to Yugoslavia to start filming only to be turned away by Tito, and we had to rebuild Russia on the back lot at Universal. It was a nightmare. I had to pay $1,000 a week out of my salary to get a gaffer to head the lighting crew because the studio was too cheap to hire one.'

Equally disenchanted was George Fiefer, who visited the Viennese lot only to express disgust at the sets, which he thought slovenly and inaccurate, and the script, which he derided for being stuffed with unintentional howlers. The only bright spot for him was meeting the star: 'Goldie is so startlingly the incarnation of Oktyabrina, the flighty adventuress with the sad past, that the sight of her before the camera squeezes my heart.'

The film which should have taken a couple of months out of Goldie's life succeeded in wiping out most of 1973. With it went the opportunity to play a more substantial role, opposite Donald Sutherland in *Day of the Locust*. Sutherland had just made *Don't Look Now*, Nicholas Roeg's chilling tale of murder in Venice, with Julie Christie, and the word was that the film was a work of genius and Sutherland's performance worthy of an Oscar. An opportunity to get alongside Sutherland, and perhaps more importantly a director of the status of John Schlesinger, might help to revive a career which suddenly looked in danger of meandering aimlessly and without purpose. Schlesinger, whose previous credits included *Darling* (again with Christie) and *Midnight Cowboy*, was keen to have Goldie balance his front-line players but in the end the part went to Karen Black. Hanging round a doomed production like *Petrovka* 'was killing me, my heart wasn't in it any more, but I couldn't get out of it.'

Maybe a different agent, an agent other than Art Simon, could have got his star out of trouble. But just as Goldie had been on a steep learning curve these past three years, so too had Simon; and there were those around the star who said her Svengali had blown it. Simon had on his hands more than just an Oscar-winning actress; he had a national treasure, someone whose very features in a newspaper photograph could bring a smile to the reader's face, someone whose daily minutiae was of pressing importance to the adoring millions. And yet, though the film-scripts were still dropping through the letter-box, they weren't getting better, and the moment to capitalise on that precociously early Oscar was receding fast. Simon's critics say he could have pulled his star out of *Petrovka* at any number of stopping-points along the way; that he should not have allowed her to agree to pay $1,000 a week to be lit properly; and that he should have chased more ruthlessly the prizes that were there just waiting to be picked up.

Goldie sensed these things but as yet did nothing, for while the magic-merchants tried to make something out of the shambles of *Petrovka* she slipped away into the shadows with the new love in her life, a handsome Swedish actor by the name of Bruno Wintzell.

Possessed of glorious Scandinavian good looks, Wintzell had auditioned for the part of a Russian army officer in *Petrovka*: he was to completely occupy Goldie's life for the next two years. Already a star in his native country with such films as *Tinto Mara* and *Miss and Mrs Sweden*, Wintzell was also a gifted singer who had opened the European production of *Jesus Christ, Superstar* in Copenhagen. An unknown in Hollywood, he none the less found himself in Los Angeles for talks with the actress Ali McGraw on a possible future project and, *en route*, landed the relatively minor part in *Petrovka*.

In between casting and shooting there had been a six-week break, and Goldie, growing restless in London, decided to visit a friend in

Sardinia. She asked around among the cast to see if anyone wanted to accompany her, and Wintzell agreed to go as her bodyguard and baggage handler. Knowing no better, they flew to Sardinia's southern airport when in fact their destination was on the northern Costa Smeralda. There ensued a nightmare journey of taxis, trains and more taxis, but one which sealed their relationship.

'She was the love of my life,' recalls Wintzell now. 'She was such a very happy, refreshing person to be around. Sometimes she had a great temper and would be very angry, and she had one characteristic which was very funny: I used to look at my watch when it was getting close to six o'clock in the evening because I knew we'd better go and have dinner. If she didn't have anything in her stomach by 6.15 or 6.30 she used to get tetchy, like a child. It was very important to have dinner at 6 p.m.'

With *Petrovka* thankfully behind them, Goldie and Bruno spent the next year travelling. Though business in Los Angeles called the star back from time to time, Bruno started to show his girlfriend hidden corners of Europe, starting with a back-to-nature stay on Hjärter Ön, which translated means The Heart Island. They stayed with Bruno's childhood friends Rune Andersen and Nicholas David Stjrftrand on their smallholding, helping out by fishing, feeding the animals, cooking, chopping wood and helping with general chores. For a girl from Takoma Park by way of Las Vegas and Tinseltown, this life was a revelation, and she gasped in admiration when Rune presented her with a jumper she had knitted using wool from sheep on the farm.

Bruno and Goldie sailed blissfully around the inlets of Sweden's north-west coast and landed on the island where Ingrid Bergman and Lars Schmidt had a house, later visiting Goldie's *Cactus Flower* co-star in France at her home near Versailles. He introduced her to opera and they spent much time listening to music together. While Art Simon continued to work ahead, fixing deals and battling to keep the lid on the constant, almost hysterical, flood of interest in his client, Goldie was able to enjoy what turned out to be the most uncomplicated relationship in her adult life. 'We were very much home people,' recalls Bruno Wintzell. 'Los Angeles has a very strange magic, and when we were in Europe, or when we were travelling, we had a much better time. In LA she was so constantly attended – there were so many people she was working with that I used to say that when we got off the plane it was like she was walking out on to a stage and playing the movie star. She was very good at that.'

The lovers continued what he describes as their romantic tour by visiting an artist friend in the mountains near St Tropez. The visit to Sweden had been an eye-opener for Goldie, since Bruno was a bigger star there than she. *Petrovka*, when it opened in Stockholm, did not go down well, according to Bruno: 'The film itself was anti-Communist and because the socialists had so much influence there, living in the shadow of Russia, it wasn't popular. I was living with a movie star from Hollywood and that didn't go down well, either.' As a friend of the future king, however, his popularity was soon rekindled and the Swedish press started to write favourably about his girlfriend. Indeed, one cinema, following her visit, dedicated itself to playing nothing but her films.

Bruno took Goldie to meet first his parents, then the soon-to-be-king, Prince Carl Gustav, at a private dinner at the Swedish royal family's castle in Stockholm. The girl who once served behind the counter in a suburban Washington DC jewellery store and came to stardom via the table-tops of sleazy New Jersey pick-up joints took it all in her stride. 'Our king is a very funny, comic clownish person and not difficult to have a good time with. They got on with each other very well indeed,' says Wintzell.

The relationship attracted virtually no publicity, even though it lasted two years. A number of factors contributed to this quite surprising news blackout – Goldie's by-now guarded attitude towards interviews (since the furore over her observations on open marriage, she had constructed an interview formula which lasts to this day, handing out only small dollops of pre-packaged personal information); the attitude of a complacent American press, happy to take whatever crumbs Goldie's publicity people gave them; and the fact that with no film to promote she could legitimately stay out of the public eye. Bruno Wintzell was happy with this and appeared to demand nothing from the relationship: 'Everyone in the business was so absorbed by her charm and her talent and the prospects of a future project with her that people were very focused on her.' Perhaps a polite way of observing that Hollywood's big-shots usually only spare time for other Hollywood big-shots, not unknown Swedish hunks.

This relationship had similarities with its precursor, in that once again Goldie was the breadwinner and star; her partner merely an also-ran. The difference was that, this time, Goldie carried no feelings of guilt over her status and Wintzell felt no jealousy. There was an understanding between them that they would live as equals and Goldie would not use undue influence to secure him acting roles. While this may have had a staying effect on Wintzell's Hollywood career it allowed him to retain a certain moral integrity. Both seemed able to live with that, but discussions got under way as to what he should do to earn a living.

Hollywood at the time exercised restrictive practices when it came to handing out acting parts to foreign nationals: if the job could be done by an American, it was. Getting a Green-Card work permit was virtually impossible, and though for a time Bruno continued to seek acting work it was clear that it would take a miracle to make the breakthrough. During this time he toyed with the idea of starting a bakery in Los Angeles with Laura Hawn. Mrs Hawn, now sixty-two and a victim to cancer, still possessed that feisty entrepreneurial streak which had taken her out of Braddock and given her two daughters a fine upbringing in Takoma Park. But by now Rut Hawn was no longer in evidence back in Takoma Park and Laura was thinking of moving to the West Coast to be near her daughter. Ever-restless, that Braddock work-ethic still deeply ingrained, she would need something to do. Bruno, with his youth, his business-training background, his Scandinavian charm and his love of her little girl, would make an ideal partner ... but it was not to be.

As the couple flew in and out of LAX airport on their world travels, Art Simon was negotiating his way towards a unique and crucial deal for Goldie. After two flops the love-affair with Universal was over; the third contracted movie would never be made. But Warren Beatty, Goldie's co-star from *Soup* two years ago, had for six years been playing with the idea of a film based on a Robert Towne TV script called *Breaking Point*, about a modern Don Juan with 'so many pretty girls and so little time'. Despite the fact that both *McCabe and Mrs Miller* and *Dollars* failed to find favour with the critics, Beatty was determined to have his two leading ladies from these films together in *Shampoo*. In Julie Christie's case it was a done deal – she merely asked where she should sign on the contract. As for Goldie, Art Simon saw an opportunity and grabbed it. Bringing all his negotiating skills to bear, he walked away from the table clutching a document giving his client seven per cent of the action.

This was an unheard-of deal in Hollywood. Leading ladies got a flat fee, a nice dressing room, and a car to pick them up in the morning. They knew nothing of percentages, of points, of shares of the action. While they bathed in the glow of publicity, posed for photographers and answered questions about their innermost being, the boys in the backroom were cutting deals on deals and getting seriously rich. Actresses, with few exceptions, did *not* get seriously rich.

But on this movie Beatty was the producer, and Simon knew how much he wanted Goldie. The deal he struck moved Goldie for the first time into the Big Earners' league, even though it could be argued that Julie Christie and not she was the main female interest in the movie. As a piece of negotiation it was brilliant and provided the basis for Goldie's future fortune, but conversely it marked the beginning of the end of the Hawn/Simon partnership, for Beatty learned at first hand how his actress friend was being represented. And he did not like what he saw.

'Art was a grotesque person, very loud and vulgar,' recalls Bruno Wintzell. 'This little girl would be sitting beside him and he would be throwing out horrible things about other people all the time. I think she felt secure with him, protected, but at her level you need a little sophistication. They'd been together for a while but the time comes when you must move on.' Those who had a fondness for Goldie worried about Simon's attitude towards his client, which one described as bordering on the obsessional. With encouragement from Bruno and from Beatty, Goldie prepared to cut herself adrift from the man who had discovered her only six years before, and to tie herself up with the William Morris agency and its undoubted star negotiator, Stan Kamen.

Word of the existence of *Shampoo* ran through the Hollywood gossip-columns like a bush-fire. Sex and Beatty were synonymous. Christie and Beatty were fireworks. Goldie and Beatty were – irresistible. The actor/producer saw something more. Having carefully set the story during the US election of 1968 he intoned, 'It was the moment when this country came face to face with the hypocrisies that *Shampoo* represents – the day we turned to each other and realised that we had elected Richard Nixon and Spiro Agnew as his number two. George, the central character, is like the country, a guy who looks like he's got the world by the tail one day and next morning he realises he hasn't.'

Critics and audiences cared less about the politics than the sex. The story revolved around a day in the life of George Roundy, top Beverly Hills hairdresser, who behind his apparently gay exterior beds his clients with a ferocious hunger. He roars from body to body on his motorcycle but as the election night party approaches so too does his undoing. Christie, playing George's former girlfriend, was at her sensuous best, crawling under the table to get at his loins. Goldie, his present amour, portrayed an altogether less sexual being.

It was probably the best movie Goldie had played in, though press attention tended to focus more on Julie Christie and on Lee Grant, who won an Oscar for her portrayal as the most voracious of the hairdresser's clients. Romantically, Beatty had time for neither of his ex-leading ladies. With a minute budget, a tight turn-round, and wearing a three-cornered hat as writer, producer and actor, Beatty worked every daylight hour. Julie Christie brought a new boyfriend on to the set, and Goldie brought her faithful Bruno: 'I was not happy with Warren, he was so uncomfortable during the whole movie, he looked so troubled, always frowning – he was running the whole thing.' When time permitted Goldie, Julie, Warren and their partners would troop back to Goldie's house for dinner but then Warren would return to the studio dressing room he had converted into an apartment for the duration. The critics, when they could spare time from ululating over Julie Christie, concluded this was an excellent performance from Goldie particularly in the concluding scene where she makes Warren Beatty tell her everything. What they could not know was that the scene had required thirty-eight takes and was shot only after Beatty had kept his co-star waiting for hours, late at night, while he worked himself up in preparation for his performance. In this regard, but only in this, it was like working with the deranged Sellers once again.

Eventually, *Shampoo* grossed more than $45m worldwide on an outlay of less than $5 million. Goldie, on seven per cent of the profits, would never again work for a flat fee, but, more importantly, she had watched closely as Beatty went about his business as actor/producer and inwardly stored the vital knowledge she had gleaned.

None the less, there remained the nagging feeling she had been upstaged by Christie and Grant: 'Making *Shampoo* was one of my toughest experiences. To start with I didn't like my role. I thought Jill was the least attractive character. She had no fire, she was a simple person. I thought she was uninteresting.' Seeking perhaps to rationalise this loss of focus, Goldie added: 'In the end, it was my character who evolved into someone. She was the only one who had the strength to change. At the end, George didn't really get her. Everyone else is left writhing around in muck. But she wasn't.' Perhaps unsurprisingly it took Goldie seventeen years before she could be persuaded once again to share equal billing with two other female stars in a film.

Meanwhile, her relationship with Bruno Wintzell was cooling. 'I would like to have married her. We were very, very close but I was sceptical about Hollywood marriages – people would marry for a year, start a life and a family and then it would be over. But we never discussed it – she was just through her marriage to Gus Trikonis. In any case I wasn't intending to stay in that place,' he says.

Compare this with Goldie's own public utterances on the marital state just a year into their relationship, and it can be seen that Goldie preferred to perpetuate the fiction that she was a free agent when, in fact, she was in a committed live-in relationship. Outwardly, she appeared to relish an unfettered single status, telling an interviewer in the summer of 1974, 'It's so marvellous to be free and make one's own decisions. I can get up and plan my day without having to consult anyone else. I can accept a film without wondering if it'll suit my husband's commitments. And if it's on some faraway location I don't have to think "Oh, God, this is going to rock the matrimonial boat." I've completed four big films in sixteen months and at the moment I'm enjoying the rest before reading more scripts. So I look out of the window when I get up and if it's a nice day I get into the car and drive along the coast for hundreds of miles on my own without a worry in the world.' Marriage may have been in the mind of Bruno Wintzell, but it was most certainly not in the mind of Goldie Hawn.

With her business relationship with Art Simon unravelling, and with the pressing need to find a vehicle to put her back as a principal leading lady, Goldie accepted the suggestion of Bruno Wintzell to look at the work of a man called Colin Higgins. Wintzell had seen his *Harold and Maud*, a black comedy about a repressed young man, fixated on death and funerals, who has an affair with an eighty-year old woman. Encouraged by this novel idea of asking writers to submit direct to her, Goldie received three scripts from Higgins, including one about a quiet San Franciscan librarian who picks up a hitchhiker who dies in her arms, but only after he has surreptitiously planted a microfilm on her person and whispered the disconcerting words 'Beware the dwarf.' After some delay, Goldie turned the script down and Higgins, nettled, walked away vowing to find someone else – someone younger, taller, blonder, someone maybe like Farrah Fawcett – to play the lead role he had so carefully crafted.

There was a lull when nothing much seemed to be happening at all. Goldie seemed to stand perpetually on the threshold of mega-stardom – stardom of the order of a Marilyn Monroe – and yet was stopped by unseen forces from crossing the threshold into that exclusive sorority. She expressed frustration at her tinselled life in a rare explosion of public anger: 'Hollywood is not a place I want to spend my life in, not where I want to raise my children. Because Hollywood is one of the cruellest places on the face of the earth. Within Hollywood, you'll meet some of the most vicious people you'll ever hope to meet – people who'll smile and stab you in the back. Your life is not your own in Hollywood, even the people who you think are your friends talk about you. You can't really confide in anyone. This town is built on gossip and it's very easy to get into that syndrome. You know there are places where you go to eat in Beverly Hills where they give you *such* horseshit ... "Oh, Miss Hawn; of course, Miss Hawn. What *can* we do to make it up to you?" What the fuck, so I'll wait, they don't have to feed me all that crap. The trouble with the movie business is that no one in it who is successful ever gets to grow. Movie people's egos get to the point where failure is the only thing that stimulates them. I just hate the place, hate what it does to people. It makes you so self-conscious; you have to be that way, or else you cut off completely. But you can never get away from it. Not long ago I was in a village in France, one I adore. I was sitting in the café there when suddenly I heard somebody whispering, "That's Goldie Hawn." Something terrible happened inside me; all the free-flowing energy inside me was just shut off. I had stopped being who I am, and started thinking about what they thought of me. It was awful.'

This extraordinary outburst says much about her mood at the time. By now Goldie had learned to shield her innermost thoughts from the public gaze and her stereotype interviews rarely gave anything away. This attack on Hollywood and the business which had validated and enriched her opened, for a moment, a door into her private world to reveal anger, frustration, unhappiness and resentment. She was at a crossroads in her business, artistic, and personal lives and it was hurting. Her critics might argue that by expressing disgust at being recognised by fans she was biting the hand that fed her; and that since world-ranking film stars lived perfectly happy lives outside Hollywood she had a choice as to her territory. More likely, though, it was the fears and frustrations of a frightened actress speaking out: Goldie had been in the headlines for nine years and was now asking herself for how much longer her luck would hold out before she was superseded by a younger, funnier, more talented version of herself. After all, no one was rushing forward with offers of work.

Into this vacuum entered the unlikely figure of Melvin Frank, veteran of a hundred big movies from the Bing Crosby/Bob Hope *Road* series to *White Christmas*. Two years before, Hollywood had made its obeisances as his George Segal/Glenda Jackson vehicle, *A Touch of Class*, swept the awards with an Oscar and four other Academy nominations, plus two Golden Globes and a further three nominations. The comic teaming of Segal and Jackson as a married businessman and a dress designer who have a very physical adulterous affair charmed and delighted audiences the world over: Jackson won an Oscar and Golden Globe as Best Actress.

Frank, at the end of a long and hugely successful career, could not resist seeing if he could make the double: he created a script for a film to be titled *The Duchess and the Dirtwater Fox* specifically as a vehicle for Jackson and Segal. But when it came to signature, Jackson, always unpredictable, always uncompromising, had other ideas. Despite the very real chance of being nominated for another Oscar, she turned her attention to other films: a dreary and forgettable drama with Susannah York called *The Maids*, a Joseph Losey period piece with Michael Caine called *The Romantic Englishwoman*, and – rather more shrewdly – Trevor Nunn's adaptation of *Hedda Gabler*, for which she did indeed receive an Oscar nomination. '*Duchess* was a poor script,' is Jackson's arid explanation today.

It was into this actress's shoes that Goldie stepped, very much a second choice, just as she would be in her next film too. But Art Simon, still stitching deals together with aplomb, secured a $350,000 guarantee – and 7.5 per cent of the profits. This was half-a-point up on her *Shampoo* deal and had the effect of signalling to Hollywood bosses that this was an actress who only made films for a share of the action. Those who did not look too closely into the casting of *Duchess* were suitably impressed.

*Duchess* was shot entirely on location in Colorado but unlike *Shampoo* Bruno Wintzell was not in evidence; however there was a happy reunion for daughter and father when Rut Hawn turned up to make a brief appearance before the cameras. Melvin Frank's story-line had Goldie playing a foul-mouthed happy hooker who falls for George Segal's cutesy cardsharp. The film's ethos was as bawdy as a dirty postcard and though her performance won her a Golden Globe nomination for Best Actress, Goldie regretted it: 'How can I say this? Everything was over-extended, all the scenes went on too long. And one thing I learned was that I should never curse in a film; it just doesn't match my image. It would be different if it was *Taxi Driver*, but it wasn't. And it wasn't Mel Brooks either.'

Back from Colorado, it was showdown time. With the assistance of a lawyer suggested by Warren Beatty, she started the painful process of dissolving her business partnership: 'I don't know what it is about this business. People become so possessive. I used to say to Art, "Go out and get some other job besides managing me. I don't want my life to become your life. I want, I *must* have some control of myself."

'It was one of those things where I was young, I had no great drive except to become a dancer, but Art saw something else in me. He pushed me, he believed in me. It's the same old Hollywood story that occurs so frequently between manager and artist – I started to grow up, to become a little wiser, I started to have my opinions on what things I should and shouldn't do. But like many managers Art started playing the artist role himself. He became dominant, sort of omnipotent. Art is only thirty-seven, we were both growing up at the same time. I found some of his manoeuvres, his impingement on my personal life, too strong. We had a seven-year contract and I didn't mind paying him a twenty-five per cent commission because he relieved me of a lot of burdens. But after five-and-a-half years enough is enough.'

Simon's response was to issue a writ for $6 million against the star whose career he created but ultimately was unable to control. As with Gus Trikonis, Goldie saw it as the ultimate betrayal that a man should take money from her; indeed there were close parallels between the two relationships. Finally she settled out of court: 'The lawyers' fees were enormous, so enormous, and it seemed that I would have to spend the rest of my life in court, so I settled for a small fortune.'

Later she observed, 'I had a manager who I adored for many years. He was part of my family. He started using me as his power tool. I didn't feel I was being represented properly. But he had found me early on in my career when I was still dancing, so I felt like I owed him a lot. People told me to get rid of him. That's a problem with me – sometimes I'm too loyal and I end up getting hurt because of it.'

One writer who met her when she was new to Hollywood, Lloyd Shearer of *Parade*, contrasted the old and the new Goldie. In 1970 she told him, 'I know it sounds naïve, but right now the whole world seems good, golden and glorious to me. I really am the luckiest broad alive. I'm here, living it up like a fully-fledged movie star – do you think this sort of luck, this kind of happiness, can last?' By 1976, observed Shearer, she was thirty and subdued; six years in Hollywood had taken their toll. The $75,000 divorce settlement, and Art Simon's lawsuit, coupled with an apparently bleak future on the jobs front had left her nerves frayed.

In addition things were not so wonderful back home in Takoma Park. Despite Goldie's public pronouncements on family values, things had gone from bad to worse between Rut and Laura Hawn. The redbrick semi-detached house in the cosy cul-de-sac saw less and less of the wandering minstrel, and neighbours noted that absences of a month at a time had turned into two, and then three. By now the Hawns had been married for forty years and Rut was sixty-seven, but seemed determined not to allow this lengthy marital legacy to hold him back. His behaviour became somewhat eccentric and later he would invite people he barely knew to go and stay with him at Goldie's house in Colorado.

'One day he just took the car and was gone,' recalls one neighbour. 'It seemed very strange for a couple who had been together for so long.' The unease, swamped by constant laughter, was over. The truth was out.

'Rut was kind of weird,' says a relation, 'a strange duck. I believe he hung an awful lot of his self-image on Goldie's success because the last time I saw him it was Goldie this, Goldie that, Goldie-Goldie-Goldie. You could talk to Laura and she'd say, "Goldie's made it!" and then she'd talk about something else. She once told me she didn't think Rut had handled Goldie's success well, and I think they drifted because of that. They stayed friends, there wasn't another woman or anything like that. I think Rut just wanted to hang in the limelight a little bit, that was his life, he played for stars.'

The curious semi-detached existence which the Hawns called a marriage was now at an end, though the couple were not to divorce.

Laura bravely overcame a mastectomy and soldiered on with the Flowers Gift Shop, but the business was running down. Now she opened up more to neighbours and seemed for the first time to enjoy their company: 'She was very, very lonely,' recalls Art MacMurdie, who lived opposite. 'She talked a lot about her schooldays and lived her life vicariously through Goldie.' Meanwhile the irrepressible Rut set up home in a city where the stars always shine, Las Vegas, and looked around for the occasional gig.

Goldie's life back in Hollywood seemed to be built on similarly shifting sands. Bruno Wintzell had helped her through the trauma of separation from Art Simon, but now Goldie could not conceive of a future with him. Though Wintzell – 'her embarrassing Swedish boyfriend' wrote Oscar-winning producer Julia Phillips in her coruscating memoir, *You'll Never Eat Lunch In This Town Again* – may still have harboured dreams of marrying her, she was emotionally in another place. With no prospect of employment as an actor in Hollywood, Bruno moved his base to London to record with reggae musician Johnny Nash; Bob Marley was expressing interest in turning the multi-faceted singer into the first white reggae star. Goldie visited him a couple of times, but she was ready for something new. Her 'turning-out year', as she called it, was reaching its climax.

Flying back from New York to Los Angeles in the summer of 1975 she found herself sitting across the aisle from three musicians who, on introduction, turned out to be the Hudson Brothers, a successful rock and comedy act who, two years previously, had been spotted by

Elton John and signed up to his Rocket Records label. By now the band – truly brothers, but Italian immigrants born with the name Salerno – had been on the road for a decade and were an accomplished act. By coincidence they had been staying in New York at the Sherry Netherland Hotel, where Goldie too had been staying. It was enough to get the conversation going. Bill Hudson, the eldest brother, had similar darkly handsome looks to Gus Trikonis but was younger by a dozen years.

By the time the plane touched down at LAX Hudson had persuaded Goldie to have dinner with him, and before too long the couple were, as the gossip columnists put it, an 'item'. For Bruno Wintzell, it was a dashing blow: 'She had been back and forth visiting me in London – then she met some guy on an airplane! I was broken-hearted, for many years I was very sad – she was a very clever girl and she had made me very happy, we'd had a good time. She was the love of my life.'

The love of Goldie's life, though, was now Bill Hudson, a man who had reached for fame with no special privileges to help get him there. He was five when his father sent him off for his first day at school, left town and was never seen again. Brought up by his mother, he and his brothers Brett and Mark pretended that their uncle was their father. They grew up living off welfare: 'We literally lived on Spam.' In their teens Bill and his brothers loaded trucks for a local produce company until they ran off to break into showbusiness. But their ties to those who remained at home in Portland, Oregon, remained close.

Goldie, now thirty, did not waste time asking herself about the relationship. By the year's end she was pregnant, though still not divorced from Gus. A self-confessed 'house freak' she set about building a dream home on the beach at Malibu to her own design, first buying doors and windows, then designing the house around them.

By contrast with her previous relationship, Goldie could not wait to spread the news from the rooftops that she had found a marriageable man: 'He's just the most beautiful person. I knew from the moment I met him he wasn't the typical Hollywood manipulator.

He has shown me exactly what love can be. I've never felt this way with any other man. You know something, I keep dreaming about him – Bill is part of my soul, my bloodstream, my kitchen table. What do you want, an inventory?!'

Bruno Wintzell had been sent packing without even a chance to collect his things. Later he discovered that 300 pictures taken of him and Goldie during their two-year love affair had disappeared: 'The bitch secretary threw them away!' he fumes. Understandably sore at his dismissal he was at pains to point out to friends that, of the men who'd been around Goldie, he was the only one who had not taken money from her and was the only one who'd actually *made* money for her. His name never again passed Goldie's lips in public. 'It was probably better for her to pretend I hadn't existed while the divorce was going through with Gus,' he observes now. Two years of true love had been airbrushed out of the star's life.

Meanwhile with no firm offers of work, Goldie settled back into a life of placid domesticity to await the arrival of her first-born. The timing, she reasoned, was perfect: if she had had children with Gus, once – long ago – a high priority, it may have saved the marriage but kiboshed her career. Now she was established, both financially and in the eyes of Hollywood, and even if the career was less focused than that of her contemporaries Barbra Streisand and Jane Fonda, things would come right. What she needed right now was to take time off to make a family, and 'family' was a concept that meant a lot to Goldie.

Of Hudson she pronounced, 'He's a very special man, a real family man, and I'm a real frustrated family woman. He's never been married and we're going to try it: the trio travels a lot and I'm going to travel with them. They're going to Japan, and I will too – luckily I love to travel. Another thing, this town has been very good to me in many ways, material ways – I have a house in Bel Air and a new Mercedes – but Bill and I aren't crazy about this town. We want a house, a farm with people working it.'

This was a dream which would go unrealised until the arrival of the real love in her life, Kurt Russell. In the meantime, Goldie was ready to give her relationship with Hudson her best shot: 'What I've learned in the past six years is a little wisdom. Success and stardom are great, they provide you with a maximum of comforts and a minimum of privacy. But if Bill Hudson makes me take a choice between marriage and a career, I'd choose marriage, a successful marriage. Because I've already had a successful career, I mean I'm still having it. But without someone to love and someone to love you, it's not all that hot.'

The joy she felt was not unalloyed: *The Duchess and the Dirtwater Fox* was released in the Spring of 1976 and confirmed the feelings of those on the production team that it was only so-so as a movie, and a sad letdown on its precursor *A Touch of Class*. With the baby now just three months away, Goldie was still wrangling with Gus over the final details of his $75,000 settlement. Though the couple had been separated for over three years, the negotiations dragged on and threatened to scupper Goldie's plans to marry Bill, not in some hideaway ceremony as she had eight years before in Honolulu, but as all young brides dream of doing, from her parents' home. This scenario played into Gus's hands and the deal was finessed to his satisfaction. 'I figure it's worth it to buy a new life,' Goldie said resignedly. 'I had a lot of success all at once and my husband worked too hard to equal it. He never made it. Gus and I will be divorced before the baby is born so it will work out all right.

'One of the reasons we never had children was because Gus wasn't ready. It's not fair to any baby to come into a world that doesn't want him, the baby doesn't ask to be born. Before I met Bill I felt I had given up all hope of having children; now I'm happy I waited because I can really appreciate this baby and everything he means to me and Bill. The past three years, since parting from Gus, have changed my life and given me time to rethink a lot of values. It's something I've wanted for a long time. I just had to be sure the daddy would be the right person.'

Curiously, her situation now mirrored that of her co-star in *Cactus Flower*, Ingrid Bergman. The older woman's career had been all but destroyed by being married to one man while having another's child and the resultant exile from Hollywood had been a warning to other leading ladies to watch their morals, or at least such morals as touched the outside world. Now there was a guarded acceptance, if not an overall delight, at Goldie's situation. She received her invitation to the annual Academy Awards, and duly turned up – Mrs Gus Trikonis carrying another man's baby. 'I am not having this baby in a closet,' she uttered defiantly, and the columnists and commentators, perhaps in fear of the consequences of casting her out into a Bergmanesque exile, drew in their horns. In any event, Bergman herself had been officially welcomed back into the fold with an Oscar for her part in Sidney Lumet's *Murder on the Orient Express* two years earlier and was now one of Hollywood's untouchables. No one wanted to open old wounds.

With a month to go to her confinement, Goldie and Bill were free to marry. She chose as the venue the back garden of her old home at 9 Cleveland Avenue, Takoma Park. The whole street was invited, with city police blocking the cul-de-sac off to traffic. Bill's family arrived, together with Goldie's own immediate family – Laura, Rut, and sister Patti – and in deference to the mix of religions both a Rabbi and a Roman Catholic priest were invited to officiate. This took care of Bill's family religion and that of Laura Hawn – no one thought to ask Rut if he'd like to have a Presbyterian minister along. One person not invited was the bride's childhood friend Sylvia Colen, the one whose house became a second home and whose folks had become a surrogate family. Sylvia had married at twenty-one and Goldie had sent a dinner service as a present, but now she was back on the home patch, the star, she did not think to call up and invite her housewife friend along. 'I didn't realise you two were still close,' rasped Laura to Sylvia later.

Back in Pacific Palisades Goldie prepared for the birth of her firstborn. During pregnancy her weight had shot up from 120lb to 170lb, which threw an enormous strain on her body. She went a month beyond her due date, and eventually she was taken into the Cedars Sinai Hospital where the baby was delivered by Caesarean section. The birth was a difficult one, lasting over two hours, giving rise to fears for both Goldie's safety and that of the child, but finally two months to the day after her wedding she was delivered of a son weighing eleven pounds. Mother and father named him Oliver Rutledge Hudson, a nice compliment to Goldie's father and to those ancestors who stretched back over two centuries, who, though they might not have signed the Declaration of Independence or been Abraham Lincoln's inamorata as Rut had variously claimed, were as much a part of the Republic's history as their more famous kinsmen.

But almost immediately the child developed pneumonia and was rushed into intensive care. Near death, and on a life-support machine, he underwent a ten-day crisis before finally pulling through. This event had the most profound effect on Laura Hawn, recalling as it did the death of her own first-born so many years before, and had the result of drawing mother and daughter even closer.

The anxiety over her daughter's confinement helped Laura make some decisions about her own life. Now sixty-three and living alone since Rut Hawn's curiously matter-of-fact departure from the family nest, she no longer had the daily support of her elder daughter Patti, who had moved from her house round the corner on Collesville Road to the West Coast. The Flowers Gift Shop had run its course, and with Rut no longer around to repair the watches and re-arrange the window displays, she had become involved in a wholesale jewellery business on Apple Street in Silver Spring; she was no longer her own boss after forty years in the jewellery business. She had talked of moving out West to be with Goldie and start a bakery with Bruno Wintzell, but Bruno was yesterday's papers and somehow the ties of quiet, suburban, Takoma Park still bound Laura. Whenever Goldie made a film, she would be there to support and, as she saw it, protect her daughter; but she was not yet ready to make the transition from the simplicity of Maryland to the ultra-sophistication of Los Angeles. Laura rented out the redbrick semi-detached house Goldie had grown up in, with its neatly-tended quarter-acre garden, to a newcomer, Donna Wulken, and moved to California. On arrival she realised it was a one-way trip she had taken, and sold the house to her tenant.

In Hollywood, life was moving into a lull. The Hudson Brothers were touring and making albums, and mostly Goldie stayed at home in their Pacific Palisades house, where she had a recording studio built for Bill as his wedding present. Dressed in T-shirt, old sandals, and with Goldie wearing no make-up, they looked like a couple of bohemians. 'It wasn't chic but it sure was comfortable,' observed one visitor. Goldie returned to her various hobbies including writing poetry and, appalled to learn of the premature death of her teenage idol Elvis Presley, bent her skills to writing a suitable epitaph. 'I was hurt, I was shocked. It was painful for me because I saw what happened to him, which is why I never wanted to be a star in the first place. He was the personification of my fears, and he abused himself *so* much. I wrote a poem about a sparrow:

The sparrow doesn't sing
Sorrow has clipped its wings
How lightly he was perched
Upon the icy birch
A lover shot a dart
Right through his tender heart
His stiffened body lies
Beneath the sunfilled skies
To make reminder of
To care for those who love

'It was my catharsis,' she said. 'It might just be the shittiest poem, it sounds like a child wrote it. But it's what I felt.'

At the age of thirty-one Goldie had achieved everything she could hope for. The nagging self-doubt which dogged the early years of her adult life was now replaced by a plateau of calm, and she felt sufficiently confident in her new role as wife and mother to bid farewell to the analyst who had seen her through some of her darkest moments. Her life had moved to another level and now she employed clairvoyants and psychics to quiz instead. This period of calm, of consolidation, was at the outset deeply enriching, but before long she started to ask herself whether Hollywood had forgotten her. Despite having William Morris's golden boy Stan Kamen as her agent, he could do little but feed her the third-rate film and TV scripts which occasionally landed on his desk. Caught on the hop by a reporter demanding news of her next assignment she answered wanly, 'I guess I'll have six months off for the baby if I'm lucky – probably less.'

It was to be more, not less; though before too long came one of the most intriguing challenges yet to be laid before her. The most discussed book of that era, Eric Jong's *Fear of Flying*, had been optioned by producer Julia Phillips, who had won an Oscar for *The Sting*.

*Fear of Flying* was a watershed book, a cultural phenomenon with paperback sales ultimately topping ten million copies worldwide and with Erica Jong's term for the ultimate sexual encounter, the 'zipless fuck', entering the vernacular. Outwardly the novel is about a struggling writer, Isadora Wing, unhappily married to a psychiatrist who, as one academic observed is 'one of literature's least sympathetic males'. She tries to bring passion back into her life by running away with another man.

It could be argued that there were strong parallels between Isadora Wing and Goldie Hawn. Isadora, almost a parody of the fifties good girl – anxiety-ridden, dominated by her mother, mocked for writing poetry, alternately obsessed with and resentful of men, and pathologically guilty about all her conflicting impulses – marries because she is sick of being single. She discovers she is expected not to desire any other men after marriage – 'then the desires come and you were thrown into a panic of self-hatred. What an evil woman you were! How could you keep being infatuated by strange men?' – but finds that there is little to be had by jumping from one man to another since they seem to share life's less attractive characteristics.

Julia Phillips saw *Fear of Flying* as a perfect fit with two other films she was making, *Taxi Driver* and *Close Encounters of the Third Kind*. These two, she knew, were destined to become box-office smashes and so was *Fear of Flying*. In addition she could take her pick of

Hollywood's top actresses because all of them were desperate to play Isadora. Another candidate for the part, for example, was Barbra Streisand. For Goldie, it was an opportunity to show something that had not been seen since *The Sugarland Express*: that she could act without laughing, that there were depths to her the world had not yet seen. But as negotiations with Columbia dragged on, she began to get anxious at the idea of stepping outside the persona she had so carefully crafted since arriving in Hollywood and which had taken such a severe dent after appearing in *Sugarland*. At a party at Bob Evans's house, she bumped into Sue Mengers, one of Hollywood's starriest agents.

Julia Phillips recalls in *You'll Never Eat Lunch In This Town Again* that the following morning Goldie asked her to drive over to her house where she recounted the events of the night before: '... and I go to the bathroom and Sue Mengers follows me in, and I put my alligator bag on the sink, and try to pee and Sue asks can she borrow my brush, knocks the bag in the sink, and while she's brushing her hair, she talks to me in the mirror and she says "You know you're ruining your career committing to Julia" ... I don't know, the whole thing has made me very nervous ...'

And with that, Goldie finally kissed goodbye to any chances of turning hers into a multi-faceted career. But Sue Mengers's advice was not wrong. Julia Phillips's own career, once so lustrous, was about to explode in an orgy of drugs and self-inflicted failure, Erica Jong ended up suing over the rights to her own book, and the film was never made.

# CHAPTER SEVEN

# *Don't Call Me Babe!*

'Then comes she to me
And with wild looks bid me devise some mean
To rid her from this second marriage'
– ibid.

It was two years before Goldie faced the camera again. The mother in her relished this opportunity to watch her baby son grow, but the actress felt cheated and frustrated. If *Fear of Flying* now seemed like a missed opportunity so too did that script she had commissioned from Colin Higgins, *Killing Lydia*. Higgins had recovered from that rebuff with another of his offerings, a mystery comedy starring Gene Wilder called *Silver Streak*, which had been released the previous year and had the critics raving.

Slowly she came round to the idea that maybe *Killing Lydia* could still be a possibility, but to her horror she discovered that the film was going ahead without her. Following the success of *Silver Streak* Higgins had taken the original script and rewritten it, incorporating new situations and characters, and retitling it *Foul Play*. Paramount had expressed interest and wanted to cast Farrah Fawcett, then at the height of her popularity through the TV series 'Charlie's Angels', as the leading lady. It was another missed opportunity.

Then, however, it was discovered that due to contractual difficulties – Fawcett was having serious legal battles with the 'Charlie's Angels' producers – it looked like she would not be available. Suddenly the door was once again ajar for Goldie. Stan Kamen negotiated the deal and soon Higgins was cooing that he was very happy that Goldie was 'available'. Goldie in turn announced that since she was always on the lookout for a good plot, and since by rewriting it Higgins had turned it into such, she had 'agreed' to take the lead part. Hollywood, being a place of elastic semantics, allowed both versions to stand.

Nevertheless there were hurdles still to jump. Paramount studio chiefs, resigning themselves to the fact that they would not be getting the lissom Fawcett, asked after Goldie's condition and, fearing she had grown fat from pregnancy and retirement, insisted on looking her over before signing the contract. 'Forget about talent!' she blistered. 'That doesn't enter into it!'

Finally, heading thankfully towards the San Francisco location where she would film for the next month, she paused to give her opinions on motherhood: 'Being a mother is the greatest experience in my life – well, actually, the *second* greatest. The first was when I played Juliet onstage at Williamsburg when I was eighteen. I'm a realistic person, so you know I'm not exaggerating when I tell you my son is a genius. He's a year old and he's already talking – believe me, he speaks! The child is like a light bulb; when he smiles, the whole room lights up. And he got the whole damned thing from his mother.'

What, inquired a hesitant interviewer, about Bill? 'Oh ... Bill is a *fabulous* father – gets up in the night, changes diapers, the works. I couldn't *design* a better father ...'

Her own public explanation for the fact that she hadn't stood in front of a camera for two years was that she stopped work because she was tired; everyone had a creative well and hers had run dry. Now she was restored: 'I've regained my creative enthusiasm and I'm really anxious to return to acting. When I was expecting my baby I travelled round with Bill on concert dates so much, my father called me the pregnant groupie! Once the baby arrived my whole life changed; I'm not the same giddy girl I used to be. The character I played in *Cactus Flower* looked like a newborn bird, I was so young and skinny in 1968. A lot of the girl essence is still there, but it will be interesting to see the new growth and maturity on the screen.'

Her two years' hibernation had given her a very pure existence: she was happy, she said, not to have had the temptation of some fabulous movie offer. But after such a long layoff she faced the return to work with trepidation: 'I'm really scared. I have all these insecurities like, am I still funny? Have I gained too much weight?

Will the audiences still believe me in a role? Thank God I function well under stress and a lot of demands. I suppose everything will fall into place after the first day in front of the cameras, but my situation is very different now. I wasn't even married when I did my last picture.'

Her fears were groundless: she looked better than ever, and if she had gained a few pounds they were to her advantage. Her face had a new maturity and, if possible, her comic timing had sharpened. Playing opposite Chevy Chase she had a moment of *déjà vu*, for here was a male version of herself a decade before. Chase was the star of 'Saturday Night Live', the US top-rated comedy show, up for his first feature film, just as she had stepped from 'Laugh-In' into *Cactus Flower*. According to one member of the crew, 'She helped him with his timing and made his humour work. She would never be short with him, or if he wanted to try something and it didn't work, she was happy to do it again. She really was caring and giving to a newcomer when others might have been less patient.'

The combination worked well and with the added talents of Dudley Moore and Burgess Meredith, together with music from the Bee Gees and Barry Manilow, *Foul Play* was a guaranteed box-office hit. The critics made favourable comparisons with Hitchcock, and Colin Higgins's decision to direct his own work was fully vindicated, even though a complex car-chase sequence ended expensively with the wrecking of twenty-three automobiles. But Higgins had working as his cinematographer David Walsh, who had filmed the mother of all car-chase sequences with *Bullitt*, nine years before, directed by Peter Yates and starring Steve McQueen. Walsh argued that an actor filmed in a car that is actually skidding will always deliver a better performance than if the sequence is faked on a studio back-lot and so Goldie was submitted to a series of terrifying switchback rides across the streets of San Francisco.

The critics applauded both the film as a whole and the choice of leading lady. The *New York Times* went so far as to discover in Goldie 'a new-found acting talent', their critic enthusing, 'Her anger, imbued with all the quivering, outraged self-righteousness Miss

Hawn can muster, is enough to make the most hardened moviegoer melt.'

*Foul Play* made over $50 million at the box office and re-established Goldie Hawn as a leading lady in her own right. Its success led directly to the making of *Private Benjamin* and to the fortune that Goldie was to amass, making her one of the richest and most successful actresses in Hollywood's 100-year history. Yet it was a film that, in her grander days, she turned down, and only finally came to make by stepping into another actress's shoes.

Despite the critical acclaim and the newfound enthusiasm for her work, once again Goldie's career was about to be becalmed. Between *Foul Play* and her next Hollywood production there was to be a gap of three years, filled only by the actress going to Europe to make a little-regarded and long-forgotten co-production called *Lovers and Liars* or *Travels with Anita*. The story tells of a forty-year old married man, Guido, who is driving home to the bedside of his dying father accompanied by Anita, an American friend of his former mistress. She is young, beautiful and liberated in her attitudes and morals. During the journey the car is involved in an accident and a pedestrian is seriously injured. Unable to continue until the man recovers, the couple are drawn closer together and inevitably into a passionate relationship. Mesmerised by Anita's beauty and sexual prowess, Guido is distracted from the object of his journey and when finally he arrives home it is to find his father already dead. Not a storyline, then, to tempt American audiences into the cinemas nor to persuade the judges at the Oscars ceremony that Goldie had found yet another new dimension to her career. But it was the only work available, though ironically her leading man, Giancarlo Giannini, barely had time to draw breath. On the set in Rome he read scripts of the films that were to follow – in 1978, when *Lovers and Liars* was filmed, he made a total of six movies.

With a script based on an idea by Federico Fellini, *Lovers and Liars* was shot in English with an eye to worldwide distribution, and based on locations in Rome and Tuscany.

Giannini, who describes *Lovers and Liars* as 'a real flop', recalls,

'She was afraid the director, Mario Monicelli, wanted to make an erotic film, especially since she had seen me in *Swept Away* in which my character was a man who was very brutal in his relationships with women.

'One day, as we were shooting a scene in bed which displayed her naked back, she turned to the camera operator and told him not to shoot below her waistline. She explained that she was the mother of a small child and some day, were he to see the film, he might judge his mother in a negative way.'

Goldie rationalised this excursion into art-house movies by pointing out that Bill was working in Britain and that husband and wife could alternate weekends with each other in Rome or London. The Italians were delighted to have such a gorgeous Hollywood star in their country and when *Viaggio Con Anita* was released *Oggi* magazine enthused, 'The delicious Goldie Hawn proves a depth of acting talent some may have believed beyond her capability. Her portrayal of smouldering sensuality puts many of the other so-called sex symbols to shame.' Be that as it may, when the film was released in Britain and the United States, it disappeared without trace.

Fortunately for Goldie as far as Hollywood was concerned the dictum that a star is only as good as her last film was applied not to *Lovers and Liars* but to *Foul Play*, and suddenly there was a new feeling abroad about her. Asked to be one of the presenters at the annual Oscars ceremonies, the veteran writer Rex Reed observed of her, 'Gone is the old Tweety-Pie expression. She's ditched the teased hair and dumb-blonde image too. At the Awards ceremony she was one of the best-dressed and most dignified presenters onstage in the middle of what looked like a Hollywood junk-yard. Goldie has grown up.'

Part of the process of growth was the knowledge that to stay fresh in the eyes of the studio bosses she had to prove that there was more to Goldie Hawn than merely an actress who turned up on time, word-perfect, looking fresh, and able to laugh when the director ordered it. The way to go was production or direction. Recently she had learned that Barbra Streisand had become part of a three-picture deal with Orion which would result in her starring in and directing

*Yentl.* Goldie looked at a property called *The Contest*: 'I like the idea of producing. Getting something good on is hard, but I think I have vision. I know what works. I have clout. And I'm becoming more interested in directing; I have a director's eye and the older I get the more I begin to trust it.'

Nothing came of *The Contest* but as 1978 rolled over into 1979 and she became pregnant for the second time, the word was out that Goldie wanted a script to produce. She was approached by a triumvirate of writers – Charles Shyer, co-author of a Burt Reynolds box-office hit *Smokey and the Bandit,* Harvey Miller, an ex-army sergeant and once President Carter's joke-writer, and Nancy Meyers. Meyers had met Goldie while she was working for Ray Stark, Hollywood's most reclusive and Machiavellian power broker. The previous Christmas, Stark had fired Meyers from her post as the studio's chief script-doctor, but she had come out of her corner fighting with her first film outline about a pampered Jewish American Princess – a favoured phrase at the time – who joins the US army and comes to the slow realisation that there is more to life than a manicure.

In partnership with Shyer and Miller she visited Goldie and extracted the promise that if the three could produce a half-way decent script, Goldie would sell it to one of the major studios with her as producer and star. 'We weren't a team,' recalls Shyer now. 'Harvey was a close friend of mine and he and Nancy were working on something together but I came home one night and they were pitching this Jewish American Princess idea back and forth and it just grew and grew. I thought we could do it in six weeks – we were still writing it six months later.'

Though Miller had served in the army, to gather added authentic military detail Nancy Meyers put a tape recorder in her pocket and went down to the local recruitment office where she pretended she was upset with her life and was thinking of joining up. 'The whole recruiting scene is a rewritten transcript of what the guy actually said to Nancy,' says Shyer. 'He was the one who said you can quit any time you want!'

With the script finished Goldie, now heavily pregnant, started touting it round the studios. Nobody wanted to buy. 'The only person who really liked it was Don Simpson at Paramount but the powers-that-be wouldn't take it. First of all I don't think anyone envisioned Goldie as Jewish when in fact she was – they didn't like that – and I don't think they liked the idea of Goldie in a feminist movie, I think it bothered people at the time. When she slugs the guy at the end of the script, I think it shook people up a little. Plus there was really no big male co-star – it wasn't Goldie and Harrison Ford or something. She was going to have to carry this movie,' says Shyer.

To a large extent Goldie's ability to treat with the studio heads was as a result of her lengthy career, her relative youth and the success of *Foul Play*. But the money-men found it hard to dismiss their prejudices that here was a dumb blonde: 'In the beginning they patted me on the head, I was cute little Goldie. But the minute you stand up, you qualify as a bitch.'

According to Nancy Meyers the money-men were unable to correct their preconceptions: 'They expected certain movies from Jane Fonda and Jill Clayburgh, but not from sweet Goldie. Sweet Goldie wouldn't call a guy a schmuck and punch him on the nose. They didn't want her to fight back.'

But Goldie felt empowered. Giving birth to a 9lb 4oz girl in April 1979 at the Cedars-Sinai Medical Center was just one of the things she was doing that week. Mercifully there was no repetition of the emergency surrounding the birth of Oliver two-and-a-half years before, and though this birth, too, was by Caesarean section, mother and daughter – Kate Garry Hudson – emerged happy and well. She closed a deal for *Benjamin* with Warner Brothers and their tough head of production, Robert Shapiro.

Spring turned to autumn, and with the script for *Benjamin* now being honed by the Meyers-Shyer-Miller team and with a barely-adequate $8.5 million budget set in place by Warner Brothers, Goldie turned her attention to the other duties which fall to the lot of executive producer: casting, set design, locations, budgets, crew hire and schedule. Filming would start in December and the schedule worried her more than anything else: with production being charged to her at $75,000 a day she realised that, even with a nine-month old child, she was going to be working all hours. Even before shooting commenced she confessed that the work was a big drain on her energy.

Nevertheless, she found time to travel to Nashville for the funeral of her uncle OD, Rut Hawn's elder brother. Rut, remembering the guidance OD had given when he was starting out as a musician in New York fifty years earlier, was uncharacteristically snappy when the local newspaper in reporting his brother's death focused its story on Goldie. 'Why did they do that?' he barked. 'He had so much in his own right.' OD had married a Catholic and converted to Catholicism and at the funeral Goldie, well known for her half-Jewish, half-Presbyterian background, shocked many in the congregation by stepping forward to take the Sacrament. 'Musta been a liberal priest,' observes a family member drily. 'Those Catholics are usually pretty sticky about letting non-Catholics partake.'

Back in Hollywood, Goldie set about hiring a director. The first choice, Arthur Hillier, was let go early on because he felt the script could be construed as being anti-Semitic, notwithstanding the three writers' Jewish birth and Goldie's own Jewish ancestry on her mother's side. This decision helped endear her to Robert Shapiro; though he admits to having been wary of the concept of actress-as-producer. Soon he was bracketing Goldie with Clint Eastwood and Robert Redford; actors-turned-film-makers who thought about the whole movie and not simply their individual contribution.

With the storyline now incorporating Judy Benjamin ending up in France, a brief visit was made in November by the producer to Paris to audition for the role of Judy Benjamin's French lover, Henri. 'He has to be between thirty-five and forty, speak English, be handsome, amusing, virile and irresistible,' she declared. A total of twenty-five actors were auditioned, including a tall blond Frenchman called Yves Renier, who in real life fitted the description perfectly; but in the end the part went to a New York theatre actor, Armand Assante. None the less, Goldie and Renier went out to dinner. Before too long they were in bed. Renier was married with a six-year old daughter, Goldie was the mother of two children aged three, and seven months. The way these things go, it could have been just a one-night stand.

Back in Hollywood fights broke out with the money-men over the storyline. There was great resistance, for example, to the wedding-night sex-scene between Goldie and the actor Albert Brooks, where Goldie and her writers wanted her character to be on the floor, degraded by what takes place. That survived, but a line at the end of the movie which turned Eileen Brennan's tough army captain into a man via a sex-change operation was dropped. A scene was shot to drop into the end section of the movie where Goldie was with her friends in a Paris museum; that too was canned. 'She lost it a little bit and had gone a bit over the edge. She started talking real fast, motor-mouthing, and it was a bit uncomfortable, a bit weird,' recalls Shyer. 'I thought it was the best acting Goldie did in the movie, incredibly brilliant. I wanted to keep it, but I was out-voted.'

Though Goldie was in overall control, and though ultimately the film's success or failure was down to her, Goldie believed in parity when it came to her writers and co-producers. She earned the respect of her collaborators by insisting that no one among them had autonomy and that decisions such as casting should be voted upon. No scene was changed without consultation, and in delivering her lines to camera she refused to alter a single one without prior discussion. An early example of their unanimity of thought was when Hal Williams auditioned for the part of Sergeant Ross. After reading just three lines Williams was brought up short by a delighted chorus of: 'Hire him!'

When principal photography started at the Warner Brothers studio in December this led to the new director, Howard Zieff, finding himself in the untenable position of his writers being able to appeal over his head to Goldie when he took crucial decisions. Either Shyer or Meyers was on set every day, making sure their director did not deviate from their original blueprint. Though Zieff said little, the crew became visibly disgruntled when Harvey Miller, the third of the triumvirate, dropped in to 'pep up' some lines. There were battles, particularly in the cutting room, but in the end, 'Howard listened to us,' says Shyer drily. 'Time heals all wounds and whatever wounds were there are healed.'

Zieff took this constant interference in reasonably good part and encouraged his girlfriend to entertain the actors who weren't needed on the set. But, unversed in chic Parisian ways, even this hospitable gesture was not without its downside. 'When he got the bill for tea at the Plaza Athénée he nearly had a heart attack,' recalled an eyewitness.

The film's most memorable sequence came from a single line in the script: 'Private Benjamin undergoes basic training'. From that simple instruction, recalls the film's cinematographer David Walsh, grew a marvellous sequence which demonstrated to Zieff and the entire crew what an accomplished extempore actress they were working with: 'When you see her with those big troopers, running and going over the hurdles, well, how do you direct something like that? Well you just yell "Go, Goldie", and go she did. She was totally game and so fit from all her dancing that all that running and jumping and climbing was nothing. She just did it.'

Walsh, with thirty years' Hollywood experience, adds, 'As a producer I would give Goldie a ten. I wouldn't do that for many of them because others make too many mistakes. But she is a smart girl. Filming *Private Benjamin* was a wonderful event. If you have Goldie as a friend you have a true friend; she will stand by you. Not foolishly, but if she believes in you and thinks something is right for the film, then that's it.'

Yet despite the pressures Goldie still had time to be a mother. One morning she received word that Oliver had been hurt at school and instantly left the set to drive straight to him. Far from infuriating the professionals it endeared her to them; she had already earned the respect of the crew by learning everyone's name and by never losing her temper on set.

Filming proceeded on the Warner Brothers' lot and in Beverly Hills, though a plan to shoot some sequences in New Orleans had to be dropped for budgetary reasons. In the trailer she made her home

Laura Hawn was usually to be found, her Gauloise-tinted voice grating out jokes not everyone immediately got. By the twelfth week the production team had moved to France to shoot *Private Benjamin*'s curious tailpiece of a finale. Though the film became a massive box-office success story, its coda continues to baffle the critics who see no logic in Judy Benjamin ending up in France. Charles Shyer concedes, 'It was an odd structure, it rambled a little bit, took her to these weird places. We didn't really know one hundred per cent what we were doing. But going to France was fulfilling a fantasy for three of us.'

That fantasy extended to Brussels in the case of one of the trio, and scenes set outside the NATO headquarters there were written in. 'I said what in the world are we going to Brussels for if it's just the shot of a building?' recalls David Walsh. 'The answer came back, "Well, I've never been to Brussels."' Walsh saved his producer thousands of dollars and many days' production by walking up a street in Neuilly and finding a nearby building which served the purpose.

To film in Belgium, or not to film in Belgium – it mattered little to Goldie, who by now was in love with France and all things French. After their initial encounter Yves Renier had followed her back to Hollywood for a screen-test; now the two of them were back together on his home patch. After twelve weeks, *Private Benjamin* was just two days behind schedule, an amazing achievement for a fledgling producer and Goldie was relishing her new-found power as well as her new-found love.

The crew of twenty-seven lined up the scene where Goldie, as Judy Benjamin, makes love with Armand Assante: those on the set remember the enormous concern she showed her fellow-actor, whose first feature-film it was. 'She was very giving to him,' recalls David Walsh. 'There was a scene where Armand is giving a lecture and she comes in and he introduces her – there was a nice sweetness about it, and she looks at him like she really cares for him – it's amazing what one look can do for an actor.'

Some, but not many, were aware that off the set life was imitating art, and that maybe that look at Assante was merely a reflection of her feelings for Renier; but it must have been a confusing time. With the benefit of hindsight Goldie's comments to the American writer Fred Robbins, who had flown over to interview Goldie on location, indicate a mind that is not yet ready to assimilate the enormity of the changes happening to her. Asked how family life was, she replied, 'Sometimes my son will just grab me happily, or grab Katie, or Daddy, if he's around, and he'll say, "Oh, we're a family, aren't we, Mom?" And, God, there's nothing more reassuring in the whole world than that. For a little child to feel those roots is the most important thing imaginable.'

In the meantime, there was a film to be finished. A last-minute row broke out between the studio and the producer over the design of the publicity posters, which showed Goldie as Benjamin with a tin-hat and her blouse undone. Meyers and Shyer were incensed, feeling this one image could destroy the underlying feminist message of the movie. Goldie went to Robert Shapiro and warned, 'If you're going to use that picture of me with my blouse undone and my bra showing I'm not doing the "Tonight" show. As for the rest of the publicity schedule, you can forget it.'

Warner Brothers backed down, but took a firmer stance when it came to the final cut of the movie: when Goldie finally handed over the finished product to the studio, it was running at an overlong two hours and twenty minutes. At that point *Benjamin* was no longer hers to play with, and by the time it was ready for cinema release Warner Brothers had lopped thirty minutes off the running-time, arguing that no comedy had ever run successfully at two hours and twenty minutes. There was no appeal against this decision, and in the anxious months leading up to its premiere Goldie and her collaborators Meyers, Shyer and Miller, had no conception of how the finished product would turn out. Goldie vowed, 'Next time it's going to be different. I'm never going to agree to another contract like this one – when you're a creative producer you need a contract that reflects that, or you just go crazy. When other people don't have the same sensitivities as you, and they have the power, it can drive you wild.' Since she had no idea of how the film would turn out, she said, it would be a picture she either loved, or disowned.

She confessed that she had had to make concessions in order to get the film made at all, and that she had not stuck her neck out or made big demands of the studio bosses because of her inexperience. But when *Private Benjamin* was finally released later that year it was, as Charles Shyer put it, 'as if we'd bottled lightning'. At a preview in Denver the audience rose out of their seats and cheered Goldie in the scene where she stands up to her parents. Robert Shapiro, the only studio boss to back Goldie and her collaborators, sat in the back row watching and smiling, realising with a rising sense of triumph that his gamble had paid off.

From day one *Private Benjamin* was a box-office sensation, eventually earning nearly $200 million worldwide. Goldie's take was fifteen per cent of gross; but perhaps more importantly for her future, this was a hallmark Goldie Hawn film, one which paid back to her fans in full measure the expectations they had had ever since 'Laugh-In' but which successive movies had failed to deliver. It was her eleventh film since the Oscar-winning *Cactus Flower* and, at last, it seemed Goldie had hit the right speed.

The film's themes were picked up and obsessively chewed over by the press; and Goldie, driving down the street in Beverly Hills, was cheered vociferously by groups of women who felt she had said something on their behalf. Most importantly, it demonstrated to Hollywood, and beyond Hollywood to the outside world, that a woman *could* be an actress and produce a smash hit at the same time. To Goldie, this was not exactly news, but she accepted the plaudits that came her way – including three Oscar nominations – with good grace. With a sizeable stake in the movie she had just made herself rich and created an investment for the future. Never again would she work without producer's points. Almost as an afterthought, she announced her price as an actress had vaulted threefold to $3.5 million.

She got a gratifyingly contrite letter from Don Simpson, the Paramount Pictures boss who'd missed the opportunity of taking up *Benjamin*: 'When we fuck up, we fuck up big.'

\* \* \*

Reviewing the box-office success of *Foul Play* it now made sense to the Universal studio chiefs to capitalise on the inspired pairing of Goldie with Chevy Chase. Rather than tread the Colin Higgins route again – he had been accused of producing scripts that were 'samey' – Goldie's producer Ray Stark chose an unusual piece by the celebrated New York playwright Neil Simon, *Seems Like Old Times*. Simon had been behind seventeen films of his work in the past thirteen years and could also be accused of formularising his work, but this one differed in that it was neither set in his native city nor was it based on real people and events.

It was an out-and-out farce, and all the more demanding on the actors because of it. 'Farce is like juggling six balls in the air at the same time,' explained Simon. 'It's very difficult to keep them all going. The pace must be very fast. It's not done often because we don't have such wonderful exponents like Cary Grant and Irene Dunne any more, you need actors who are facile enough to do this kind of comedy. Luckily for me, Goldie and Chevy can do it.' Chase played the part of a novelist forced into robbing a bank by a gang of thugs, who then has to seek refuge with his ex-wife, played by Goldie, who now lives with a law-abiding new husband who is standing for political office.

Filming, straight off the back of *Benjamin*'s post-production, took seven weeks in June and July and centred on the picturesque coastline of Big Sur in California. Once again the cameraman was David Walsh, who had filmed *Benjamin* and *Foul Play*, and though Goldie's private life was, at this stage, becoming extremely complex it was a happy shoot. Once again Laura Hawn showed up to support her daughter, and Goldie struck an upbeat relationship with Jay Sandrich, an inspired comedy director who had come from TV and whose first feature film it was. The rapport between her and Chevy Chase was better than ever. 'He's an off-the-wall guy but she handled him well and I think he thanked her for that by behaving himself and not playing up,' recalled Walsh. 'Goldie is always prepared and she always brings much more to the table than the part requires – so many good ideas and so much vitality. Chevy had also grown by that time and Jay Sandrich was perfect, a no-problem director who really knew jokes. Having come from TV, he doesn't get one laugh, but three laughs out of every joke.'

On the set Goldie got the chance to meet one of Hollywood's great characters, a woman named Margaret Booth who had been at MGM in the 1930s with the legendary director Irving Thalberg and, despite the fact she was now eighty, was overseeing the edit of *Seems Like Old Times*. Walsh recalls, 'She was the most vital person I have ever known – she would go to the basketball game and to the races, and was very, very outspoken. I remember doing dailies* with her and Herb Ross and she didn't like something. She said to the director, "Well, Herbert, that certainly isn't very good!" She would tell it like she saw it and even at that age was a powerful lady.' With authority and power still new to her, Goldie cherished such rare moments when a woman was allowed her say, and respected for it.

With filming of *Old Times* wrapped by July, what happened next was in complete contradiction to all Goldie's stated perceptions of family life and the one-woman-one-man idyll. She disappeared with Yves Renier, abandoning her cherished family and flying in the face of everything she had ever uttered regarding the importance of family cohesion as she set off on a round-the-world odyssey.

Renier, an acclaimed actor in his native France and a national celebrity for his TV cop show 'Commissaire Moulin', was in many respects a re-run of Goldie's affair with Bruno Wintzell. Unlike Wintzell, he walked away from a top-rated show to pursue his affair with Goldie and their bumpy, sometimes volatile relationship was to last the next three years, leaving behind a wife and daughter and spending, he says, all his money in keeping up with Goldie. After a brief spell in South Africa following his failed screen test in Los Angeles, he called Goldie and told her he was coming to live with her in America.

Still married, still sharing a house with Bill Hudson, both appalled and excited at this magnificently Gallic gesture, Goldie dispatched a

* Viewing footage.

limousine to pick up her lover from the airport and had him installed in a state-room aboard the old Atlantic liner, the *Queen Mary*, now moored at Long Beach and transformed into a floating hotel. Though their reunion was as passionate as it was romantic, almost immediately Renier came to understand the disparity between the earnings of a French TV star, albeit a successful one, and those of an Oscar-winning international actress. He was spending above his head.

Reports leaked from Bill Hudson's camp suggested that back in the Spring Goldie had insouciantly brought her lover back to the marital home and introduced him to her husband. 'She introduced him ... although Bill didn't know what was going on,' the source, so close to Hudson it might almost have been him, revealed. 'She is so brazen. Bill found out eventually, through friends he has in Paris, that Goldie was having an affair with this two-bit Frenchman. It killed him. Bill is an easygoing man. But it's hard to forgive a woman when she throws an affair in your face.'

It emerged that soon after Goldie auditioned Renier the previous November, the pair had been seen dining and discoing in a series of chic Parisian night-spots. In May there was a confrontation at home between Goldie and Bill, and by the end of June Goldie was established in a flat in Regents Park, London.

Goldie's original intention had been to take the children with her over to Europe, but after further discussions and an insistence by Hudson that they remain with him, she left empty-handed with Renier. From there the couple flew to Paris again, and by mid-July they had made their way to William Holden's safari park in Nairobi. Their travels continued onwards, without children, to Hong Kong and Tokyo. A production team which had flown out to Paris to prepare for a 'Goldie Hawn in Paris' TV special were told to pack their bags and go home again – Miss Hawn was 'too shaken up' with her personal affairs to be able to tape the show. Renier, according to French writer Michele Stouvenot, 'always had the reputation of being a Romeo, but since his marriage he seemed to have calmed down. He seemed to be terrified of his wife Virginie, who had done her best to keep a tight rein on him.'

*Above:* Arguably a great movie, undoubtedly a great performance: Goldie as poor white trash in Spielberg's *Sugarland Express*.

*Below:* 'When you look at the money I want it to be an orgasmic experience.' Goldie tries her best in *The Heist*, 1971.

*Left:* Almost a husband: Goldie with Bruno Wintzell, 1974.

*Right:* Julie Christie may have been the star of Warren Beatty's *Shampoo*, but Goldie got the percentage points.

warren beatty
julie christie · goldie hawn

*SHAMPOO*

*Left:* The star and her agent: Goldie out on the town with Stan Kamen.

*Below:* The one she loves to hate – husband number two, Bill Hudson.

*Left:* Yves Renier.

Bottled lightning: Goldie as Private Judy Benjamin, 1980.

*Above:* Guiding, protecting, pushing – the ever-present Laura Hawn nursed dreams of her daughter becoming a star.

*Below:* A pensive moment on the set of *Seems Like Old Times*, caught by cinematographer David Walsh.

*Left:* Without a wedding ring, the magic lives on: Goldie and Kurt have been together since 1983.

*Below:* The Hawn-Russell spread in Old Snowmass, Colorado.

*Above:* Happy families: Goldie with Oliver, Wyatt, Kurt and Kate.

*Right:* For once, no glamour: Goldie kitted out in Flabbercast in *Death Becomes Her*.

*Right:* Gorgeous at fifty: posing at the Deauville Film Festival.

*Below:* Over-the-top vintage Goldie: her classic performance in *First Wives Club,* 1996.

For most of the summer of 1980, then, Goldie was separated from her children. By September, bitter words were tumbling from the Bill Hudson camp: 'She has hardly been home for the past year. She just plays at being mother; Bill has been raising the kids for the past twelve months while she's got everyone round her telling her she's the perfect mother. She went off with Renier in July and said she'd be back in five weeks – she's still away.'

Hudson, who some years later was to mount an attack on his ex-wife for her behaviour at this time, played it cool to start with: 'I don't have anything bad to say about her. She's a great human being. I still love her. Maybe Goldie didn't feel she could turn to me, but I'd still take her back. Being married to Goldie is the best time I've had in my life.'

But the frustration soon mounted and to another interviewer he confessed, 'I'm still willing to work things out but right now I'm juggling so many emotions. I'm sitting here like a lame duck while she's out there playing, deciding my fate. I feel as though I'm waiting for a verdict to be handed down.'

The verdict for the hapless Hudson was a thumbs-down and by the time Goldie was back in Tinseltown to announce that she was going to do a film version of the show *Chicago* – an ambition that would take another twenty years to come to fruition – Hudson had filed for divorce, citing irreconcilable differences. He chose not to cite Renier as a co-respondent, probably because by now he was having a relationship with Kelly Lange, a Los Angeles-based TV reporter.

In October Hudson opened his heart to the gossip-writer Liz Smith, pledging there would be no bitter contested divorce or custody battle: 'We aren't fighting over anything, we're going to do the best for our two children, including having joint custody worked out around our separate career needs.' He added that it wouldn't need a court to work out the financial settlement and continued, 'Our divorce is not tragic, it is sad because there are children and six years involved, but tragic it's not.'

Smith commented drily, 'He is either completely sincere or an awfully good actor.'

Hudson's contention that the divorce was nothing more than a sad parting of the ways carried the customary gloss of sophisticated PR campaign management, but behind the scenes emotions ran higher. It was the third consecutive long-term relationship Goldie had pulled out from, and once again there was to be a bitter battle over money.

Goldie was deeply involved with Yves Renier – involved to an almost frightening degree. Following her round-the-world odyssey she was now showing Renier the delights of Hawaii, where she had married Gus Trikonis eleven years before and where she had dallied with Hudson subsequently. Back in Tinseltown friends predicted that, as Elizabeth Taylor habitually did, Goldie would go the whole hog and marry her latest lover. Speculation increased when she started to wear a single diamond necklace which, she explained, had been given to her by Renier's grandmother.

As Christmas 1980 approached, the relationship seemed to have grown even stronger. Goldie arrived back in France to travel to Orleans, seventy miles south-west of Paris, to stay at Yves's country house. At the same time, *Seems Like Old Times* was released in America and did a record $10 million business over the holiday period. To her embarrassment Goldie found an over-enthusiastic Ray Stark placing adverts all over the Hollywood trade press in support of her nomination for an Oscar. Whether this had any effect on Goldie *not* winning the 1981 Best Actress Oscar – it went instead to Sissy Spacek for *Coal Miner's Daughter* – is hard to say. Stark was pushing Goldie as *his* actress for her part in *Seems Like Old Times*, whereas the natural nomination within the time-frame would have been for *Private Benjamin*.

In the end, the nomination did come, but the almighty Academy did not like being told by a producer whom to honour.

*Benjamin* had to be promoted abroad, and by the beginning of 1981 Goldie prepared to capitalise on the film's undoubted international appeal by embarking on a world tour. First stop, predictably enough, was France, where a year before she had sealed her love for

Yves Renier and shut the door on her marriage, as well as shot the curious tailpiece to her film. She flew into Paris and booked into the Plaza Athénée hotel but, according to local reports, though Yves was now officially 'Mr Goldie' he was fearful of press attention and the consequent reaction of his wife if he were to move in with his mistress.

The relationship was not without its ups and downs. In Paris Renier very publicly stood her up on a date, though finally the couple were reunited at the exclusive jet-set nightclub Castel's, favoured by the likes of Princess Caroline of Monaco. Here, though, the couple proceeded to have a very public row. 'He was arrogant and he didn't even have the courage to have an honest fight,' reported an eye-witness. 'He treated her like dirt. It was all innuendoes, and very embarrassing to other people nearby.'

At issue was the next stage of Goldie's international promotional tour, South Africa. She had two first-class tickets and expected Renier to accompany her. In the end he relented and flew down with her to Johannesburg, where the couple installed themselves in adjoining suites at the plush Ladrost Hotel. But much of the time Goldie was openly cold towards her lover, and on one occasion after an interview in the hotel she snapped, 'I'm fed up, I'm going to bed.' Renier, who had waited outside during the interviewer, said, 'Oh come on, Gold, let's go to a restaurant.' But Goldie snapped back: 'You do what you want. I'm going to bed.' A chastened Renier confessed to an accompanying photographer, Mike McCann, that their love had grown cold. The couple were scheduled to fly on to Australia but next morning Goldie took the first flight back to Los Angeles saying she missed her children: 'I've had enough of this travelling. I don't need it at all. I've been away from home too long.'

It was the first of many separations and ultimately many rows. Because of the difficulties over her divorce from Bill Hudson and Renier's own delicate domestic arrangements – he was trying to back out of his marriage with as much grace as could be mustered – the affair was kept as far away from the press as possible. To this day Renier is convinced that virtually no one knew of the relationship, even though he had walked away from a top-rated French TV show and his public wanted to know what had happened to him. He describes it as 'a very underground situation'. Certainly the newspaper clippings libraries in both America and France are remarkably empty of any detailed accounts of the runaway romance and the people of Hawaii, who became quite used to the sight of Goldie and her Frenchman during the years 1980 to 1983, were far too discreet to talk.

Back in the States when asked about Renier, Goldie snapped back, 'I divorced because of another man, and he let me down. Frenchmen are macho and hypocritical. I've been married twice and twice it failed, but now for the first time I'm free to do as I please, and I'm going to enjoy it.'

Later a spokeswoman was to 'clarify' her statement that she had divorced Hudson because of Yves Renier: 'Goldie's divorce is not purely because of Yves. There were problems with her marriage before she ever met him.'

But, in time-honoured Hollywood tradition, it was not the whole story.

# CHAPTER EIGHT

# *The Dividing Line*

*'And what says my concealed lady to our cancelled love?'*
*– ibid.*

If 1980 was the busiest year yet for Goldie, with the shooting of two films, *Benjamin* and *Old Times*, and with post-production and promotion of *Benjamin* an added burden on her time, 1981 was, by comparison, an oasis of calm professionally speaking. Ahead was the finalisation of her divorce from Bill, and a money settlement which would include sacrificing the house on the beach at Malibu. But as an actor and producer, Goldie was not in demand.

The only drama in her life was the divorce. Bill Hudson went to court saying that, although he had started proceedings the previous July, by January 1981 Goldie had still failed to respond. Could he now have his divorce by default? Goldie's people said she had been 'too busy' to do anything about it. She herself went public, saying that Bill had 'resented' being second string in the marriage insofar as money was concerned

Back came Hudson: the divorce was off. 'We've gotten back together. I think we have worked out most of our differences. I'm going to nullify my divorce action in court this week. I'm convinced we can all work it out now, and Goldie agrees.' This was news to Goldie's legal team, but to observers it was a signal from Hudson that he was prepared to forgive and forget. His wife, unfortunately for Hudson, was not.

To the stop-go nature of her acting career was now added the extra burden, as a producer, of convincing the money-men there was more where *Benjamin* came from. In theory she was now Hollywood's golden girl, having brought home a surefire hit; but the reality was that there would be a four-year gap between producing this film and the next. There were meetings with expectant studio bosses at Warner's who, infuriatingly, contrived to be at the same time enthusiastic about Goldie making them millions more dollars, and wary about making decisions. Goldie mentioned a property she had her eye on, a wartime drama set in a factory which highlighted the role of working women, but there were precious few jokes in the treatment and that frightened the money-men. The talks reached *impasse* and Goldie looked for something more commercial.

As ever, the gap between public perception and professional reality remained wide. Goldie had plenty of credit to trade on in Hollywood, though a new movie would have helped to calm her ever-present fears; but *Newsweek* magazine, not privy to this latest *impasse*, presented her with a bouquet. She was, they asserted, the most popular actress in America: 'She makes audiences unreasonably happy. The comic pleasure she provides moviegoers – a pleasure to which men and women, children and critics seem equally susceptible – is generous and direct. She combines the babyfaced sultriness of Brigitte Bardot, the girl-next-door familiarity of Jean Arthur, the daffy dithering of Judy Holliday and the madcap perkiness of Tweetie Pie, the cartoon canary. If Barbra Streisand wears her stardom like a tiara and Jane Fonda wears hers like a merit badge, Goldie wears hers like a borrowed raincoat thrown over the shoulder.'

This critique accurately summed up Goldie's appeal, but failed to make the point that of the dozen or so films she had made to date, very few of them had been a suitable vehicle for her exceptional talents. Though in some regards it was flattering to be compared with other Hollywood funny-women – Lucille Ball and Marilyn Monroe were also often cited – the truth was that hers was a unique talent, one which, when utilised properly, outshone all Hollywood's funny women, both of the present day and of the past. It seemed that circumstances had conspired to keep the *real* Goldie Hawn off the screen for most of her career. In this Goldie, her agents and her producers were all in part to blame: her first four breakthrough films for Columbia under Mike Frankovich slowly deflated the bubble which had escaped from 'Laugh-In', and the following pair for Universal – *Petrovka* and *Sugarland* – did nothing to bring back that wondrous, madcap joyousness which had brought the nation to its knees in adulation a dozen years before. *Shampoo* had its focus on Julie Christie (and Lee Grant won the Oscar), *Duchess and the Dirtwater Fox* was a shallow follow-up movie which Glenda Jackson had wisely sidestepped, and not until *Foul Play* and *Benjamin* had Goldie really come face-to-face with her potential. Yet all these ups and downs were lost to view; the US press continued to treat her as a star as if every movie she had ever made had Oscar potential.

Compared with the two actresses the columnists liked to bracket her with – Barbra Streisand and Jane Fonda – she would always come a poor third. Against Goldie's twelve movies Fonda had made thirty-five, and though Streisand had made fewer they were, unlike Goldie's, of consistently high quality, from *Funny Girl* and *Hello Dolly!* to *The Way We Were* and *A Star Is Born*. From her first agent, Art Simon, there had appeared to be no attempt to forge a consistent career-path; the studio system did little to give her screen persona a shape, and her own inclinations to prove to the world that she could be a serious actress were all impediments to a greater success.

In one sense, very little of this mattered. By 1981 Goldie Hawn was a multi-millionaire, an Oscar-winner, a trailblazing producer and a world-class heroine loved and adored far beyond the reaches of the English-speaking nations. She had left an indelible imprint on Hollywood's hundred-year old history. Yet on the other hand, those who analysed these things were in no doubt she was capable of far greater things, conscious the while that comedy is the hardest entertainment of all to pull off, and that scriptwriters tended to think that only men did jokes. The male-dominated industry of which she was now a lustrous part had done Goldie no favours, nor was it about to do so.

Norman Jewison, gifted producer and director of such films as *The Thomas Crown Affair*, *Rollerball* and *Fiddler on the Roof* was looking for someone to cast opposite Burt Reynolds in a piece called *Best Friends*. Reynolds, who had briefly been married to Goldie's 'Laugh-In' stablemate Judy Carne, was a multi-faceted male lead churning out movies at an astonishing rate. He had just finished *The Best Little Whorehouse in Texas* with Dolly Parton, but his repertoire extended to such disparate pieces as *Smokey and the Bandit*, *Cannonball Run* and John Boorman's stark vision of man, *Deliverance*.

Jewison was working out of Warner's as a producer and at least *Best Friends* would keep Goldie on the lot while a production deal of her own was found. With an asking-price of $3 million a film and with an expensive divorce on the way, it seemed like a useful stopgap. The plot of *Best Friends* centres on two writers who have enjoyed a peaceful professional relationship but encounter problems when they get married and visit their respective families. Shooting was due to commence in Buffalo, New York state and Vienna, Virginia, in the spring of 1982. Meanwhile Goldie signed to make a TV special for ABC, 'Goldie and the Kids – Listen To Us'. This show had the virtue of displaying Goldie's natural warmth and empathy with children, rising above the standard song-and-dance format to allow her to spend most of the hour conversing with children at their level.

It was during filming of *Best Friends* that Goldie discovered her father was suffering from emphysema; he had been taken ill at home in Las Vegas and as his condition worsened the seventy-three-year old musician was rushed into the Cedars Sinai Hospital in Los Angeles. Soon it became clear that he was dying, though the process was to be a lengthy one lasting nearly three months. 'They kept him alive for all that time, eighty-one days, and Laura went to the hospital and stayed with him almost all day long, every day,' recalls his sister-in-law Mary Hawn. 'She was still devoted to him even though they were no longer living as man and wife. That's the way it was.'

Naturally the press focused on Rut's daughter racing to the hospital between takes on set. Warren Beatty came by to add his support, to hang around the intensive care ward and to bring Goldie soup, but Rut continued his grip on life and it was not until June that Edward Rutledge Hawn, musician, eccentric, inspiration and support to his golden daughter, finally died. Rut Hawn, not the glorious descendant of a signatory of the Declaration of

Independence, but the son of a humble railroad telegraph operator, breathed his last on a sunny June morning.

The woman he had abandoned as his wife seven years before, the woman he had been married to for nearly fifty years, now stepped forward to take control of events. Though Rut was born Presbyterian Laura Hawn insisted on a Jewish funeral. 'It was a Hebrew service,' recalls Mary Hawn, 'then after the body had been taken care of we had a service in the sitting room of Goldie's house and there was a Protestant minister who came and held a celebration of Rutledge's life, rather than mourning his death. People in the family told stories about what they remembered of him.' Goldie paid her own tribute to the man who, if not the driving force behind her career, had provided insight and succour as she made her first tentative steps in showbusiness.

The final voyage of the man who had bus-and-trucked his way across the United States during a half-century of making music was, extraordinarily, to the Hillside Memorial Park on West Centinela Avenue in Los Angeles. Extraordinary, because the cemetery is Jewish. That the Presbyterian Rut Hawn, a man who held strong anti-Semitic views according to one son-in-law, should end in a Jewish grave was conceived by some to be a ghastly act of revenge by Laura for having been abandoned. Others merely saw it as a preparation for the day when she would lie alongside him, the act of a wife who had never stopped loving her querulous, restless loner of a husband. To those Hawns back in Arkansas, deep-died Presbyterians all, the choice of their cousin's final resting place merely raised an eyebrow or two; but for the benefit of the brothers who turned out for Rut's funeral, if not for Rut, there was at least a Presbyterian minister present. A lone fiddler played him out of this world and he was laid to rest alongside the likes of Jack Benny, Eddie Cantor and Dinah Shore.

Her father's death affected Goldie profoundly. At this time she determined to follow a broader career path, aiming for more serious roles. To this end she pitched for the lead in *Sophie's Choice*, Alan Pakula's adaptation of the William Styron post-Holocaust novel about a Polish concentration camp internee finding that her past still haunts her. The script was one of the darkest and most unsettling pieces ever to be made into a Hollywood film; but it suited Goldie's mood. In the end the part went to Meryl Streep, earning her an Oscar. To those closest to Goldie, comparing what she might have done with the role as against what was achieved by Streep was rather like comparing Goldie's version of 'Carey' against the original sung by Joni Mitchell. When it came down to it, she just wasn't in the same league.

For someone who had come so far so fast, the star clung tenaciously to her roots, nearly always in interviews citing the halcyon days of childhood in Takoma Park, and gathering her extended family about her whenever she could – Laura Hawn was now a permanent fixture on any film-set, the Praetorian guard at the gate of her dressing-room, and was soon to emerge as a bit-part player in some of Goldie's movies. Rut had landed the odd walk-on before his demise, and even sister Patti had been dragged in. A former social worker, it turned out she was a deft and charming publicist and her skills were to be utilised on future Goldie projects.

Since the days of watching Warren Beatty take control of his destiny by becoming producer of his own films, Goldie had seen this as the only way forward. To be fully empowered, the actor must have control of the whole film, not just the part they were playing. Laura's atavistic entrepreneurial skills were born anew in her daughter, and the child who had counted out the change in the Flowers Gift Shop was now able to marshal multi-million budgets.

Since *Private Benjamin*'s colossal box office success, Hollywood was looking to Goldie to see how she could match or beat it.* *Benjamin* had been the brainchild of Nancy Meyers – a brilliant concept forged in the heat and pressure of working long years for Hollywood's biggest fish, Ray Stark. But now there was a vacuum. No scripts which

---

* As if goading her into action, *Life* magazine ran a front-cover story carrying Goldie's picture and the headline, 'Shrewd and Sexy – the third most powerful woman in Hollywood'. Numbers one and two were Barbra Streisand and Jane Fonda. The pressure was on to live up to this sobriquet.

matched Nancy Meyers's for originality and verve were forthcoming, yet the money and support and enthusiasm for a new Goldie-produced product were all in place. All that was missing was a script.

Goldie had formed the Hawn-Sylbert Movie Company, with offices on South Buena Vista Street in beautiful downtown Burbank, not a million miles from the 'Good Morning, World' studios where she had started on the short path to stardom nearly fifteen years before. Anthea Sylbert had made a name for herself as a costume designer for such movies as *Rosemary's Baby, Carnal Knowledge* and *Chinatown* before meeting Goldie on the set of *Shampoo* in 1974. She was a true Hollywood insider; uniquely, she was known, liked and highly regarded by all who did business with her. Her costume work had won her two Oscar nominations, one in 1974 for *Chinatown* and again in 1977 for *Julia*. But she was much more than a woman who worked with clothes, and soon after *Julia* she was head-hunted by Warner Brothers to become their vice-president in charge of production. She was a woman with a reputation for sorting problems, as best exemplified by her first assignment at Warners – trying to get the film of *Greystoke* out of writer (and on that occasion director) Robert Towne while he had become obsessed with making another movie, *Personal Best*. She and Goldie had been neighbours in Malibu and had a high regard for each other.

Following the runaway success of *Private Benjamin* Warner's had looked to TV for a spin-off series. CBS picked up the option, trying out a four-show pilot which left the critics with their heads in hands – for fear of upsetting middle America's cornball brigade, Judy Benjamin was no longer a Jewish American princess, nor did she espouse the feminist cause. Goldie's part as Private Benjamin was taken by a virtual unknown, Lorna Patterson, whose only known work at that time was as a screwball air stewardess in the disaster spoof, *Airplane,* and the part written for her reflected that previous experience. The show was dismally produced by Don Reo and *On Cable* magazine reported, 'His product was so ill conceived and poorly edited it was difficult to follow the mere twenty-odd minutes of flimsy plotting.'

Reo was fired and the 'I Love Lucy' production team of Madelyn Davis and Bob Carroll Jr were drafted in. Charles Shyer, who would have liked to stay with his pet project, was dropped by CBS at an early stage: 'We were told that CBS wasn't interested in doing the same kind of TV show, not interested in the message of the film, they wanted a female Gomer Pile.*

'They told us that the female lead wasn't going to be Jewish – they just dropped the whole Jewish element. They took the substance out of it and it was just a piece of a shit. It was a terrible show, embarrassing, it demeaned the movie and it made us feel bad.'

Though TV's 'Private Benjamin' continued to be a sorry tribute to its Hollywood progenitor it at least had the virtue of providing ongoing employment to two of the film's stars, Hal Williams as Sergeant Ross and Eileen Brennan as Captain Lewis. Brennan had felt warmly towards Goldie since the good old, bad old days of 'Laugh-In' but their association developed into a close friendship during the shooting of the original *Benjamin* and continued as the actresses went their separate ways. Though others hated the TV 'Benjamin', Brennan had cause to be grateful for continued employment: her elder son, aged three, had learning disabilities but because of her ongoing role she was able to afford to send him to special schools even though she was a single parent.

A couple of months after Rut Hawn's death Eileen and Goldie arranged to meet for dinner at a Venice Beach restaurant. Goldie was an hour-and-a-half late but eventually the pair met up and had dinner. They spent some time talking about the future of the 'Benjamin' TV series as it had been closed down for a week because the scripts were not good enough. Later as they walked outside and were saying their goodbyes, a passing car struck Brennan, throwing her up on the windshield. The actress suffered broken legs, a fractured skull, facial fractures and internal haemorrhaging. Police later said the driver had not seen his victim because a power cut had blacked out street lights. 'Goldie saw the whole thing coming,'

---

* Well-meaning but dumb US sitcom character.

recalled Laura Hawn, 'but was too paralysed to call out. She went to the hospital and stayed until five a.m. Then she went home and stayed in bed for two days.

'I've seen Goldie go through a lot,' continued her mother. 'I've seen her divorces, I've seen her defeats, but I have never seen her unable to get out of bed before.'

Eileen Brennan was near to death and recovered only after a two-year convalescence. 'Later Goldie told me she had a premonition and was going to stop and call the restaurant and say let's do it another night,' she says now. 'As it was she saved my life, she ran back in the restaurant and raised the alarm. Then she stayed all night in the emergency room. She had to deal with what she saw herself and that, I think was quite shattering for her: it was a horrible, horrible thing for her to have to witness. She had to deal with why it didn't hit her; she is a very deep and complicated, metaphysical soul.'

The guilt associated with this appalling accident, coupled with her father's recent death, consumed Goldie and she retreated behind the walls of her Pacific Palisades house. With Yves Renier only a part-time companion in her life there was no one close with whom to share this particular burden and she reflected bitterly, 'Some day I hope someone will come along who I can share this wonderful life with. One who is not threatened by what I am or who I am, someone who has a deep satisfaction in whatever work he does, someone with a strong sense of his own worth. These things are very important for a relationship, they have nothing to do with love. They have to do with self-esteem.' It was not what Renier wanted to hear.

She was within months of having her prayers answered, but did not know it. Goldie took consolation from the annual awards of the National Association of Theatre Owners who 'honoured' her, her *Foul Play* co-star Dudley Moore – now a national treasure since his drunken performance in *Arthur* – and her director from *Sugarland Express*, Steven Spielberg. 'I've never been honoured before,' was Goldie's *sotto voce* observation as she accepted her bouquets.

1982 rolled into 1983 and the gossip-columnists, unable to grasp the reality that Goldie's transatlantic affair with a Frenchman was still limping on were expressing their dissatisfaction that there was no one new in her life. They managed to raise a brief flurry of excitement in February when the *New York Daily News* was able to report, 'Perhaps not coincidentally, Warren Beatty and Goldie Hawn popped up in Manhattan at the same time, and they were both registered in the Carlyle Hotel, where they had what one might describe as some very interesting get-togethers.' But Warren and Goldie were old news – and with Goldie finally moving towards her next full movie production, it was only a matter of time before she would meet the real love of her life.

For several months she had been trying to persuade the moneymen at Warner Brothers to look seriously at *Swing Shift*, the project she had been burning to produce for many long months. With echoes of the 1943 *Swing Shift Maisie* starring Ann Sothern, the script had been commissioned from Nancy Dowd. The storyline follows the arrival of a female workforce in a World War Two aircraft factory and the dilemma of one woman who has seen her husband go off to war and then falls for the charms of her foreman. In common with *Private Benjamin*'s story-line, the chief protagonist matures from subservient housewife to confident and assertive factory forewoman. *Newsday* commented that it 'seemed likely to result in a mass-audience movie with dimension,' adding portentously that up to now, 'Goldie's movies have been fluff'.

Certainly there was a new purpose to the producer/actress: the film was budgeted at $14.5 million and after much dithering Warners finally offered to put up half. Goldie snapped, 'No, dammit! I'm not gonna show up half the time for work!' To avoid a standoff with their star there was a reluctant agreement from the studio to go ahead.

Her first choice to direct was Jonathan Demme, a stylish, intense film-maker who had already been acclaimed as one of America's finest directors for his quirky, sensitive, bittersweet social comedies. He arrived on set having just been voted Best Director by the New York Film Critics Circle for his latest film, *Melvin and Howard*; but insiders expressed their doubts as to the wisdom of putting a director who had yet to make a commercial success, and one who had never worked with an established mega-star, in the same room with the likes of Goldie Hawn. With Demme as part of the team came the experienced cameraman Tak Fujimoto who had worked on Demme's début, *Caged Heat*.

With casting taken care of – she picked a young unknown called Holly Hunter for a walk-on part, a promising actor named Kurt Russell for the role of factory foreman, and even found a cameo role for her mother Laura – filming proceeded on location at the old Firestone factory at Downey, where a production line was set up and old airplanes brought in, and on the Warner Brothers lot. As filming got under way, a limousine bearing the fragile form of Eileen Brennan stopped by the lot. Still unable to walk, she smiled bravely at Goldie and wished her luck with the new movie. 'She saw me and was just weeping copiously because she felt that, at last, I was out of danger,' Eileen says. 'It had been the most magical friendship I ever had.'

Back on set, tense technical discussions took place over the crucial ambience of the film. Tak Fujimoto recalls, 'They wanted to make Goldie look young and, dare I say, virginal, and her producer supplied the key phrase, that she wanted her to look like peaches and cream.' This contrasted with the general thrust of the piece, which was to show the ordeal of ordinary women doing factory shiftwork – warts, curlers and all.

'It had to have an older yet romantic look to it. Through a combination of filters and lighting and production design and wardrobe, these things came together to recreate that feel,' explained Fujimoto. 'It had to be shot with a more romanticised glow, rather than other approaches to this subject-matter which would have been more realistic and tougher – but we were dealing with a person who was a big star who was carrying the movie and, anyway, it was *her* movie!'

The shooting schedule was completed, and post-production began. During this time Goldie kept away from the rough assemblage, and by the time she was ready to look at the film it was in a loosely-edited form. What she saw then appalled her: 'They made me look like a prostitute,' she complained. Neither did she approve of the film's balance which, according to some, appeared to favour

Goldie's co-star Christine Lahti. After seeing the film through in a viewing room with visibly mounting agitation, Goldie got in her car and drove to co-producer Anthea Sylbert's house and threw herself on the lawn: 'When she came home I was lying there face-down, crying. I didn't know what to do. I was devastated.'

Recovering her *sang-froid* the producer decided to assert her powers – 'When you need to be tough, yeah, I'm tough' – and called in Robert Towne, the louche and laid-back writer whom she first met on the set of *Shampoo.* Towne was given the task of writing extra scenes to beef up the love interest between Goldie and the factory foreman played by Kurt Russell, and a half-hour of new footage – directed by Demme – was shot. But once he got back to the cutting-room, Demme could only see two minutes' worth of film that, to him, added anything of merit. He declined to edit in any more.

By now *Swing Shift* could have been retitled *Free Fall.* The money-men at Warner Brothers, never a jovial bunch, were extremely unhappy at what was going on between their producer and director. In order to win their support, Goldie first relinquished her executive producer's percentage, then gave away her producing credit, and with new investors watering down Warner Brothers' exposure, she buckled under and submitted completely to the orders from the money-men. In return for this capitulation she won their support against the maverick director, but it was an ignominious defeat. From being the film's progenitor and producer, she had been seen to be reduced to the status of a mere hired hand, and not a particularly reliable one at that.

There followed an unprecedented war of words between Goldie and Jonathan Demme: from his camp came accusations of a power-hungry egomaniac who shanghaied his rough-cut and demanded rewrites and re-shooting because she hated the way she looked and was appalled at the thought that she may have been upstaged by Christine Lahti.*

* Her fears may have had some foundation: even after drastic recutting, *Swing Shift*'s only Oscar and Golden Globe nomination went to Lahti as Best Supporting Actress.

Goldie's self-defence and counter-attack was more leisurely; it underlined the cultural differences between her and her director: 'I worked on getting *Swing Shift* together for two years. I thought it should feel like a musical, that you almost wouldn't know whether it was the forties or the eighties – the costumes, attitudes and love affairs all had to have a real element of sexuality. It had to capture that sorority feeling that happened during the war.

'I thought Demme was just the guy who could bridge the forties and eighties. He walked into my office one day and looked adorable, very hip, dressed absolutely right. I really saw great talent there, so I called the studio and everybody said great, and they made a deal. But it turned out that when Demme made *his* deal, he wanted a lot of my powers reduced, although I didn't know that then.

'When we got on the set I realised there were certain things wrong. He got a script going, but scenes were being written as we were filming. Also we were shooting very little coverage* which is insane, because lots of movies are virtually *made* in the cutting room. Also, I need to let a director direct me. I have no problem with this power thing of mine. Once I give somebody the ball, I just want to go home and learn my lines.

'Jonathan, though, was very uneasy about working with a movie star. But just as we have a tendency to protect the men in our lives, we also have a tendency to protect men who shouldn't be protected. So I said nothing. Then he very sweetly asked that I should not go to the dailies. I said fine, if it makes you nervous – I didn't want him to feel he was working with a movie-star tycoon. He also asked Anthea Sylbert not to go, so ultimately neither of us saw any dailies.

'I also let slip a lot of things I would normally have discussed with a director – collaborative stuff like "Should we shoot it this way?" or "This is how I feel about this scene."'

In the end, as the cameraman Tak Fujimoto succinctly summarises, 'The director was fired. When the director was off, I was off. They let me come and see one print, and that was it. None of us had

---

* Linking material.

anything to do with the finished product – it was a studio picture.'*

The proof of this very expensive pudding was in the eating. *Swing Shift* failed to ignite the imagination of the cinema-going public – 'The best 1944 movie made this year', said the *Boston Herald* sardonically – and the original shooting budget of $14.5 million had been exceeded only to bring in US box-office returns of just $6.7 million. Warner Brothers, and those last-minute backers, lost their collective shirts.

Just why the film was such a failure is contained, her critics argue, in Goldie's own words on the subject. As producer she had ultimate responsibility to the studios to bring in a satisfactory finished product on time and on budget – a feat she had more or less achieved on *Private Benjamin*. On *Swing Shift* some fundamentals of producing were let go – perhaps most important, that she disliked the way she looked: if the producer had attended screening of the dailies, even some of them, she would have known much earlier what Demme and Fujimoto were trying to achieve with their lighting. Instead, even though she had a multi-million dollar responsibility to Warner Brothers, she and Anthea Sylbert politely acceded to Demme's request for them to stay away.

On the same grounds she allowed the director to assemble a rough-cut version of the film without setting foot in the editing suite. Her declaration that 'once I give somebody the ball, I just want to go home and learn my lines' works perfectly well for Goldie Hawn, actress, but according to her critics Goldie Hawn, producer, should have intervened at all times and stayed with her decisions until they were enacted. Ultimately, say the critics, the idea she would wish to protect a director points to a fallibility which could only cost the studio dear. Robert Towne, the writer brought in to provide additional post-production material, observed that Goldie was too fearful. 'She let him do what he wanted to do. She said to him "This would be better" and he said "OK", and then didn't do any of it, and she didn't argue about it.'

* Edited and completed by the studio with no further reference to director or producer.

On her fatal choice of Jonathan Demme, Goldie reflected later, 'It was like meeting a man in a bar and thinking he's the greatest thing you've ever seen, making promises, then coming out a loser.'

Yet Demme was no loser: within a few years he would sweep the board with an Oscar, a Golden Globe and a Directors Guild of America Award for *Silence of the Lambs*.

One main reason that Goldie's concentration on fine detail was less comprehensive than when she produced *Private Benjamin* was that she had fallen in love again. The object of her affections, like Yves Renier at the time of *Benjamin*, was an actor who had presented himself for audition before his producer. Kurt Russell, however, was unlike most other men Goldie had known in that his ethnic background was all-American.

The son of a well-known and much-loved character actor Bing Russell, who for fourteen years played Sherriff Coffee in *Bonanza*, Kurt was born in Springfield, Massachusetts in 1951 and raised in Colorado. By the time he was eleven he had already made his film début, as the Boy Who Kicked Elvis in *It Happened At the World's Fair*, yet another of the King's woeful schlock movies. Later, Kurt had the chance to use this close-up experience to good effect when he sensationally impersonated Presley in a TV biopic, *Elvis*, for which he received an Emmy award. In between he managed to cram in more than a dozen projects for Disney before turning professional baseball player. An injury sent him back to the screen in 1979 and by 1983 his career had started to zoom with appearances in *Escape From New York*, *The Mean Season* and, opposite Meryl Streep, *Silkwood*.

Among the list of forgettable Disney projects he worked on – *The Computer Wore Tennis Shoes* was a typical title – was one called *The One and Only, Genuine, Original Family Band* which could best be described as Buffalo Bill meets the Family Von Trapp. Filmed in 1968 its credits included a non-speaking role, Giggly Girl, ascribed to one Goldie Jeanne Hawn. At the time, the dancer from Takoma Park via Las Vegas had thought this was a break into the big time, coming as it did so soon after her arrival in Los Angeles. Then she turned over the pages of the script to discover that she was required to speak not one word. It would require a season or two of 'Laugh-In' before she would be allowed to show Hollywood whether she could cut the mustard. Instead, she did what was required of her and went home; and a seventeen-year old actor, six years her junior, went back to thinking about girls of his own age.

Now, though, things were different. And as she looked over her prospective leading man – blue-eyed, tough, charming – there was an instant attraction. As Russell left the room he hazarded, 'Even if I don't get the part, can I take you out some time?' The answer was – sooner rather than later. And on Valentine's Day 1983 the couple first stepped out together after the newly-hired male lead suggested it might help their work if they went out in search of a 1940s big-band to dance to. Their quest got no further than the Playboy Club where they talked for hours and did not dance once.

Later they went to look at Goldie's Pacific Palisades house which was undergoing reconstruction and gave a patrolling security guard a surprise when his flashlight came upon the naked couple lying giggling on the floor of what would be the master bedroom. They finished the evening in the comparative privacy of a nearby motel.

As the couple parted with whatever expressions of devotion first-time lovers are able to muster, Goldie lifted the telephone and dialled Paris. Yves Renier was not surprised to hear from her; their relationship had become one of interminable long-distance calls as he tried to make what he could of an interrupted screen career. What made this telephone conversation different was that, though Goldie was calling, it was Renier paying for the call – she had phoned reversing the charges.

Still flushed from her night of passion with Kurt Russell, she told Renier the affair was over. It was a carbon-copy of her termination of the affair with Bruno Wintzell – a chilly, and very final, transatlantic call. 'We had arranged to be together again the following day,' recalls Renier, who had his bags packed ready to return yet again to the States. 'I must admit it was an awful shock. I was in despair and when I heard soon after that it was Kurt Russell she'd fallen in love with, it made it even worse.'

Renier is nothing if not a man with a sense of humour. His friends believed that Goldie may have stayed with him had he proposed marriage – but that offer was never forthcoming. When she telephoned him with the news that she had found someone else, he believed it was because she had given up hope of ever marrying him. And her perceived anger helped him to understand why she had reversed the charges when she called. It was a long and very expensive call. 'Cela m'avait coûte les yeux de la tête,' he said sorely. 'It cost me an arm and a leg.' He then sat down and wrote a song, 'PCV',* which helped to help ease the burden.

Having despatched her unsatisfactory Frenchman Goldie embarked on the most physical affair of her life. But however important the intimate side was, one other factor clinched the long-term viability of this relationship, and that was Russell's attitude to Goldie's fame and fortune, and to his own relatively lowly status in Hollywood's pecking-order. 'To go on about acting as an art is ridiculous,' he said. 'If it is an art, then it's a very low form. You don't have to be gifted just to hit a mark and say a line. As far as I'm concerned, hitting my marks and saying my lines is ninety per cent of the job. Anyone who finds acting difficult just shouldn't be doing it.'

Sadly exactly the same could be said of producing *Swing Shift*. 'The film was mutilated,' was Jonathan Demme's damning verdict. 'They took a very fine film that had something important to say and turned it into a schizophrenic mish-mash.' But for Goldie, there was a consolation for all the professional heartache and the lost millions: 'It was a major disappointment, yes. Nothing ever happened in that movie. I expected it to be funny and it didn't turn out that way. But oh my gosh, I met Kurt on that picture. Are you kidding, I'd do that again!' Whether the money-men at Warner's shared her joy is a moot point.

Seven years earlier, seated at a table in an Italian café, Goldie had come up with the idea of a satire on the life and exploits of those who

* 'Reverse Charges Call'.

toiled in and around the White House. Primed by the sardonic views of Rut Hawn, who had seen the protocol and the parties at close quarters, she decided that what was needed was a film which showed Washington DC in its true colours.

During the intervening years Goldie's thoughts had crystallised into the idea of a satire on Capitol Hill and its people. But this was no *Primary Colors* or *Wag the Dog* – rather, it was old-fashioned, flag-waving stuff, with Goldie as Sunny Davis, a cocktail waitress pitched into the public eye when foiling an assassination attempt on a eastern emir, and subsequently winning the hearts of watching TV millions with her scatterbrained frankness. It was, to all intents, *Private Benjamin II*, with the 1980 team of Nancy Meyers, Charles Shyer and Harvey Miller hauled in to weave the same magic as before. The order of battle: Goldie as star and executive producer, Miller and Meyers as producers and Shyer as director.

But something went wrong. Between the first script-draft and the first day of filming, Meyers, Shyer and Miller were all uncere-moniously dumped. In her actions could be seen something of the cold, calculating shark that Bill Hudson had seen in his ex-wife, but in the end there was a film to be made and the end justified the means. Maybe it was the fear of repeating the disorganisation and lack of purpose which characterised the making of *Swing Shift*, maybe it was that the heady spendthrift days of *Benjamin* had gone and the triumvirate didn't see it; whatever, they were fired amid much rancour. In as the rewrite man came Buck Henry, who had an awesome array of hits to his name including *The Graduate*, *Candy*, *Catch–22* and *What's Up, Doc?*

Veteran director George Roy Hill, who had made *The Sting* a decade earlier, was drafted in to replace Shyer but having surveyed the battle-field, decided to withdraw. His place was taken by a name from Goldie's and Laura's past – Herb Ross, whose sister had lived with Laura during the war years in Maryland and had turned go-go-ing Goldie away from the Copacabana fifteen years before. Ross had, by this stage, progressed from choreographer and stage director to movies, and had directed such hits as Neil Simon's *California Suite*,

*The Goodbye Girl, The Sunshine Boys* and Barbra Streisand's *The Owl and the Pussycat.*

Filming took place around Washington and in Auburn, California before finishing up in Tunisia; the production came in on time and more or less on budget. However, there were chilling echoes of *Swing Shift* when Warners ordered the end to be re-shot after target audiences expressed their disappointment with the film's conclusion. Whether the film's central theme was ill-conceived, or whether changing writers mid-development holed it below the waterline, *Protocol* opened to chilly reviews. Nor did the end-product meet with Charles Shyer's approval: 'We wrote a script for *Protocol* but it wasn't *that* script: I thought it was a really poor script, it just didn't work for me at all. They took our movie, which was basically an anti-war movie, and turned it into a dumb comedy. It bothered me a lot.

'They ruined the movie,' he said, echoing Jonathan Demme and his verdict on *Swing Shift.* 'It was awful. It wasn't a happy conclusion.'

The critics felt a similar unease but the movie pulled in a $26 million gross, which meant that if nobody made a lot of money, nobody lost any. As a producer Goldie was no longer a one-hit wonder, and with some pride she was able to dedicate *Protocol* to her father, Rut: 'Because of Dad, I never look at what I've got, but what I don't know, what I haven't done, and how I can do it. Daddy taught me to be complete, to ask myself at night "Did I give enough quality time to my children? Did I call my mother today? And did I take time to go outside and look at my rose bushes?" If I can keep that balance I can be satisfied with myself.'

Talking of the money she earned from *Protocol* she added, 'I have more than I ever dreamed of, but I will never let it reign over me. If I lose it all, put me in one room with my family and I'm gonna make it. Money buys me the freedom to choose my work and if, God forbid, anybody in my family is sick – and my father was *very* sick, I can say, "I don't care what it costs, I want my father well!"' This generosity extended to those outside her family – one friendly psychic she consulted when she first arrived in Los Angeles was taken care of, years later, during her last illness.

There now followed a period of happy readjustment for Goldie. The stable, unruffled Kurt Russell turned out to be the ideal life-partner. Divorced from the actress Season Hubley, he was the father of a five-year old son, Boston, and amiably took to Goldie's children Oliver and Kate, now nine and six. Soon the couple travelled to Kurt's home-from-home in Colorado near the celebrity ski resort of Aspen and Russell introduced his new love to the life he preferred – riding horses, roping steers, cooking in the great wide open. While this would never be Goldie's preferred way of life it added a dimension to her own existence which until now had been bounded by first suburban, then metropolitan, life. Invigorated by the clear air and high altitudes the couple hunted for, and found, a piece of land upon which to build their own home. Behind Aspen at Old Snowmass they discovered down a long track a seventy-two-acre plot with woods, fields, and far-reaching views across rolling rivers to the snow-capped mountains beyond. Russell set about supervising the construction of a guest-house – designed by Goldie, named Someday, and perched over a tiny manmade lake – which was to be followed by completion of a sprawling 5,000 sq ft traditional log-framed main residence, designed by him, nearby.

Early on, a decision was reached by the couple that their finances should remain separate: Goldie was determined that the pleasure and contentment this new relationship was bringing should not be overshadowed by the threat of messy financial disentanglement further down the road and, given her preoccupation, bordering on obsession, with the idea that men might take money from her it was a shrewd move by Russell to concur. 'We signed an agreement. We had both been through some rough stuff with divorces and I wanted to make it clear that if we ever split I wanted nothing from her and Goldie wanted to show she wanted nothing from me,' admitted Kurt some years later. 'People say it's not romantic but I wanted Goldie to know I wanted to be with her just because of herself.' And to the raised eyebrows at this almost clinical entry into a relationship he shrugged, 'If you can't cope with discussing what would happen if you split then your relationship has little chance of surviving. A contract takes a great deal of pain away, it takes things out of your hands.' And of the likelihood of the couple ever legitimising their relationship, he added tersely, 'Marriage is a prelude to divorce.'

A dividing line was drawn down the middle of the property, named the HR (Hawn Russell) Ranch, with Goldie's house – green and white, with wraparound windows two stories high – on one side and Russell's, separated by a tennis court, on the other. Though they would live in the main house, on Kurt's land, the division of the property – thirty-six acres each – was a clear and unequivocal one. 'When I live in his house, that's his home, and we're respecting of it. When he's in Pacific Palisades – the house I bought before I met him – he respects *my* home.' Whatever bonding was necessary between the couple's children could be achieved much more satisfactorily after days spent under Colorado's clear blue skies, rather than in the stuffy hothouse atmosphere of Hollywood.

*Swing Shift* was released in April 1984, followed by *Protocol* in December. It was fortunate that these two films, made back-to-back, came out in the order they did, for with box-office grosses of $6.7 million and $26.3 million respectively, it looked as though Goldie was on an upward curve. Warner's made light of their *Swing Shift* losses – heavily laid off as they were – and indicated publicly they were content to continue with their star as a producer. There remained, after all, the vestigial hope that she might be able to pull off another *Private Benjamin* even though by now she had learned enough caution to no longer speak in superlatives, saying merely of her last film, 'I wish it had gone through the roof, but it didn't. Most films don't.'

But whatever the outward appearance, the relationship with Warner's was all but over. Goldie would only make one more movie with the studio before moving on by mutual agreement. Though she was rapidly approaching her fortieth birthday, she desperately wanted to have a baby to cement her relationship with Russell and was spending more time at home, both in Pacific Palisades and in Colorado.

From the Rockies she expatiated on their life together: 'We're very different politically. He's very conservative and verbose about his opinions, I'm a quiet liberal. But the things we do agree about are much more important – raising children, family, loving, responsibilities, adventure. Plus we have similar dispositions. We're basically not moody people, we wake up quite happy in the morning.'

She went on: 'Any time, day or night, this man is a real joy to be around. And he's so much fun, which is a key element a lot of people leave out of their relationships. When fun stops happening it's time to close up the shop – I refuse to live my life, as long as I have my health, without joy and happiness.' The key to the success of this still relatively new relationship lay in Russell's fatalism when it came to the acting business. Having survived being a child actor he had no stars in his eyes and knew intimately the fleeting nature of the business; therefore, according to Goldie, he was able to sidestep the common problems of jealousy and competitiveness.

She continued to look at scripts in the hope that there was out there, somewhere, another *Benjamin*. Because of her breach with Meyers, Shyer and Miller during the pre-production of *Protocol* it was unlikely that the triumvirate would once again lay a golden egg for Goldie. Eventually she fixed on an idea written by a relative unknown, Ezra Sacks, whose only previous claim to fame was a revisitation of his Harvard days, *A Small Circle of Friends*, released five years earlier to a round of polite indifference. But since she and her partner Anthea Sylbert saw this as a rare gem among the scripts they had sifted, they hired a director, Michael Ritchie, and started in on pre-production.

With the working title of *First and Goal* it certainly appeared to have the potential of another *Benjamin*: Molly is a track coach at a Chicago inner-city high school who wins the job of coaching an ill-disciplined male football team and, triumphing through tribulation, brings them success by her gutsiness and determination. In place of *Benjamin's* feminism there was now a care for the underprivileged; for *Benjamin's* Jewish voice, there was now a black accent; for that stirring sequence of basic training in *Benjamin* there was now Goldie racing round the football park, shouting in the faces of her recalcitrant pupils.

As near as was possible it contained the same elements of her blockbuster of five years before, and expectations ran high that Goldie the actress and Goldie the producer could equal or exceed *Benjamin*'s financial and critical triumph. With James Keach playing her kid-snatching ex-husband, with a small part for an upcoming actor called Woody Harrelson, and with director Ritchie weaving the same magic that had made a success, a few years before, of Redford's *The Candidate* and Lee Marvin's *Prime Cut*, filming took place on location in Chicago during the summer of 1985 and the film was set for release in the New Year.

The announcement that Goldie was pregnant happily coincided with her milestone fortieth birthday in November, after filming on the newly renamed *Wildcats* had been completed; and though doctors had warned Goldie of the risks, she was more than content to let the pregnancy run its course. The world's press awaited the announcement that she and Kurt would marry, but despite his presentation of a symbolic 4.5 carat diamond 'love ring' no announcement was forthcoming. Unlike her previous relationship with Bill Hudson, neatly seguéd into marriage in the weeks leading up to her first confinement, there was to be no repetition of that happy family scene in the back garden of 9 Cleveland Avenue, Takoma Park nine years before.

Gradually the plot of land at Old Snowmass became a ranch, with the acquisition of horses, cattle, sheep, pigs and chickens. Already in residence were flocks of magpies. A separate house was built for live-in staff and a further small house constructed for the children to play in. Dining out meant a visit to the ten-stool Charcoal Burger diner in Basalt or, if they were feeling adventurous, the Barking Pig – complete with real stuffed hog strapped to the roof – made famous by their neighbour, the self-styled gonzo journalist Hunter S. Thompson. Only one note jarred in this scene of bucolic harmony: a pet parrot bought to swell the ranks of the burgeoning Hawn/Russell zoo was named Rut, after Goldie's father.

'Moving here has been good for all of us, especially the children: you can fish or take long horseback rides in the mountains.

Those are the kind of memories that you own in your heart for ever. That's what I want for my kids, and they love it here,' Goldie said contentedly as she prepared for the baby, and the critical reaction to *Wildcats*.

The critics came first. *Wildcats* opened in February 1986 and back in Chicago, where the film had been made, it received an unprecedentedly chilly welcome from the *Sun-Times* newspaper whose writer Roger Ebert, in awarding just a half-star in its star rating system of 1–5, commented, 'They thought they could clone *Rocky* one more time. At the end of *Wildcats*, whadya know, Hawn's team beats the cross-town rivals. I've seen that ending before.'

In vain Goldie parlayed her film to passing interviewers, pointing out it had done better business in its first week than had *Private Benjamin*. She could not make the critics like it though the public, in small measure, did. Eerily, *Wildcats* did exactly the same box-office business, $26.3 million, as its predecessor two years before, *Protocol* – far better than the sorry $6.7 million pulled in by *Swing Shift* and with a dramatically reduced production cost, a profit-generating movie to be proud of. But back in Colorado Goldie could not hide the frustration that her bid to match *Benjamin's* success had failed: 'If a movie doesn't turn out the way you expected you can work out your disappointment faster here, if for no other reason than there aren't as many industry people around to remind you.'

Here, maybe, there was a lesson to be learned – that Goldie and her advisors were not the best people to pick a star vehicle for her. Kurt Russell argued, as she herself had done vehemently so many times before, that her love for film-making was based on the hope that her choice of subject-matter could make a difference – opening eyes or shattering stereotypes, or saying something new about relationships. What had so far escaped all those who surrounded her was that Goldie Hawn was loved the world over for the stereotype she herself had come to dread – the cutesy, lovable, screamingly-funny blonde. She didn't need to come with message attached. People were prepared to forgive her second-rate movies and would come back, again and again, in the simple hope that, this time, she would make them laugh. And when it came to making the world laugh, no one could do it better than Goldie.

Meanwhile back at the ranch, Goldie prepared for her summer baby by digging further into the rural life, interesting herself in such hitherto arcane issues as the purchase of a manure-spreader to fertilise the acres of hay and bunchgrass on which the animals would graze. Laura Hawn came to stay, helping with the housework, answering mail and keeping her daughter company. It said much of Kurt's easy-going tolerance that he welcomed his *de facto* mother-in-law as a permanent guest under his roof.

Finally in July the family decamped back to Los Angeles where Goldie entered the Cedars Sinai hospital to give birth; delivered by Caesarean section and with his father assisting, the 8lb 4oz Wyatt Russell made his arrival on July 10. Originally, if a boy, the child was going to be called Henry, but Kurt was searching in his mind for another name, which was supplied by an intuitive friend. 'Oh, I love it!' said Goldie.

'That was the first time I even began to think about having a boy because up till then I very much wanted to have a girl,' recalls Kurt. 'I wanted to have a daughter to even things out in the family, and to have a daughter of my own from birth. Although when the day came, I was fifty-fifty and as Goldie was taken in to hospital and I was going in with her she asked "What's it going to be?" and I said I was pretty sure it would be a girl. But it was a boy and part of me so much wanted a boy.'

Married or no, the family circle was now complete with Oliver now nine, Kate now seven, and Boston Russell now six. For the rest of the year they stayed close, either in Pacific Palisades or in Colorado, with the ever-present Laura, now seventy-three, helping her daughter with the new arrival.

The relationship with Warner Brothers was over, even though as recently as the summer of 1986 Goldie was declaring, 'I have a great relationship with Warners. I've been there for seven years. I have a value to those people right now. If my movies were a disaster, I wouldn't have value. They might like and respect me as a person but

I wouldn't have the power I do now. I can get five million dollars to do anything I want right now, I assure you.' But both Goldie and Warners wanted more than the other could give, and a planned follow-up, *Babe West*, about an entertainer in Vietnam, was abandoned.

Other projects which failed to bear fruit were *Honeysuckle Sue* for her old mentors Columbia, and a film which, for the first time, she would produce without appearing in, *Sisters*. But waiting in the wings was a delectable script, ripe for the talents of not just Goldie, but Kurt too.

*Overboard* was written by Leslie Dixon, who was shortly to make a further name for himself with the Oscar-winning *Mrs Doubtfire* starring Robin Williams and the Bette Midler comedy *Outrageous Fortune*. The storyline is of a rich bitch who falls off a yacht and, suffering from amnesia, is claimed from hospital by a loutish carpenter and his brood of noisy children. Before regaining her identity she turns round the mayhem that is the carpenter's shambolic home life and, in doing so, discovers hidden depths within herself.

To Goldie, always keen to have a subliminal message, ever searching for a film's *raison d'être*, the script was a winner: 'I know this is comedy but I didn't relate to it as if it would be making a joke. Kurt and I believe in the rewards of family, and so we like the script for that reason.' Be that as it may, it was an out-and-out farce in which Goldie, as the bejewelled Joanna Stayton, and Kurt, as the horny-handed Dean Proffitt, counterpointed beautifully.

The film was directed for Metro Goldwyn Mayer under the United Artists tag by Garry Marshall, soon to make *Pretty Woman*, and executive-produced by Roddy McDowall, who also played the butler. 'It's all about what happens when a spoiled rich girl gets together with a no-frills, real American man,' McDowall explained. 'The theme is what really counts is your personality, not where you come from or what you own.'

Not everyone came willingly to the first day's shoot in Fort Bragg, a quaint fishing village on the California coast. 'I was really very worried about doing it,' said the star. 'I didn't know if I could pull it off.' Others believed Goldie was struggling with her self image, doubting whether she should be cast as a bitch. Director Marshall also had reservations: a forthcoming directors' strike presented him with a dilemma which was only overcome by the size of MGM's paycheque, and by the prospect of working with Goldie.

The chemistry between Goldie and Kurt worked better than anyone had hoped. The cameraman John Alonzo, who had met Goldie when re-shooting the ending of *Protocol*, recalls, 'The whole shoot was a terrific family affair. On the weekend we would go over to where Goldie and Kurt were staying and have a barbecue. They'd rented a house and Patti and Laura were there, and the kids as well.' Patti had been recruited as unit publicist, and the shoals of positive press clippings which came out of the shoot around Mendocino bear tribute to her deft footwork in keeping reporters and stars happy.

Despite reports that Goldie proved difficult on certain scenes, cameraman Alonzo states, 'The ocean photography when Goldie had to dive into Malibu Bay, where the water is not the world's best – you saw no prima donna. It's amazing what a trouper she is.' Her only moment of doubt was when the script called for rich-bitch Joanna Stayton to metamorphose through a photo-montage. 'Goldie is used to seeing herself in that one hairstyle she liked to use – and the montage of her in a swept back look, a real tight look, overly made up with a long cigarette holder – we had a problem. She didn't want to do it. We had to talk her into it,' recalls Alonzo. She had worn her 'bangs' on her forehead since those modelling days in New York twenty years before, and they were still her professional security blanket.

Alonzo created a hallmark joke which carried over into the next film he did with Goldie, *Housesitter*, by leaving the camera running as the star walked away, focusing in on her zebra-swimsuited *derrière*. 'It was a gentle joke for the boys in the laboratory When the dailies were finished I would send them to the lab and call them in the morning and ask how everything was, and they'd say, "John, Goldie has the cutest butt in the world!" They loved her, just from those scenes they got in the lab. She took it very graciously. She said, "Oh that's nice, I'm glad they like it. I'm still good!"'

There is a curious coda to the filming of *Overboard*. The finished product contains high-octane Goldie, fizzing with comedy, yet when Marshall took the footage back to MGM they hated it. Those who witnessed the dramatic action around Mendocino and in the Raleigh studio on MGM's lot were convinced they were seeing vintage Hollywood being re-created. Marshall's direction and the principals' acting put them in mind of the Frank Capra and Preston Sturges blockbusters of yesteryear like, but it was not what the studio bosses had in mind.

'MGM was not charmed with my finished product,' said Marshall. 'It turns out they wanted an adult movie they could market to a sophisticated audience. At that point I didn't have much clout, and so they sent me back to the editing room with instructions to cut down the film and push the relationship between Goldie and Kurt. I ended up trimming all of the characters' back-stories, and so I was left with a lot of characters who look like sticks.'

Excluding *Wildcats*, this was the third Goldie film in a row which had to be expensively re-stitched at the end, though on this occasion no blame could accrue to the actress. By the time the finished product had been polished up and was ready for distribution, Alan Ladd Jr, chairman and chief executive of MGM Pictures, was expressing his satisfaction at the way things had gone: 'There's no question of Goldie's drawing-power. I would be very disappointed if *Overboard* didn't do at least $60 million at the box-office.'

In the end, though, *Overboard*, without doubt Goldie's best movie since *Benjamin* seven years before, managed to gross just $26.7 million, less than half Ladd's low estimate. Some ascribed this relative failure to the cinemagoing audience's lowered expectations of their star – they had paid good money to see Goldie in a string of second-rate movies recently, and didn't want to pay out more to watch another turkey. This theory gains support when the phenomenal income from video sales is taken into account: word got around too late that *Overboard* was prime, vintage Goldie, and by the time the public was ready to see the film it was no longer in the cinemas. It is also underpinned by the fact that by the time her next movie came out, the public's disappointment had evaporated and they were back, bums on seats, in their millions.

The critics, too, had their part to play in the disappointing initial response to *Overboard*. The opinion-forming *Washington Post* dismissed it as 'banal', a hard word to justify by any standards unless, by chance, they had been listening to any of the star's homilies on the sanctity of the family. Goldie was quite capable, in some circumstances, of shooting herself in the foot.

'It was the biggest disappointment I ever had,' she said later. 'It's like having a big fish on the end of the line, you bring it up and it kind of wiggles off the hook. We were both very depressed, but we went on. We looked at the reviews, I made dinner, and we went on and had our life.'

For years now, since the angry parting from Art Simon, Goldie had been represented by Stan Kamen, considered to be the greatest agent Hollywood had ever known. Kamen, the colossus of the William Morris Agency where once Art Simon had been a humble junior, had represented them all – Robert Redford, Warren Beatty, Jane Fonda, Sylvester Stallone, Al Pacino, Barbra Streisand, Diane Keaton, Kirk Douglas. But during the past couple of years the bachelor Kamen seemed less assured, less energetic on behalf of his clients. And slowly, like the first rumblings of a volcano, they started to leave – first Redford, then Burt Reynolds, then Stallone. Next went Jane Fonda. Most were leaving to join Mike Ovitz, the new power in the land at Creative Artists Agency.

Some, though, stayed with Stan Kamen, and not just in the belief that he was still the best in town. Word had begun to spread among a very small group that Kamen was suffering from AIDS and, quite quickly, his life started to draw to a close. Goldie visited his home, so too did Barbra Streisand.

Kamen had long been a energetic supporter of Israel through the United Jewish Fund, and for the previous two years had masterminded visits to the homeland of prominent Hollywood figures: Walter Matthau, Jack Lemmon and others would tour army bases and meet political leaders in heavily publicised gestures of friendship and solidarity. Israel had much to thank Kamen for, and just before his death the agent had been honoured by a dinner at the Beverly Hilton attended by *le tout* Hollywood. Now, with Kamen dead, Goldie moved to CAA but retained her affection for her mentor and flew to Israel for the dedication of a Tel Aviv cinematheque in Kamen's name.

After visiting the Holocaust museum she declared, 'I can't believe it took me so long to get here. I've dreamed of this trip, to fulfil the dreams of two people I loved dearly.' These turned out to be her mother and Kamen. For the first time she aired the question of her Jewishness in public, declaring that her Presbyterian father Rut 'almost converted – but didn't', which would have brought a wry smile to the faces of his fellow musicians who had never heard him express that wish, or anything like it.

Of her upbringing, she revealed that although hers was not 'a classically Jewish household' her mother had made sure that she and Patti had been aware of their Jewish origins: 'I thought of myself as half-and-half when faced with people who might have thought that it wouldn't be great to be Jewish,' she conceded. But on this visit she visited a day-care nursery, climbed into archaeological digs, visited the Wailing Wall where in time-honoured tradition, she put the name of her 'grandfather', and had a meeting with the Prime Minister, Yitzhak Shamir.

'Now I understand more about who I am and why I feel the way I do and do the things I do,' she declared, saying that she had at last resolved her feelings about being half-Jewish. 'For the first time in my life, I felt really Jewish. To think that I ever classified myself as half-and-half for the sake of others! The one thing I've learned here is that I would never do that again, because I am very proud now. I understand *the best* of what it means to be a Jew.'

# CHAPTER NINE

## *Cold-Eyed Shark*

*'Then, window, let day in, and let life out'*
*– ibid.*

The press's love affair with Goldie, now twenty years old, showed no signs of abating. Extraordinarily few critical articles had ever been written about her, and when Kurt's former wife Season Hubley made the headlines at the beginning of 1988 over unpaid child maintenance it was unlikely to be to her advantage. A typical headline was that from the London *Daily Mail*: 'Gold-digging – the woman who was ousted by Goldie Hawn'.

The nub of the story was that Miss Hubley, by now divorced from Kurt for five years, was seeking increased child maintenance payments for their son Boston, now seven. The present payment of $2,000 a month was insufficient, she argued, and it should be increased to $10,000. Court papers revealed that the support payments should be based on the respective incomes of her and her ex-husband, but this brought a sharp response from Kurt's lawyer. 'Asking for $10,000 a month for the support of a seven year old child is absurd,' he said. 'Even $2,000 is too much.'

Behind this rare splash of controversy in the Hawn-Russell household lay a lengthy tale which did not always show Kurt in his customary good light. He and Season Hubley had met on the set of the Emmy-winning *Elvis* when Kurt played The King in an inspired impersonation and Season played Priscilla Presley. 'At the time,' recalled a friend, 'Season had been working a long time and her price was about three times Kurt's. They didn't bother to take the make-up off, they just carried on the love affair offscreen and got married pretty soon. She was pregnant within a couple of months and it was only after the child was born that she realised they had absolutely nothing in common.'

Their son Boston weighed a mere 4lb at birth and doctors warned immediately after that if he did not die he would be retarded, possibly severely. Season put her career on hold to look after the baby and by the time he was two she had decided to file for divorce. 'Kurt was aggressive around her. She didn't want Boston to grow up with that constant fighting,' said another friend. The couple had already been divorced a year when Goldie walked into Kurt's life, and to begin with relations between the couple and Season were polite. 'Goldie brought her own kids round to the house one day with Kurt when he went to pick up Boston,' recalls the friend. 'I guess like all women she wanted to have a look-see. She wore a laurel wreath in her hair and tried to give Season a hug.'

Relations soon began to sour, however, through Kurt's reluctance to pay child support. 'He said to Season, "You've got the kid, you pay for him",' continued the friend. 'She was asking things like $500 for Boston to go to a kindergarten and he was saying no.' The child, added the friend, was extremely fragile, had undergone surgery and continued to require constant medical attention during the first seven years of his life, making a nonsense of Kurt's lawyer's declaration that 'The boy is not ill in any way.'

'After he met Goldie, Kurt was working more and more while Season was working less and less. But though California law says that the child should be able to live in the manner of the more affluent parent Kurt didn't want to pay for private school. The thing was in court most of the time, but what got to Season was that here were Kurt and Goldie claiming that Boston was part of their extended family, posing for photographs and so on, while at the same time he was doing the bare minimum in supporting the child. In the end, Goldie was subpoenaed to appear in court because Kurt kept saying, I don't know how many staff we have, I don't know how many cars we have, the house isn't mine. He hid from her that Goldie and he were planning to build a massive new mansion in Pacific Palisades. Goldie was subpoenaed because supposedly she knew everything that Kurt didn't. That was the day the matter was settled – Goldie didn't like the idea of getting publicly drawn into a slanging-match and you can't blame her for that. What's astonishing is that she didn't tell Kurt to sort it out sooner.'

Though the matter was concluded to the satisfaction of the courts it was not the end of the story. 'As an actress Season had been on the studios' A-list,' explained the friend. 'Now, she wasn't. And inevitably she asked herself whether it was the power of the Goldie machine which had caused that change in her fortunes. Bitter? Wouldn't *you* be?'

Today, Kurt Russell commands $20 million a film while Season Hubley has, for the time being, withdrawn from acting.

Controversy continued to dog Kurt's footsteps after it emerged that he was organising a celebrity shooting-party at Grand Junction, Colorado, near the Old Snowmass ranch. He charged three dozen big-game hunters $7,000 a head to take part in the event in which it was planned to hunt down dozens of deer, elk, moose, foxes and birds. Animals rights campaigners persuaded Hollywood stars to join their protest against what they described as a 'bloodbath', while an unmoved Russell cheerily pointed out that the event was a fundraiser for the World Wildlife Fund. The plan was that while Russell and such stars as country singer Johnny Cash and rocker Ted Nugent blasted away, Goldie would stay at home and entertain the wives.

The 'Cheers' actress Kirstie Alley thundered, 'It's absolutely appalling and monstrous. I can't think why slaughtering innocent animals is so appealing to some men."

When it was suggested that perhaps some of the proceeds should instead be channelled into feeding homeless people in Colorado, the actress Betty White from TV's 'Golden Girl*s*' started a petition and begged, 'I am asking all people not to eat anything purchased with this blood-tainted money.'

Russell, a committed countryman, refused to budge: 'It's completely silly. What's the difference? I can't imagine why this publicity happens – it's like all publicity, cannon fodder. I think as long as you don't have a picture of you strangling your kids everything is OK.'

And so it proved: Russell's career, strengthening and broadening with every film he made, was unharmed by the fuss. Goldie stayed out of the argument altogether, and pretty soon the dust settled.

She returned to production, for the first time launching a film in which she would not star. *My Blue Heaven* was a workmanlike enough piece, starring Steve Martin as a fun-loving Mafia stool pigeon assigned to the FBI's witness-protection programme who has difficulty maintaining an appropriate distance between himself and his former colleagues. Directed by the old family friend Herbert Ross, it was produced not only by Goldie but by a raft of other so-called producers including Ross, the film's writer Nora Ephron, Anthea Sylbert, and one Andrew Stone. Businesswise it did modestly, grossing $23.5 million – but the money-men at Warner's backed it because of Steve Martin's massive popularity at the time. The movies Martin made which sandwiched *My Blue Heaven* – *Parenthood*, made immediately before, and *Father of the Bride* – tell the real story. *Parenthood* grossed $100 million and *Father of the Bride* $132 million. Counting up the production costs of *Heaven*, Warner's were left with small-change and no one came out of it feeling good.

The original idea was that Goldie would play the part of an uptight district attorney but according to reports was bothered by the fact that the men's roles were juicier, and she eventually dropped out. One person who worked on *Heaven* observed, 'She says she wants to do ensemble movies but she doesn't really understand what that means.'

Goldie countered this, saying: 'I have no problems taking a smaller role. It's really about the content of the role, not the size. In *My Blue Heaven* the character had no moments – maybe she will in the finished film, but I didn't find her that interesting.'

Nothing was said publicly, but Warner's had made up their minds – no more Goldie-produced movies. They were a headache, they made no money. She tried a couple more ideas out on the studios – *Last Wish* was the celebrated tale by Betty Rollins of her cancer-stricken mother's assisted death, and writer Warren Adler had put forward a promising script called *Madeleine's Miracle* – but the party was over.

The difficulty for Goldie was that she had now become, in many women's eyes, a quintessential role-model. She was the woman who kicked in Hollywood's glass ceiling, the enabler in whose footsteps lesser fry could now tread with confidence. Every interviewer marvelled at how Goldie managed to be mother, lover, actress *and* producer all at the same time, and it was beyond Hollywood's rules to tell the truth and say that producing may bring its rewards, but it brought its headaches and heartaches, particularly when, as was the case at the moment, she couldn't get a single project off the ground. To those who persisted in asking about her producer status she offered, 'I've relegated a lot of my production company duties to other people. I still plan to produce my own movies, but I don't want to work as hard as I used to. I'm more domesticated now.' But as everyone in Sharktown knew, there was no such thing as a *domesticated* film producer.

With Warner's not returning her calls, negotiations opened with Disney to see whether the pastures were greener on their side of Hollywood. Eleven years earlier, when making *Foul Play* at Paramount she had met Michael Eisner and Jeffrey Katzenberg who now ran Disney. They, remembering Goldie at her best, were now prepared to offer her a seven-picture, eight-figure deal to star and produce for their new division, Hollywood Pictures. Poo-poohing the wiseacres' warnings, Ricardo Mestres, president of Hollywood Pictures, declared stoutly, 'It's not like we're trying to revitalise a flagging career. She remains one of the few females in the world who can "open" a picture. We're viewing Goldie as an actress of depth and latitude.'

At Warner's they shook their heads in disbelief. There, they had come to the conclusion that what Goldie was good at was making people laugh. If being an actress of 'depth and latitude' meant she was going to make more serious films, then Disney were welcome to her. And the idea that she should be offered seven pictures to make when the ones she had produced, with the exception of *Benjamin*, had proved exceptionally tricky to complete, seemed to them foolhardy in the extreme. Others put such negative thoughts down to jealousy.

But analysts did issue a warning that Disney had made a reputation for itself in recent years of going into business with actors whose careers were faltering. Bette Midler had been Disney's most striking success story, but the studio had tried the same kind of makeover with Richard Dreyfuss and Tom Selleck with less financial success.

Beyond the fact that it was worth a notional $30 million, whatever that meant, no details of the 'eight-figure' aspect of the deal were revealed. However most movie analysts took it to mean Goldie would receive a 'golden hello' sweetener, plus a piecemeal payment per film. The big bucks would come only if she could come up with blockbusters found through her own production company. 'I'm really excited about this next chapter,' said the newly-revitalised producer. 'It's a great relationship with Disney. They believe that you can't just play the same part over and over. If you're capable of doing other things, then why not run the gamut?'

However, the new kid on the block slightly put her foot in it when she declared that she would not make 'fuzzy movies, movies that are about nothing, like *Outrageous Fortune*'. For Touchstone Pictures, the 'adult' division of Disney, were delighted at the success of Bette Midler's madcap hit, and saw nothing fuzzy about it at all. What's more, as they pointed out, at $52 million gross *Outrageous Fortune* had done twice as much business as Goldie's last two efforts, *Wildcats* and *Overboard*. It was not a propitious start.

Goldie and Kurt continued to share their time between Colorado and Pacific Palisades and in March 1989 made their now routine visit to the Oscars' ceremony. What happened as they took to the stage as co-presenters electrified the 1.5 billion people in ninety-one countries who were watching the ceremony live – or at least it electrified those who were sufficiently conversant with Goldie and Kurt's domestic arrangements. The couple, who by now had been living together for six years, had made it clear in numerous interviews that after their previous marital excursions they had no plans to marry.

However, as Goldie made her introductory remarks at the start of the presentation of the Best Director Award she said of Kurt, 'We are co-stars, we are compadres, we are companions and we are a couple.'

He responded, 'There's only one thing we're not … married.'

Goldie ad-libbed, 'Is that a proposal?'

Russell appeared to be thrown. He stuttered, 'Whaaaat? You're putting me on the spot. Listen, we'll talk about it later tonight, OK?'

Suddenly, the newspapers had their story; no one cared about who won Oscars that year.

The debate raged – should they marry? Why hadn't they married? Wasn't it better for the children from three unions to feel some sense of harmony living under the roof of Mr and Mrs Kurt Russell? The gossip-columnists and the pundits refused to leave it alone, and for two months the story stayed alive with one magazine even running a voice stress analysis test on the videotape: they came to the conclusion that Goldie was 'crushed' by Kurt's reply. What nobody wanted to know, but what every actor and actress watching the Academy Awards ceremony instantly knew, was that it is dangerous to deviate from a pre-rehearsed script. Ad-libbing, as the old saying goes, needs rehearsal.

Still, the focus swivelled round on to Goldie once again, just at the moment when the producers of a new Mel Gibson vehicle were turning over in their minds a suitable leading lady. Gibson was at this stage thirty-three years old and would expect at the very most that his opposite number would be the same age. Goldie was coming up for her forty-fourth birthday and had had three children. Yet the match, when put to the test in *Bird On a Wire*, was perfect.

Gibson had established himself as the hottest young actor in Hollywood in *Lethal Weapon* and *Lethal Weapon II*, his most recent outing. Sandwiched in between had been *Tequila Sunrise*, directed by Goldie's old friend from *Shampoo* days, Robert Towne, and co-starring Kurt Russell. On paper, the matching of Gibson and Hawn in a film which combined action and comedy looked unbeatable, and filming under director John Badham began in Vancouver in the summer of 1989.

The storyline was simple enough: a former FBI agent who has kept his new identity secret for fifteen years after a dangerous drug bust accidentally bumps into his old girlfriend. Pretty soon the bad guys are on to him again and together the couple flee. There is, *inter alia*, unfinished business in the bedroom to be sorted between them.

Robert Primes, director of cinematography on *Wire* recalls, 'Goldie was wonderful. She wore a great deal of perfume and you would always know when she was on the set – she was very sexy and would come up and greet you with a big kiss, you would be a little light on your feet after that. It was exhilarating and just a joy to work with both of them.'

Devoted to his star, Primes reveals some of the trade secrets which help to make a wonderful-looking movie star look marvellous. 'For this romance to work it was essential for Goldie not to look older than Mel. So if Goldie expresses herself by shrivelling up her face or screwing up her features, it makes wrinkles – as it would do with anybody. Particularly, she could get wrinkles round her eyes and nose if she made the wrong expressions. I would watch carefully – and I loved her – and if she made one of those expressions I would say, "Goldie, you squinted!" And she would say, "Oh, thank you, thank you!" and immediately do the take again and find another way of expressing the same emotion.'

For Goldie's skin-texture the director John Badham wanted a filtered film, and a thin black net was placed over the camera lens to provide some diffusion. But, says Primes, 'We didn't want the Doris Day syndrome of suddenly the female star comes on and she is all pretty – and fuzzy.' The star was lit with very little contrast which helped smooth out the skin textures but as Primes pointed out: 'The camera loves Goldie.'

*Bird On a Wire* was a mixture of romance, action and comedy. Goldie was uncomfortable with the original script because it called for explicit love-scenes between her and Gibson, and demanded changes. 'I saw the whole thing as being quite innocent. It just wasn't right to see these two people go at it together. I felt, for the audience, it would be a turn-off.' As a result the love-scenes contained more humour than sex.

Bob Primes recalls, 'She wasn't shy and Mel wasn't shy – an enormous amount of love-scenes feel self-conscious because the actors or director is self-conscious about them, but what Mel and Goldie did was to add humour to it. He was teasing her and they were laughing – it was charming, just charming.'

The script required a lot of stunt-work and Gibson relished his work astride a motorcycle. A rig was built so that the bike could be towed by a camera car. 'We checked the light and we were doing a take and as we went round a corner something went wrong and they just disappeared off our screen,' says Primes. 'As the rig twisted round the corner at high speed the bike fell off – it was horrifying. Mel went down on his back and pulled Goldie on top of him – a total gentleman. Gradually we came to a halt. The stunt co-ordinator, the special effects people and the assistant director all rushed out, but Goldie said she was fine and Mel just laughed it off. It shook up John Badham quite a bit, though, and he awarded them both stunt pay.'

There was another heart-in-mouth moment when, filming twenty-two storeys up, for a moment it looked as though Goldie, held only by a thin safety wire, might plunge southwards; but the star held her nerve and the scene was completed.

As with *Overboard*, cameraman and director found themselves lingering on Goldie's rear-view. 'She has gorgeous legs and we did a shot of her going up a ladder with Mel following her – we knew this was going to be a popular movie!' recalls Primes. So much so, that the *Washington Post* in its review said *Wire* was a battle of who had the cutest butt.

When the first cut was screened for various focus-groups there was a marked consumer-resistance to the ending, and the producers ordered it to be re-shot. This now made four out of Goldie's past five films which had to have the ending altered, but as a mere actress she was happily free of responsibility. Indeed, by the time the production team could be put together again she was at work on her next assignment in New York and filming had to be dovetailed around her other commitments. But the new ending made no difference – the critics hated *Wire*. The *Australian* newspaper pulled no punches: 'An ugly, witless, hyperactive film which tries pathetically hard to outdo Spielberg or Lucas* at their own game.' Fortunately with a budget of $20 million and a box-office gross of $71 million – and, more to the point, with many of Goldie's fans crowding back into the cinemas delighted in the knowledge that she was back on top form – nobody gave a damn what the critics thought.

Filming *Wire* was a wholly enjoyable experience for Goldie, marred only briefly during shooting by the pronouncement by Francis Ford Coppola, director of *The Godfather* and *Apocalypse Now* and one of the true Hollywood heavyweights, that he could not conceive of making a shallow movie. To illustrate his point he described such an eventuality as 'making a Goldie Hawn'. One technician on the set recalled, 'She threw a tantrum. It really hurt her. But she called him up, and he really apologised to her. He'd stigmatised her roles and her movies as being lowbrow and he realised he'd made a mistake.'

It was nine years since Goldie and her second husband Bill Hudson had parted. Now, suddenly, in the midst of an apparently anodyne interview with *People* magazine, Hudson launched an extraordinary broadside against his ex-wife.

Apparently inviting the magazine into the Malibu home he once shared with Goldie to demonstrate the domestic bliss he now enjoyed with new actress wife Cindy Williams, and their children, six-year old Emily and three-year old Zack, Hudson started out by declaring, 'When Oliver and Kate are with us, it's like all the kids are brothers and sisters.' But this interfamilial 'quality time' came, apparently, all too infrequently for Hudson, whose alternate-weekend visiting rights were applicable only when the children were in Los Angeles. 'When they're in town we have them as often as we can,' he continued, 'but Goldie travels a lot. She's a megastar, she flies round the world. That's fine, but my kids are in this whirlwind with her, and it's hard for Cindy and me to plan anything for all of us together as a family.'

Even when Goldie wasn't travelling, he went on, his visiting rights

---

* George Lucas, director of *Star Wars*.

were often brushed aside because Kate and Oliver were at the Old Snowmass ranch, a thousand miles away. 'I don't want to do battle with Goldie over the kids,' he said, 'but I don't want to chase them all over the country. I've asked her to let me have them on a regular basis, and she tells me she'll think about it.'

The second Mrs Hudson took up the story: 'The last time we went to get the kids, Goldie and Kurt were gone – and when we left with Oliver and Kate, Wyatt, whom we all love, wanted to come with us. But we had to leave him behind with his nanny. Everyone felt terrible.'

To the readership of a moralistic middle-market magazine like *People*, such revelations rained hammer-blows upon Goldie and her much-vaunted concept of domestic harmony. But once Hudson had started, he was not about to stop: 'Cindy knows how to balance her family and her work. I never had that in my marriage with Goldie, no matter how much she came on after our divorce as this abandoned little creature who was taken advantage of by men.'

He implied that at the start of the marriage in 1976, his wife's career was at a low ebb while his was riding high. She was determined to return to the spotlight. 'She was on the comeback road and didn't want to fail. Her priorities shifted when she started filming *Foul Play* and our kids were sort of left as number two priority. I couldn't believe that I was seeing that.' He, or the magazine, fell short of bringing up Goldie's unmotherly behaviour – at least to *People* readers' eyes – during her 'lost weekend' with Yves Renier after *Private Benjamin* had finished filming in 1980.

Hudson finished by comparing his wives. 'Unlike Goldie, Cindy doesn't have to be "on" all the time. Goldie perceives herself as Goldie Hawn, the star. Cindy does not see herself as a star. She's an actress.'

He returned to the attack on television, complaining in an interview on 'Entertainment Tonight', 'It's horrendous. One of the reasons I wanted to speak was because Goldie has always said how wonderful she is, and how protective she is of the children – well, tell me how protective she is if she comes out and says these things?'

He repeated that his visitation rights were a couple of days a year, adding, 'Everything else is at her discretion. When she's happy I can see them; when she's not happy it can affect seeing my children. I see them all the time, as often as I can, but it's very difficult. Who do I call when Goldie's away? Kurt? What right does he have to tell me when I can see my kids? None.

'Goldie takes cheap shots. The press has been very kind to her but there's another side to this woman. She wants to take the issue off the children and my inability to see the children because of her lifestyle and because basically she doles out the time – she's the judge, the jury and the executioner.'

He added that it was Goldie's need for total control which resulted in the child custody settlement which limited most visitation to times when the children were in Los Angeles – yet in previous interviews, Kurt had made it clear that he wanted the family to live for half the year in Colorado.

'I don't want my kids to be subjected to that horrendous battle in the press, but I also can't continue to let this woman steamroller over me. It's enough already.'

If Hudson's purpose in airing this dirty linen was to get more access to his children, he was so far gaining little ground. Again he complained that the visiting arrangements effectively left him seeing Kate and Oliver only three days every two years. He added, 'I've asked her to let me have them on a regular basis and she tells me she'll think about it. What I want is a specific amount of time when I do have them. She does not encourage the relationship between myself and my children. The kids don't call me. I call them, and I have the phone bills to prove it.'

No doubt added to his fury and frustration was the fact that he and Goldie, once equal partners in love and marriage, were now living at opposite ends of Hollywood's spectrum. Disney had given Goldie $30 million to come and be their celebrity producer, while Hudson and his wife were earning straight salaries – and not large ones – from the same company, to turn out a weekly sitcom called 'Just Like Family'. The irony was not lost on anyone.

It was now Goldie's turn to attack: 'In the nine years he has been away from the kids he hasn't seen them very much at all. He never calls to see how they are, they always have to call him, so that's the relationship,' she stated. 'He is acting like a woman scorned. We were married for just three-and-a-half years and it seems like I've got to live with this for the rest of my life.'

Hudson bounced back. 'Here is a woman who says she promotes the relationship with the father of her children but whose actual agreement says that I can't see them unless it is totally under her control.

'If Goldie's in control, she's happy. Right now she's in control of her relationship with Kurt, she's in control of her children – my children – and she's in control of my finances to some degree, which means she's kind of in control of my other kids and Cindy. And she believes she's untouchable. She believes the press will always believe her and come down on her side.

'As long as she believes she can continue to promote the image of Goldie Hawn she can keep a happy face. As soon as that bubble is burst – and I have seen it burst – that image turns into a cold-eyed shark.'

As the battle raged back and forth it emerged that a secondary argument between the couple was over the Malibu house, now occupied by Hudson and his wife, which had once been occupied by Goldie and Hudson. She claimed that under the terms of their divorce settlement he should keep the house but pay her $550,000, completion of payment to be by 1991. With that date rapidly approaching and with an income but no large capital sum to repay the debt – but wanting to stay in the property – Hudson had asked his ex-wife if she would guarantee a bank-loan so he could repay her under the terms of the court order. 'I was advised by a lawyer, and then I said to him "I'm no longer your supporter",' revealed Goldie. 'He is still trying to live off me.'

This, to *People* readers, would have seemed a trifle harsh, given the palpable difference in their relative wealths, and here their sympathies would have lain with Hudson – but for the fact that he then disclosed that he had been invited to write a kiss-and-tell book about their life together for which he would receive $500,000.

Through gritted teeth he explained, 'I don't make $550,000 a year and neither does my wife. I would love Goldie to be fair and compassionate and big enough to say, "Forget it. Why pay the $550,000? I spend that on my staff." Anyway, the money is a ploy by her to take the issue off the children and off my ability to see the children. She takes cheap shots at me. I've had enough.'

Eventually the matter was resolved, but the open battle between Goldie and her ex-husband gave her fans a rare sight of something awesome, like an iceberg looming out of the mist. Miss American Pie, the nation's sweetheart, had for a second allowed her guard to drop. Just for a moment, the press which had said only nice things about Goldie Hawn for the past twenty years, which had allowed the Goldie view to prevail, which had decorously averted their eyes at the sign of any reverse in her life, be it professional or personal, lost the plot sufficiently to allow her to show her teeth. Furthermore they allowed her ex-husband to call the 'Laugh-In' girl 'a cold-eyed shark'. Pretty soon they would be reprinting the bit from Oscar-winning producer Julia Phillips's autobiography which read, 'Goldie, with the cute face and cute ass and cute laugh and the heart made of stone ... Goldie [who] has a cold, hard streak to her ...'

It was a crucial moment. The public's goodwill can be withdrawn without notice, irrevocably. The twentieth century is littered with public figures, in entertainment and elsewhere, who have spent their latter days asking themselves where they went wrong. If the public sensed there was another side to Goldie, that they had been hoodwinked all along into believing that she woke every day of her life with a giggle, that fragile thread of confidence between actress and public could be severed in an instant. But somehow Goldie came through, events took another turn. Bill Hudson disappeared back into obscurity, and the matter was laid to rest.

Freed at last from the suspicion and indifference which marked the final days of her production arrangement with Warner's, Goldie was ready to start afresh with Disney. But she did not leave without a parting shot at Warner's money-men. Recalling her dog-days on

*Swing Shift* and her disagreements with Jonathan Demme, she commented, 'The studio never backed me up. They were using me to catch the shit.'

Over at Disney, it was hoped, no such thing would happen again. The first vehicle on which studio and producer could test each other out was a script called *The Mrs*, a psychological thriller about a happily-married New York woman who, after the supposed murder of her husband, discovers that he is not the man she thought he was. Goldie and Anthea Sylbert impressed upon their new Disney bosses that this was just the right vehicle to show a broader, more mature Goldie to a public waiting to see her take on a meatier role: after all, hadn't some of the critics paused in the general slating of *Wire* to say Goldie was getting a bit long in the tooth to be playing the perpetual kook? Convinced, Disney gave the go-ahead, though to save money they ordered the 'New York' based movie to be shot in Toronto.

Goldie chose as her director Damian Harris who had previously made *The Rachel Papers*, an adaptation of Martin Amis's novel starring Jonathan Pryce. Because of the dark and brooding atmosphere which pervades the film she ordered a 'reverse screen test', trying out the deeply respected cinematographer Jack N. Green to see whether his work would fit. Green, who had made over twenty movies with Clint Eastwood, good-naturedly submitted himself to this unusual test and passed easily enough.

Green, known for the exceptional way he lights his subjects, says that Goldie, now forty-four, was perfectly happy to look a mess when the part called for it: 'There was a scene where she was in the hospital thinking her husband had been killed and was crying and tearful. I wanted the light to be very stark and very brutal – it hurt me to put her into that light, but I knew it was what the picture demanded. But she agreed that it was right for the picture.'

But though Goldie had supposed that life would be easier producing under Disney, she had reckoned without the money-men who invade all major film productions. From the start of the eleven-week shoot there was tension between the unit up in Toronto and the studios back in Hollywood. 'It was a them-and-us situation. The studio was interested in making one kind of movie and we all shared a vision of the movie we wanted to make – and we used every trick in the book to keep them off our backs,' recalls Green.

Maybe the Disney men were panicked by Goldie's bitter *envoi* to Warner's; maybe word had belatedly reached them that things did not always go smoothly on a Goldie production; maybe they weren't happy to see the family being rolled on to the set, with Laura Hawn being given a bit-part and the children becoming a permanent part of the backstage scenery. But the star, the director, and the cinematographer all knew what they wanted and they worked in unison to achieve it. 'We all knew we were getting what we wanted. Disney was afraid of dark movies – they had had no success with movies with lots of darkness in them,' says Green.

The film, soon to be retitled *Deceived* by the power-hungry men back in Hollywood, was structured in three parts: a light, airy beginning; a moody, painful middle; and an almost black-and-white denouement. 'They thought it was a good idea but when they started seeing it, they started pulling back little by little,' recalls Green.

Goldie went to battle with her new bosses over the script while Harris started to reschedule filming so that the dailies sent back to Los Angeles for inspection appeared haphazardly.

'We would schedule some lighter photography for the first part of the week when we knew they would have a screening in LA, then we would schedule two or three days of dark shooting, when over the weekend the labs would be closed and due to shipping complications they would get three days of dark photography all at once. Every Wednesday or Thursday we would expect a phone call when they'd seen the previous week's dark work and they would try to play good-cop-bad-cop with Damian and I – it was so silly,' says Green.

Harris agreed. 'Disney likes to divide and conquer,' he observed. 'They changed the name of the film, they changed lots of things. It made us all club together – like being at school and saying, "What dicks they are."'

The men in suits at Disney were appalled at this rebellion. The film's writer Mary Agnes Donoghue refused to do rewrites and a substitute had to be called in. Memos and phone calls started to bombard the set, and the production remained under fire until filming completed after eleven weeks. *Deceived* grossed $28.7 million when it opened in 1991, about on a par with *Overboard, Wildcats* and *Protocol,* leaving the money-men less than thrilled with their new $30 million producer; and the critics, to a man, declared themselves underwhelmed by Goldie's return to serious acting, reasoning that others could do it better.

But Goldie was not yet ready to be talked out of it, and she pitched for a place in an upcoming movie to be directed by the British-born Ridley Scott, who had just had a hit with *Someone To Watch Over Me* starring Tom Berenger. Scott had his hands on a much talked-about property, a story by an unknown called Callie Khouri to be called *Thelma and Louise.* Essentially a road-movie with two evenly-matched female leads, this would have been a departure for Goldie since it was generally believed in Hollywood that she disliked playing opposite stars of similar stature and, in any event, never women.

That she was prepared to pitch for *Thelma and Louise* sent out various messages to the pundits in the Hollywood Press – that Goldie was determined to carry on with her unpopular 'serious' streak; that Goldie finally acknowledged she could not carry a film by herself; that Goldie was now begging for parts rather than waiting for them to be offered. None of this was particularly accurate, but some unpleasant speculation forced her to counter the wordsmiths with a statement, laying the blame at her agent's door: 'Ronnie didn't want me to do it. He had moral problems with the script. I wanted to do it with Meryl Streep.'

Ron Meyer got his client a meeting with Scott but it became clear that the director wanted none of the baggage that went with a Streep/Hawn headline act. 'He thought she would overshadow the movie,' said an aide. In choosing Geena Davis and Susan Sarandon he steered clear of audience preconception, and the resultant movie won an Oscar for Callie Khouri, five other Oscar nominations and a brace of Golden Globes for the lead actresses.

'Parts like that don't come along very often,' mused Goldie, 'and

I'm not usually considered for these roles. A lot of times, directors don't want to deal with the baggage. They don't know where Goldie Hawn stops and the actress starts. In general directors don't like it when the star is bigger than the piece itself, they think the focus will be on the star rather than the movie. I think that happened with *Thelma and Louise*.' This rare piece of frank self-analysis was only what Scott was saying, but industry opinion shifted as a result.

On the domestic front, 1990 came to a close bearing good news and bad news: the row with Bill Hudson had ended with his lawyers demanding Goldie adhere to an agreement that either she or Kurt should be in the house with Oliver and Kate at all times. Up till now the children had often been left in the care of their long-serving nanny Rosalva, or Laura Hawn if she happened to be staying. It meant no more get-away trips for the lovers, and the start-date of *Deceived* had had to be delayed since Kurt was away filming *Backdraft*. But the couple were almost ready to move into a new $10 million, ten-thousand-square feet home down the road in Pacific Palisades and Goldie, an inveterate home-maker, turned her mind to decorating the place with relief and pleasure.

Perhaps it was the ongoing, nagging battles with her ex-husband which prompted Goldie's next big idea. She announced that she was proceeding with plans to produce a movie provisionally called *Green vs Green* – 'a black comedy with some real bite to it' – about divorce and the effect on the children and stepchildren involved. Given the press's determination to read into fiction the real lives of the artists involved in any Hollywood movie, the news would hardly have been greeted with joy by those of her extended family including Bill Hudson and Kurt's ex, Season Hubley. But Goldie enthused, 'It's about what we do to our children in that extended family. We're living in a world where people get married two and three times. They have stepchildren all over the place, and the children have to learn to get along, and the ex-wives have to learn to get along, and sometimes they don't. The pity of it is what we're doing to the kids.' Maybe because of what the film might have done to the real-life kids in the Hudson-Hawn-Russell *ménage*, *Green vs Green* was never made.

Goldie and the men in suits at Disney regarded each other warily. Both had reason to be disappointed with the other, but were bound by a sweetheart deal that was not yet two years old. However, as those close to Goldie were happy to point out, Disney did not regard her as their exclusive property and were happy to let her out to rival studios. 'We've invested in Goldie's long-time career,' Disney's Jeffrey Katzenberg protested when it was mooted she might make a movie with Universal. 'If she makes great films elsewhere, it only enhances the asset to us. To be supportive is incumbent upon us.'

Now, 'supportive' is not a word much used in Hollywood. It implies helping the weak, thereby suggesting weakness in both parties involved in the transaction – the helper and the helped – and if there is one thing Hollywood has no time for it is weakness. So pundits felt it safe to read into Katzenberg's remarks that Goldie would not be making another movie for Disney in the foreseeable future, and that other studios would be welcome to her services.

The Hawn-Sylbert office was still energetically brainstorming production ideas. One that caught Goldie's fancy was another *film noir* about a one-parent family caught in the poverty trap, where the mother goes out to strip in order to make ends meet and the teenage son becomes a drug dealer to rescue his mother from her thankless task. How much of this Goldie saw as personal experience, stripping aside, is hard to estimate. But in talking-up the *CrissCross* script she repeated much of her earlier commentary on *Green vs Green*, adding, 'I saw it as a love story about a mother and son who don't always do what's right.'

With a script by Scott Somer, and a British director in the shape of Chris Menges, Goldie was ready to go ahead with *CrissCross* in the summer of 1991 with production credits shared between the Hawn-Sylbert Movie Co., and Metro-Goldwyn-Mayer's United Artists label. Filming would be in and around Key West in Florida.

As with *Deceived*, there were script problems. 'There were different visions of the movie,' reported someone on the set. 'Goldie felt it was too dark, too rough. She wanted an upbeat message, she wanted the kid to do good. Originally it was more the son's story, but her part was increased significantly. But that wasn't really the problem. Sometimes in terms of the tone of the piece there were disagreements – can't we be more poignant here, more *hopeful?*'

That was only the start of it, for the film was built on shifting sands. 'The reason it flopped was because Goldie was originally going to take all her clothes off and that is why the studios agreed to bankroll the film in the first place,' recalls one person involved in the production. 'They thought, "Oh my God, Goldie Hawn stripping! Everyone's going to pay to see that!" And then she didn't do it and it made a nonsense of the storyline – the kid was supposed to be completely appalled by the fact that his mother was a stripper, it didn't work just making her a dancer. We were amazed she had agreed to do it – certainly Chris Menges was given to understand she was going to strip – but once she wasn't taking her clothes off and all she was doing was dancing in front of a whole lot of men in a club, it didn't seem such an appalling thing to do. There's a big difference, for a boy of twelve, between his mother wearing a one-piece and wearing nothing at all.

'Nobody knows what made her change her mind, maybe it was a vanity thing, maybe she got scared of shooting her fluffball image out of the water.'

Tension on the set increased when after the third day the gaffer* walked out. 'He was used to lighting a room and then the actress walking into it and being filmed, making her stand in the best position for the lighting. The gaffer said he wasn't going to spend the whole movie making Goldie look gorgeous. The best boy** was promoted to gaffer and he turned out to be an objectionable character with no experience; the camera operator wanted to kill him, the transport manager wanted to kill him – it was extremely unpleasant.

'The crew were under immense pressure from Goldie and from Anthea Sylbert to make her look good – obviously nobody wanted to make her look like an ugly old hag, but she was incredibly vain – and

---

\* The chief lighting electrician.
\** The gaffer's assistant.

there was constant pressure to keep up with the schedule. These two factors ran counter to each other.'

In addition the hotel which had been gutted and converted into a film set for the movie was hit by lightning, and because of the volatility of the weather around Key West, every time a storm blew up filming had to be abandoned for fear of another lightning strike.

Neither did Goldie take to her co-star, David Arnott, chosen by Chris Menges after some agonising: 'He was a little boy from San Diego and was a bit wild. He came from a real problem family and subsequently ended up in prison. He was actually rather good at acting the part but he was a difficult child, and Goldie didn't get on with him very easily.'

The producer had brought the usual family entourage on to the set: Kurt, Patti, Laura and the children were all there, but following the costly re-shoot on *Deceived* as a result of the producer/star never seeing the dailies, Goldie now turned up to every screening, despite having her usual family entourage on set with her. 'It was a bit nerve-wracking for a cameraman,' recalls *CrissCross*'s cinematographer Ivan Strasburg. 'Especially when you have a star who is very, very aware of her image and not that young any more. So it was a particularly hard job for me and it took me some time to figure out how to light her. She needs very soft lights from the front and the main lighting needs to come from behind through her hair. She's got quite a difficult face to light, it is flattish and a slightly strange shape, and if you don't get the lighting right she doesn't always look very good.' Strasburg found himself under attack occasionally and was made to re-shoot one scene when Goldie made her feelings known about the way she looked.

If those on set felt uncomfortable with the film's progress, based as it now was on a false premise and with conflicting demands from the producers to spend time getting Goldie lit right, but also to keep to schedule, those on set found themselves bowled over by Anthea Sylbert. 'She was a very canny operator,' remembers one of the crew. 'She is a plain-talking girl who has been in the business a long time; she knows everybody and is very smart politically. She attended every recce, she helped find every location, she was there for every minute of shooting and if there was a problem she would sort it out.'

But in the end *CrissCross* – a dramatic film without any drama, as one of the crew sourly described it – suffered the same problems as *Deceived*: the public, sensing another 'serious' Goldie movie, stayed away in their millions. A pattern had been established, if anyone had bothered to look, that after a laughter-filled Goldie movie, the public would rush to see her next offering; but after a 'serious' movie, they stayed away. If the Hollywood trade press had bothered to make an analysis of this very wavy graph which Goldie-produced films were describing, and had bothered to question the wisdom of Goldie Hawn making 'serious' movies, then the pattern might have been altered in time. As it was, Disney had silently withdrawn from their much-trumpeted $30 million, seven-picture deal soon after *Deceived* and with *CrissCross* similarly disappointing, Goldie's career as a producer was effectively over.

Undoubtedly Goldie was in part to blame for this state of affairs: her choice of subject-matter and the determination that her films should carry some underlying message did not help. She had failed to recognise that, while there were few truly gifted practitioners of the art of making people laugh, Hollywood had a million 'serious' actors, directors and producers. She had failed to make an accurate self-assessment and had spent her time pushing hard in the wrong direction.

It was also the fault of the studios. Warner Brothers and Disney had allowed their star too much licence in choosing her own material; or maybe it was that they just didn't care. But since ultimately they provided the money which made the films, and maximising that investment was their duty to shareholders, they could be accused of careless disregard towards their star and her activities.

*CrissCross*, when it opened in 1992, turned out to be Goldie Hawn's biggest flop, with a box-office gross of just $3.1 million. Disney sighed with relief and the hatchet-faced money-men at Warner's laughed their hollow laughs.

It was hard for the girl whose Juliet held a rainsoaked audience of thousands in Williamsburg, Virginia, spellbound through a long, hot summer night to come to terms with the fact people only wanted her to make them laugh. 'People feel so good when she's giggling,' declared Anthea Sylbert. 'I want her to do comedies.'

Was this the same Anthea Sylbert who had excitedly enthused just a few short months before, 'Disney believe it is smart business to use *all* of Goldie. They want her to go beyond her old image'? Though Sylbert called her partner 'schizophrenically ambitious' there was clearly no premium on duality of thought in the Hawn-Sylbert office when it came to career direction.

Universal may have lost their shirts on *CrissCross* but they now had the undivided attention of Goldie Hawn, particularly since her friend Meryl Streep was cooing over a project she had involved herself in called *Death Becomes Her*. The powers-that-be at the studios knew that Goldie would shine in this absurd caper about a middle-aged actress obsessed with youth and beauty who finds the elixir to eternal youth by unorthodox means. The film's unique selling point was its special effects and make-up, ballooning Goldie up to Michelin-man size and allowing Meryl's head to twist 180 degrees on her body. The starry line-up, also including Isabella Rossellini, was completed by the arrival of Bruce Willis, a late substitute for Kevin Kline and, as it turned out, only fourth choice after Jeff Bridges and Nick Nolte had been approached.

Though the onscreen chemistry worked perfectly, the news that Goldie would have preferred to work with Kevin Kline provoked an extraordinary attack from Willis's wife, Demi Moore. Goldie snapped back. The Hollywood gossip columns, usually pretty accurate on such encounters, delighted in reporting, 'Goldie commented how unattractive she thought Demi was without make-up. Demi told Goldie she didn't care what she thought of her, but Bruce was a big star and should be treated with respect. Goldie replied: 'Why? Neither of you is in my league.'

Whatever the truth of this, director Robert Zemeckis presided over a harmonious shoot. One scene showed Goldie consuming tins of vanilla cake frosting as she ballooned up to 250lb, an innovation that required the construction of a 'fat suit' and, for the breast and buttock region, the use of a quivering urethane rubber called Flabbercast which moved like the human body. Zemeckis was in complete control of the project, something outside the acting sphere of both Hawn and Streep, having cut his teeth on the revolutionary *Who Framed Roger Rabbit?*

*Death Becomes Her* took seventy-five days to shoot on sound studios at Universal, Paramount, and an independent stage. Under Zemeckis the film came in on time and on budget – $45 million. Editing, normally an eight-week turnaround, took twice as long because of the special effects. Zemeckis employed as his cinematographer Dean Cundey, the most experienced special-effects cameraman in Hollywood. 'When I read the script I realised we were going off on a pretty bizarre adventure,' he says. 'Nobody had done a black comedy which went to these extremes, and the challenge was to lead the audience somewhere they'd never been before. Goldie was intrigued by the prospect of being seen at different ages and with different looks – she had always played beautiful women and to put yourself as fat, old, ugly was difficult. But she saw it as a lot of fun and a challenge.'

Goldie's make-up would take at least two hours before she could even face the cameras: 'She really enjoyed it. She'd walk on the set and everyone would go, "Oh *God*, Goldie!" She enjoyed being put through the ordeal because for once she was allowed to do something and look something as an actress she'd never done before.'

The special effects meant long wearying days hanging around on set, but the shoot was remarkable for its good humour. At a crucial point in the film Goldie has a hole blown through her stomach which the camera then 'sees' through. The edges of the hole were sculpted on to Goldie's costume, then the scene was shot twice, once with Goldie acting and once with no one in the camera-frame. Then the background film from the second take was 'pasted' over the top of the hole. 'You ended up with the impression of seeing the background but actually it was stuck on the front of her, giving the illusion of a hole,' explains Cundey.

'There are actors who are very good at creating characters but when they get into a special-effects film they feel like a glorified prop because of the mechanical stuff. Others, like Goldie, realise they have to become technicians like the rest of us. She readily went along with what was necessary and found ways to make it even better.' Cundey's end-of-term report on the star reads like that of virtually every other senior cameraman she has ever worked with: 'She was always there on time, always fun, she enjoyed hanging out with the crew and wasn't one to run back to her dressing-room the moment she was done. If there was a wait until the next scene or rehearsal she would sit on the stage and chat to us all; some actors are very temperamental and stand-offish but that could never be said of her.'

The result of these combined efforts was a resounding box-office success. *Death Becomes Her* grossed $149 million at the box office – more than Goldie's previous five movies put together. In it, she demonstrated that she was capable of making people laugh in more ways than one, and the ticket-buying public were relieved to see her back in something which made them feel easy about her. More than anything else, it convinced Goldie of three things: that she was still an artist who could command a multimillion dollar fee every time she stepped before the camera, that people were as happy to see her as they ever were, and that it was more fun acting in films than producing them.

It was make-up-your-mind time.

And yet, though the evidence pointed to the fact that Goldie could have more fun simply acting in other peoples' movies, she felt unable to step back from the idea of herself as a producer. Someone at her production office took the decision to cough up $175,000 for the rights to a piece called *Mrs Faust*, in which a woman from a small town weighs up the merits of selling her soul to the Devil. A script was commissioned from Callie Khouri 'about family'. Altogether another ten projects were in development at the Hawn-Sylbert Movie Co.'s offices; not one was to see the light of day.

On the heels of *Death Becomes Her* came word that another excellent comedy script was in preparation. Brian Grazer, producer of

Kurt Russell's smash-hit *Backdraft*, was working on a film idea with writer Mark Stein about an architect who builds his dream house in the country in order to propose marriage to his girlfriend, who turns him down. Back in the city he meets a girl on a one-night stand who goes to find the house, then moves in claiming to have married him. Aptly titled *Housesitter* the film was envisaged as a vehicle for Steve Martin and Meg Ryan, but Ryan, fresh from the sensation of her faked orgasm in *When Harry Met Sally*, was hot; with offers flooding in from everywhere including an invitation to play opposite Tom Hanks in a piece called *Sleepless in Seattle*, she wriggled off the hook.

By that stage a number of other actresses were in contention for the part and, given that Goldie was sixteen years older than Meg Ryan, things did not look hopeful. Finally some deft footwork by Goldie's agent Ron Meyer secured her the part and any initial misgivings the producers at Universal may have had melted once Goldie and Steve met under the studio lights. 'At first everyone was saying Meg Ryan replaced by Goldie *Hawn*?' said a Universal executive. 'But when you saw her and Steve together, it all made sense.' Indeed it is hard to see how Ryan could have bettered Goldie's portrayal of the compulsive liar Gwen who invades Martin's dream home.

Filming took place on four locations in a rainswept Massachusetts. Once again, cinematographer John Alonzo, reprising his joke from *Overboard*, allowed his camera to linger on Goldie's denim-clad *derrière* (aficionados of the film were to count thirty close-ups in the final version). Though the atmosphere in the film was supposed to be light and sunny, the weather was exceptionally cold: 'It was freezing but Goldie had to wear this light clothing – she was shaking and had goosebumps all over her face, so we had to film the close-up later.' On another occasion the crew turned up at the specially-built house which features in the movie only to discover it flooded: it had been sited in a shallow field.

Alonzo remains astonished by the film's leading lady. 'I must tell you for a lady at that stage in her life she looks extraordinary even without make-up. What's in Goldie, and not in a lot of other actors, is this inner beauty – it comes out, and the camera likes that. That's something that no technical tricks can help, you can just enhance it. There aren't many actresses where you can say, don't bother about fixing anything, she'll look just right anyway.' He describes her performance on *Housesitter* as 'masterly'. The public thought so too: though *Housesitter* does not come into the blockbuster category, it managed to notch up nearly $90 million in box-office and rentals and once again re-confirmed to the viewing public that Goldie was worth turning out for.

This, surely, was the moment to capitalise on the revitalised interest in her. Now past the watershed age of forty-five, Goldie Hawn was still in demand while many of her contemporaries were rewriting their curriculum vitae or struggling to find work in television. But it was the last movie she was to make for nearly four years.

Laura Hawn, the fire in the belly of Goldie's ambition, the spirit of Cherry Alley and custodian of the memories whose repetition were calculated to drive her daughter onwards and upwards, had suffered a heart attack. By 1992 she was nearing her seventy-ninth birthday and, as became apparent by her stay in hospital, extremely unwell. Heart disease was diagnosed and it was clear that her life was drawing to a close. *Death Becomes Her* and *Housesitter* were both released to critical acclaim, but Goldie stayed away from the limelight, sitting at home in Pacific Palisades with her mother, who had moved in permanently. Recently the family had moved to a new 10,000-square feet house nearby and Goldie's old home, a third of the size but overlooking the ocean, was sold for $2.5 million. The ranch in Colorado was closed up, the house on Broad Beach in Malibu abandoned, and the family closed in around Laura.

During this period Kurt took extended trips away, making the films which were bringing him ever closer to superstar status: if one career was put on hold, the other most certainly was not. He made *Captain Ron*, a forgettable adventure which nevertheless boxed $22.5 million – close enough to many of the infinitely better-known Goldie's movies of recent times and seven times the gross of *CrissCross*. Next he made *Unlawful Entry*, a crime thriller which brought in $83 million in box-office and rentals, before landing the lead in *Tombstone*, playing Wyatt Earp opposite Val Kilmer's Doc Holliday. Shot on location in Arizona, this finally established him as a leading box-office attraction and was followed by another Arizona-based production, the sci-fi thriller *Stargate*. *Tombstone*, made at a fraction of the cost, trounced Kevin Costner's vastly more expensive film on the same theme, *Wyatt Earp*, which struggled to make $25 million at the box-office.

The irony was that, while Disney had stalled on allowing any more Goldie Hawn productions through their doors, they were more than happy to lay down the red carpet for Kurt. And Kurt was delivering for them – *Captain Ron's* profits went to Touchstone Pictures, the Disney subsidiary which had produced *Deceived*, and *Tombstone's* $82 million combined gross went to Hollywood Pictures, the Disney subsidiary Goldie was originally meant to make movies for, but so far had yet to do.

Just as Kurt, earlier in their relationship, had been unusually relaxed about his partner's superstar status, as Kurt's income started to zoom past Goldie's there were no complaints. For a woman who all her adult life had felt an unusual unease about her partners' lowlier financial status, there was a sense of relief that the burden of earning was no longer on her shoulders. With her mother desperately unwell, at least there were no financial worries on this expensive-to-run life and, as she had said of her father in his demise, whatever money could do to ease the pain, it would.

Not only was Kurt's total income surpassing Goldie's – he was by now averaging a film a year as against her average of a film every other year, but his price had surged past hers: Goldie was stuck on around $3 million a movie, plus producer's points if she was lucky enough to get them, while Kurt had got a staggering $7 million for *Stargate*. His price was to rise to $20 million in 1998 for *Soldier* – but both realised the inequity of the Hollywood star system, which forced women out and, of those that remained, grudgingly handed out small change in return for their equal services.

Laura Hawn's days were drawing to a close. Raised in the abject poverty of Braddock, Pennsylvania, soothed by the gentility of Maryland and finally warmed by the sun of southern California, she ended her life surrounded by her own flesh and blood – Patti, Goldie, and their respective children. In those shadowy days before her death in the fall of 1993 she may have marvelled at the distance she herself had travelled, from grinding poverty to great wealth, from obscurity to fame, from an absentee father and dead mother to a loving coterie which included her two daughters and six grandchildren. Maybe there was a moment, too, to remember the baby son, her first-born, who died within a month but for those few short days bore the name of her husband. It had not been the son, however, who had burnished the family name, nor yet her next child; but the Goldie named for Goldie Hochhauser, who dreamed of leaving Braddock but never did, who had brought fame and glory to the bloodline. Goldie Hawn, the star who made millions laugh, had been Laura's invention and she died proud and happy in the knowledge of it.

# CHAPTER TEN

# *Back ... and Bad!*

*'Look love what envious streaks*
*Do lace the severing clouds in yonder East'*
*– ibid.*

Laura Hawn came home to Takoma Park to be buried at the Jewish
Mount Lebanon cemetery at Adelphi, Maryland. Though it had
been Goldie's plan to reunite her estranged parents in the grave,
something happened to make her change her mind. So it was that,
five years after Laura's death, the Presbyterian Rut Hawn still lay in
the Jewish Hillside Memorial Park cemetery in Los Angeles, two
thousand miles away. Next to Laura, the specially-purchased plot for
her husband of forty-six years remained eerily empty.

After the funeral service Goldie and her children, together with
other members of the family, trooped up Cleveland Avenue to view
the semi-detached house at number nine where she had grown up.
Finding no one home but discovering an open rear window, she and
the children climbed in to take a look around. However, when they
tried to leave via the front door they found it deadlocked and were
forced to shout and bang on the windows to call for a key-holding
neighbour to let them out. 'I didn't find out for a while and I was
actually a bit miffed about it,' says the house's owner Donna Wulken.
'I thought it was presumptuous and intrusive, but I never did
anything about it.'

Despite her vast wealth and the comparatively modest nature of
her childhood home, Goldie has increasingly returned to Cleveland
Avenue on a series of emotional pilgrimages. During her affair with
Bruno Wintzell she took the Swede to visit, similarly with Yves Renier
she turned up and knocked on the door. In 1997 she surprised
Donna Wulken by rolling up unannounced in a limo with Kurt

Russell by her side. This visit was more emotional than all the rest.

'She came in and immediately started to cry,' recalls Mrs Wulken. 'I was unwell and in my robe, but they asked themselves in anyway. They were here for a long time – this is a very small house but they were here for over an hour.' Goldie led Kurt around the house, pausing in each room and telling tales of her childhood. 'She cried the entire time, she was really emotional and very much missing her mother. Every bush in the garden was planted for an anniversary or a birthday and Goldie told me there were a lot of memories for her in this house, I have never seen anyone so attached to a house. She has never called or announced herself and I don't think quite frankly she even knows my name, but still she comes.'

After the mourning came a period of fundamental re-assessment. 'My mother was a big part of my life, and a big reason why I did what I did,' Goldie reflected later. 'I was so proud to show her what I'd done. When she was gone, I suddenly thought, "Why am I doing this? For whom?" Losing my mother was really hard for me, the hardest thing I've ever gone through.'

The work ethic, until now part-driven by Goldie, part-driven by her ever-hungry mother, deserted her. She travelled, talked to her clairvoyants, stayed close to her children, opened up and aired the houses on the Colorado ranch: 'When my mother was alive I was a daughter first and everything else second. That's what made her death so painful. There was a lot of devotion on my part for what she did for me and how she encouraged me.'

The following summer she started to pick up the reins. Since before the death of Laura Hawn, Goldie had been sizing up the possibility of doing a remake of *Mame*, the story of a fun-loving eccentric and her nephew's adventures through the Roaring twenties and subsequent Depression. It had been a Broadway stage play, a musical, and had been filmed twice, with Rosalind Russell in 1958 and Lucille Ball in 1974. Despite the abject failure of *CrissCross* the Hawn-Sylbert Movie Co. was still in operation and if Disney weren't interested in making another movie with them, then Warner's just might be. Surprising as this might seem given the history, Hawn-Sylbert was able to dangle the carrot of Whoopi Goldberg – then a hot property after two *Sister Act* movies – as the star of a story traditionally associated with a middle-aged WASP leading lady.*

Also in development was *Stealing Hearts*, a comedy in which Goldie was due to play a manic depressive who escapes from a hospital and ends up robbing a bank. She continued to travel with Kurt and during a trip into Canada they discovered a beauty-spot in Ontario, next to Lake Rousseau, and bought a parcel of land to build a summer residence.

Back in Hollywood and in conjunction with Bette Midler, Goldie made a bid for the rights to 'Absolutely Fabulous', the funniest and most original programme to appear on British television since 'Monty Python's Flying Circus' twenty years before. The brainchild of comic and writer Jennifer Saunders, 'AbFab', as it became known, was wayward, wanton and rude. It tackled with Bohemian indifference the issues of single parentage, warped egos, drug-taking and alcoholism, sex – and fashion. It was an instant hit, a comic triumph which took TV where it had never been before and made lasting heroines of Saunders as the sulky, faddy, obsessive Edina and Joanna Lumley as her amoral sidekick Patsy. If such a uniquely English show could be transported successfully across the Atlantic, then the only two people in Hollywood to play Edina and Patsy were Midler and Hawn. For once, Goldie the producer trod gently in someone else's footsteps, allowing Bette to lead the way, negotiating through her own company, All Girl Productions. Their spokesperson Bonnie Bruckheimer cooed, 'It's a wonderful show. Bette and Goldie would love to work together on it.'

One reason it was All Girl, and not Hawn-Sylbert, leading the way was because negotiations were being conducted through Disney's Touchstone Pictures, the very group who had endured Goldie making *Deceived*. That débâcle may have been four years ago, but the

---

* An added incentive was that Warner's had made both previous filmed versions of the story and were reluctant to let 'their' property go to a rival studio.

dust had not sufficiently settled for either side to want to undergo further skirmishing just yet. In the end, for whatever reason, the deal fell through. An insider told the *Daily Express* William Hickey column, 'Jennifer is worried it would be diluted to get rid of all the politically incorrect references, and that would make it unfunny.' In the end it was Warner's who picked up the option, turning all Jennifer Saunders's worst fears into nightmares and making her wish that Hawn and Midler had won the contract after all. In conjunction with smaller production companies, including Roseanne Barr's Ma Productions, Warner's put together a show which they named with staggering ineptitude 'High Society' (the original had been set firmly in the professional classes, a different world altogether). The publicity blurb billed it as 'An upper-crust comedy of manners which borrows its air of decadent chic from the hit British export "Absolutely Fabulous". The show's milieu is a dizzy Manhattan demi-monde of penthouse duplexes, double martinis and designer everything.' Mary McDonnell, better known as Kevin Costner's love-interest in *Dances With Wolves*, played Edina as a well-financed divorcee who is the publisher and best friend of Jean Smart (Patsy) who is now a romantic novelist on a permanent bender.

*People* magazine gave it a firm B minus adding, 'the atmosphere of this sitcom can only be described as swank. Brittle and thin, but definitely swank.' It was whipped off the air after a short run, with Jean Smart complaining that the audience hadn't had a chance to catch on to the show's 'bizarre' style. It was an out-and-out disaster and Jennifer Saunders was glad to take the money and pretend it had never happened. Since no one in their right minds could connect the sorry 'High Society' and her own inspired creation, she lived in the hope that the whole episode could be forgotten as swiftly as possible. Certainly the British press were in no hurry to hear ill of their favourite comic writer.

London was a second home to Goldie at this time. The British had a special affection for her, and all doors were open to her, save perhaps that of the *Daily Mail* who entered her for their 'Mutton Dressed As Lamb' awards. Having seized on the over-optimistic dressing habits of a number of women *d'un certain age*, including Elizabeth Taylor and Joan Collins, the newspaper now sought out Goldie who was dining at the Dorchester Hotel in Park Lane, scene of her jet-lagged resistance to Peter Sellers's fumbled seduction more than twenty-five years before. Dressed in a svelte black dress costing several times the writer's weekly salary Goldie posed for photographers. It was perhaps a mistake, since the *Mail* writer adjudicated, 'Our male judges, viewing the star purely from the front, argued that she looked distinctly sexy. With her tousled locks and California smile, the slinky little black dress gave the impression of someone half her age. Which is almost fifty, by the way.

'Then they saw the back view – and had to agree that it had all been a transparent mistake. From behind, the see-through mesh back-and bottom-hugging band did little to disguise the fact that, in Miss Hawn's personal battle of the bulge, it is perhaps time to admit defeat. Lovely she is. But twenty-five she isn't.' In the Mutton Dressed As Lamb category, the *Daily Mail* awarded Goldie four lamb chops out of a possible five.

Frivolous nonsense of course, but hurtful, and more importantly worrisome to an actress still trading on looks and figure apparently unaltered over a quarter of a century. The *Daily Mail* had done what no other newspaper in America or anywhere else in the world had yet done in Goldie's lengthy career: criticise and question. Those who opposed her, and there were only a few, continued to marvel that an individual who had been in the public eye for nearly thirty years could receive such an uncritical press. 'It was as if she walked on water and we stood there applauding instead of looking for the plank under the surface,' commented one veteran showbiz correspondent in London.

But it was a one-off. When soon after she dined *a deux* at Christopher's, the exclusive Covent Garden restaurant with her old friend Charles Glass, veteran of a Hezbollah hostage drama in Beirut, *Today* wrote an amused piece about the pressing attentions of the capital city's greasy-necked *paparazzi* as they tried to infer by the cock of a camera-angle what no gossip-columnist dared imply in words, that Goldie was exercising her much-vaunted sexual freedom. She was back to being the press's eternal pin-up; second only to the Princess of Wales as a surefire adornment to their pages, no matter what state her hair was in.

But if her appeal to press and public remained undimmed, it failed to kindle the same emotions in the stony-hearted money-men back in Tinseltown. Despite all the brave words and the detailed plans, Disney, Warner's and the rest refused to pick up another Goldie-produced movie. To the men in suits she was Typhoid Mary.

For sure, the Hawn-Sylbert Movie Co. looked as though it was still doing business – Callie Khouri, whose *Thelma and Louise* had evaded Goldie's grasp, had written *Something To Talk About* for Hawn-Sylbert. Julia Roberts and Dennis Quaid co-starred, and it went nowhere. Goldie had an end-title credit but had little hands-on involvement. 'Goldie was named executive producer as it was co-produced by her company but we did not meet or have discussions on that project,' recalls Callie Khouri.

The year came to an end and it seemed that there was little point in carrying on with the Hawn-Sylbert Movie Co. Though its two named partners were both exceptionally talented in their own right, they were working in a male-dominated industry which belittled their experience and, when there were faults, homed in on them. The exasperated hiss of 'Women *drivers*!' could be heard all over town and there seemed no way forward for the duo. A press release was issued, quoting the two women speaking as if in unison, 'We part with great love and affection and wish each other great personal success.' In over a decade together the two women had made a handful of films and failed to rediscover the magic that had made *Private Benjamin* such an elemental hit. There were others, men, who'd done much worse, grossed much less, but of course in Hollywood no one mentioned their names.

If this was a low point in Goldie's professional life, there was at least some consolation back home. She learned through her house-keeper that the Princess of Wales, whose personal troubles had caused her to view the United States more and more as a safe haven, wanted to bring her sons Prince William and Prince Harry out to the Rockies to savour Amercia's great outdoors. An invitation was issued: would Her Royal Highness – the world's most photographed woman yet at the same time a woman on the run from the photographers – like to take advantage of the Old Snowmass ranch's privacy and use it as a base for her and the princes for as long as she liked? The answer was yes.

The two women barely knew each other except by reputation, but it was a perfect fit. The princess, in an uneven frame of mind, needed to escape the attentions of the world's press. Not long before she had learned, via the mass-circulation *News of the World*, hitherto-unknown details about her husband's adultery. Prince Charles's former valet Ken Stronach lent his name to an article whose headline read 'Charles Bedded Camilla As Diana Slept Upstairs', and though by now she herself had committed adultery with an army officer, James Hewitt, and another man, such revelations had the effect of sending her off-balance. She needed to get away, and Old Snowmass was the place to forget the humiliations and pressures that constantly dogged her in London.

With Prince William and Prince Harry she spent the long days of July wandering among the wild flowers and sunshine, white-water rafting and watching the boys as they drove quad bikes around the ranch and out into the public roads beyond. 'Diana can relax and be her own person here,' said one of the US special services officers assigned to the party. 'Colorado attracts the sort of person who enjoys simple things in life: the skiing, the scenery, the air, the walks. We let people alone and the Princess likes that. It's also a great place for the boys.'

Meanwhile Goldie and Kurt had been travelling in Europe secure in the knowledge that a brace of films were waiting for her when she came home. The failed partnership bid with Bette Midler over 'Absolutely Fabulous' had triggered a mutual desire to work together, a squaring the circle that had started nearly thirty years before when two young would-be actresses started out as go-go girls at opposite ends of town in New York. *The First Wives Club*, a novel by

Olivia Goldsmith about three middle-aged women reunited by the death of a college friend, who seek revenge on their ex-husbands for going off with younger women, was about to be made by Paramount. Midler wanted Hawn and another old friend, Diane Keaton, in the starring roles and filming was scheduled to roll in New York City at the end of the year. Before that, she had secured a place in a new Woody Allen movie called simply *The Woody Allen Fall Project* but which was to become *Everyone Says I Love You*.

During their travels the couple visited Monte Carlo and stayed to watch the Monte Carlo Tennis Open where, by coincidence, they bumped into Kurt's predecessor in Goldie's life, Yves Renier. 'I don't know what she told him but I couldn't go to the official dinner, because Kurt said that if I was invited, he would leave the table,' recalls Renier. 'He is very angry with me. I would say he was sick; he is not reacting normally. I should be the one who was upset because I was with Goldie for three years, it was as if we were married, and one day she says don't come to America any more because I have found another guy. *I* am the one who should be upset – but *he* is upset, he can't stand me. Maybe Goldie said something, I don't know what, you know women are weird. If Kurt was not there we would be very good friends, but the fact that Kurt is jealous makes things difficult.'

Back home filming started on *Everyone Says I Love You*. Allen had waited until a fortnight before the cameras turned to tell his cast of Alan Alda, Drew Barrymore, Julia Roberts and Goldie that they were expected to sing and dance as well as act in his satire on the complexities of romance. Goldie burst out laughing at the challenge while others were more fearful for their reputations. She played Woody Allen's ex-wife, now married to Alan Alda, and was required to sing and dance her way down the River Seine; an act which won her rave reviews but as she pointed out with a wry smile, 'It's where I come from.'

Curiously Allen confessed to not knowing Goldie's work, finding himself unable to name one film he had seen, and for which she won an Oscar, and another which he saw merely as a big-screen version of a Broadway show he may or may not have attended (*Butterflies Are Free*). This studiedly offhand manner towards 'stars' and the implication that the only movies of note were those made by Allen himself could easily have caused offence but Goldie chose to turn the other cheek. And when Allen offered, 'I thought she was always amusing and had always wanted to work with her,' it might have been a reference to his grandmother for all the enthusiasm with which it was delivered. It barely mattered. It was the first film Goldie had done in four years. Being a Woody Allen production, it was unlikely to bring her a fortune. It was, however, a useful limbering-up for a much more exacting role immediately ahead. If at the end Allen had trouble trimming down a three-hour-plus opus to make it assimilable to the cinema-going public, who could blame the actress if she experienced just the tiniest tingle of *schadenfreude*?

*First Wives Club* was now ready to roll. It was to prove a staggering return to form for Goldie, a comic tour-de-force which demonstrated just how little Hollywood cared about finding vehicles for mid-life women stars: for if this multi-billion industry could make one *First Wives* there was no reason why it should not make another, and another, if it were so inclined.

But those arguments would come later. The most important thing for the producers, Paramount, was to make sure that their three female stars – Goldie, Diane Keaton, and Bette Midler – were all safely on board. It was at this point that Nora Ephron, sassy writer, director and producer, remarked with uncharacteristic bitchiness that if this was to be an ensemble piece where all three stars would receive equal billing it would never happen with Goldie. 'That is the meanest thing I ever heard,' snapped the newest ensemble-player on the block. 'I am a chorus girl. I started out that way and I still have the mentality that I don't kick my legs any higher than the girl on my right.' And yet the word started to spread that, on Day One, the production would not be graced by Ms Hawn's presence. The star, for whatever reasons, had changed her mind. After a stiff talking-to by Paramount's awesome chairwoman Sherry Lansing, however, all thoughts of a *volte-face* were abandoned. Maybe it was the threat of a lawsuit if she pulled out.* Certainly this last-minute power struggle hardly filled the director Hugh Wilson, watching from the sidelines, with much confidence for the success of his movie: 'I remember thinking, "Oh great!" Some big star is going to be coming in here mad as hell. This could be real bad!'

In the end his fears were groundless. The three fifty-year olds who between them had won or been nominated for every acting and film award going, forged a partnership which seemed to avoid rivalry and one-upmanship. Behind the camera, Goldie confessed, 'We've all been around so long, you get to a point where you just want to have fun. Our careers have come and gone and come and gone.' Once committed, Goldie gave what some critics claimed was the performance of her life as Elise, the abandoned actress who bemoans to her plastic surgeon, while begging him to pump up her lips with collagen, 'There are only three ages of woman in Hollywood. Babe. District Attorney. And Driving Miss Daisy.'

If she delivered the line with extra sting it merely added to the over-the-top character she was playing with high-octane vitality. The result was a *tour de force*, though it might have been watered down by an inclination of director Wilson to 'do a Goldie' and turn up the message. 'I wanted to make a movie where the women in the audience would rip the floorboards out of the theatre, they'd be so angry,' he said. 'I think it could have packed a much bigger punch about ageism and genderism and the unfairness of one partner just packing up and leaving.' Fortunately the film's producer Scott Rudin kept a firm hand on the tiller and the tone was kept light and sardonic. His instincts, as far as the filmgoing public were concerned, were entirely correct. Released just before Christmas in 1996, *First Wives Club* was a box-office smash, grossing sufficient in its first few

---

* Lansing said to Goldie: 'Does the name Kim Basinger mean anything to you?', referring to a celebrated Hollywood lawsuit after the actress backed out of a verbal commitment to star in *Boxing Helena*. Basinger filed for bankruptcy and was forced to sell for a knockdown $1 million a small town, Braselton, in her native Georgia which she had purchased for $20 million not long before.

weeks to earn Goldie a $1 million bonus in time to buy her Christmas presents. And if there were no Oscars to be shared out between three actresses whose combined age was 151, then at least Goldie picked up the Blockbuster Best Comic Actress award from the chain of video stores. Not quite that futile fifteen-inch statuette covered in twenty-four-carat gold plate, but not a smack in the face either. She was in euphoric mood as she triumphantly told an ever-adoring press: 'I'm back – and I'm *bad*!'

During filming of *First Wives* Goldie celebrated her watershed fiftieth birthday. This was a moment to pause and reflect, and plan for the future. But she had an early call the next morning so Kurt flew up from Los Angeles and took her out for a celebratory dinner. 'It made me look forward to mine,' recalls Kurt. 'It was a simple occasion, just the two of us, we went to a great restaurant in New York and took a hansom cab and did a little romantic thing. We have an apartment which is absolutely fabulous but because she was working it wasn't going to be a real late night.'

Russell wrote her a series of birthday cards, nine in all. 'Just thoughts about her, streams of consciousness, poetry. Unlike forty, when you are at a realisation, at fifty it's more of a letting-go time and for me, that was the most important thing about her birthday.' Borrowing from a line he wrote into his latest movie he said, 'That was my realisation from Goldie's fiftieth birthday, the future for me is now. I've been building for this future and now I'm in it.'

There nearly was no future. For the past nine years Kurt had indulged his passion for piloting light aircraft, enjoying the freedom of flying from Colorado to the new house in Canada, then down to Los Angeles and back. On this occasion he had flown from Toronto to Grand Junction, Colorado, then taken off again for Los Angeles. Over Las Vegas and at 24,000 feet he ran into a storm: 'I was in the storm for forty-five minutes before it got really bad. I wanted to see how far I could get. All of a sudden I got into heavy icy conditions, there was lightning and I was getting bounced around pretty good – I was really in the shit. Then all of a sudden I noticed my instruments started to rack over, and I couldn't determine where I was in the sky.

I began to go through a procedure you learn to determine what's going on with the aircraft, but I'm not coming up with the answers. It was a horrific moment where you have to hold on to your panic – and then I lost power in my left engine. I had to get down, but I was in the mountains. So I got down to 14,000 and I finally landed in Las Vegas.'

Russell, with his jaunty devil-may-care attitude, told this story to Goldie. She insisted he never fly again without a co-pilot. Russell agreed, then insouciantly went about his flying as he always had done.

His film career was on a roll, and after making *Escape From LA*, a re-tread of his earlier success *Escape From New York* and *Executive Decision*, he went on to take a role as a husband whose wife disappears after their car breaks down in the suspense thriller *Breakdown*.

None of these movies appealed particularly to Goldie even though, despite her present immersion in high-class comedy with *First Wives* and *Everyone Says I Love You*, she was not immune to making turkeys herself. In a moment of unusual frankness, Kurt confessed in the Paris Ritz, 'To be honest, the movies I do for the most part are not movies that Goldie understands, or cares to understand. Vice versa, it's not true. When she's got one going on, we'll start talking about it and sometimes I'll even start goofing around and writing one or two lines. I honestly *do* take an interest in her work. She's not *un*interested in the work I do, but she's not connected to it. She has a different outlook on the business in that she has a day-to-day connection with it, she goes in to the office, she has a production company, she develops material, she's constantly working. I don't have a secretary or a publicity person, so in those regards we're different – but I feel when I get involved in a project, my involvement is much greater than hers.'

To retreat to being a mere actress was not something Goldie would ever countenance, despite the knockbacks from the major studios, so, summoning the spirit and will which Laura Hawn had forged in the steeltown of Braddock, she began again with a new company which, significantly, she called Cherry Alley Productions. For some, not privy to the connection, the title raised a smirk or two; but buried deep in Goldie Hawn still is a picture of that long, narrow, unmetalled street in Braddock, Pennsylvania, with a string of mean terraced cottages down either side, each belching smoke from coal fires; while outside ill-dressed, malnourished children played on Belgium block paving. It was here that Laura Hawn, a kid with no parents and no shoes, started her fight for better things, and here, in her heart and mind that Laura's daughter would start her fightback.

Childhood memories of growing up in the Cold War had prompted Goldie to start writing. For children of that era, in the United States and across Europe, there seemed to be something permanently just beyond the horizon, some dark shadow, which caused their parents to talk in riddles and change the subject when quizzed. The fear of nuclear attack touched every young life and was the more frightening because it seemed such an inexplicable threat. Stirred by that memory, Goldie wrote a story outline called *Duck and Cover*. 'This story was my story. I would run home and ask my mom over and over again "Please explain why the Russians are going to bomb us". I wouldn't go to school when I knew there would be an air-raid test because it frightened me so much on such a deep level. When I was twelve, my girlfriend and I had heard that oilcloth would protect us from radiation. So every time we would hear the air-raid siren, we'd run down to the basement, cover ourselves in oilcloth, and scream that we were going to die. It made me aware, for the first time, that I was mortal and that I was going to die. I didn't think I was going to live to kiss a boy, fall in love, or learn to drive.'

Soon after completing her story, the Cherry Alley offices, situated on a bustling pedestrian thoroughfare in Santa Monica just three blocks from the ocean, received a script called *Hope* which told much the same story; of a young girl growing up in the early 1960s in the South, facing the same fears of nuclear attack coupled with other issues of the time, principally the race problem. The story, written by Kerry Kennedy, touched on the very emotions Goldie had explored in her own tale and the decision was taken to make it, not as a big-screen movie, but as a made-for-TV movie. On the cusp of fifty, with the door marked Producer remaining obdurately closed to her, Goldie pushed open another, marked Director.

Robert Zemeckis, who had directed *Death Becomes Her*, warned Goldie that if she intended to take this new career path she must know her script inside and out. But *Hope* had by now been five years in development and Goldie knew the story in a very personal way: 'I identified with the girl to the point that the whole time I was developing the script, I kept referring to her as me. Like her, I was terrified of the bomb, I was terrified my mother was going to die.'

TNT, the Ted Turner cable company, bankrolled the production and filming of *Hope* took place in a monsoon-like Thompson, East Texas, with a tight twenty-eight-day shoot. 'I had been warned I would probably be answering six hundred questions a day and that it would be difficult,' recalled Goldie of this new challenge. 'But I saw the movie as being like building a house. First I had to get the plans right, then I had to get the foundation right. When I had those things together, then I had to go ahead and decorate it.'

Evidence of a new maturity emerged towards the end of shooting when a can containing five hours of a complex fight scene had been accidentally exposed. 'Instead of panicking I just went into a little thirty-second trance,' said Goldie, who decided to reshoot the fight scene in modified form that night. 'In the end it was all we needed.'

*Hope* received the desired reviews, and was even nominated in the Emmy awards, TV's equivalent of the Oscars, and the Golden Globes. Cyndi Stivers, who so famously had put Goldie's face on the front page of *Time* magazine as one of the three most powerful women in Hollywood, now observes: 'Directing a cable movie is really smart. TV wasn't necessarily the only place she was going to direct, but TV companies have the money, there is a lot less baggage you have to wade through to get the green light, the management structures are simpler. There aren't as many people trying to put their creative scent all over your project.'

In February 1997 the film world, which had not handed Goldie Hawn too many plaudits of late, suddenly realised their mistake. It was, after all, thirty years now since she had burst into the public consciousness with 'Laugh-In'; and for every year since she had provided something to keep the public amused, either on the big screen, the small screen, or in the newspapers. She was a walking entertainment, a 'national institution' as Kurt Russell had proudly but not inaccurately described her. The Academy Awards being such a lottery, she had never received another Oscar to keep her first, for *Cactus Flower*, company on the mantelpiece. Maybe she should have been recognised for *Private Benjamin*, though her chances had been weakened by Ray Stark's determined publicity campaign to get her elected. Almost certainly she should have won an Oscar for *First Wives Club*, and might so have done, had it not meant driving a wedge between her and her two co-stars. Maybe in the future, the Academy complacently convinced itself, that if no suitable vehicle came along which would give her a crack at Best Actress, then a Lifetime Achievement Award would be a suitable adornment to her lustrous career.

The American Museum of the Moving Image wasn't prepared to wait that long. A banquet was proposed in her honour in New York at the Waldorf-Astoria hotel: there had been only eleven previous Museum 'honorees' and these included James Stewart, Sidney Poitier, Robert de Niro, Mike Nichols and Steven Spielberg. Now, Goldie was the first woman – actress, director or producer – to cross this all-male line and it spoke volumes that she beat those two lifetime Hollywood rivals Barbra Streisand and Jane Fonda, along with other candidates such as Meryl Streep and Glenn Close. The reason given by the Museum's director Rochelle Slovin for singling out Goldie was because of the length and range of her career, and the fact that it had spanned film and television. 'It's very easy to underestimate a comic performer – and highly unlikely that a comic performance wins an Academy Award. But it requires no less skill than a dramatic performance; in fact for a woman in particular to be a successful comedienne as well as a sexy woman is a balancing act very few people have ever succeeded in achieving.'

But, as Cyndi Stivers observes, 'In the movies, women will go and see men, but men won't go and see women.'

*Time*, also returned to the theme in an article deploring the gradual loss, over the years, of first-class female talent. 'Sixty years ago the screens teemed with movies about women. Strong women, saintly or desperate ones, but always smart. Greta Garbo drove men to their doom; Barbara Stanwyck did the same and went along for the ride. Carole Lombard traded quips and punches with her co-stars. Rosalind Russell ran giant corporations, Katharine Hepburn, a cool goddess, came to earth to cuddle with Spencer Tracy.'

Now, *Time* argued, with film having surrendered its mass-medium primacy to television in the 1950s, it had bequeathed to TV most of the female audience. From then on, female stars from Lucille Ball to Roseanne would hold sway on TV, while the big screen continued to create the male stars. Actresses who stayed in films found themselves playing minor or makeweight roles, or taking the bimbo route. 'Hollywood wants women to fit these stereotypes, if only to prove the rules of its game: that films must be tailored to the appetites of young men; that women will go to male-oriented movies but men can't be dragged to women's pictures; that an actress's bloom as a box-office icon (Julia Roberts, Jodie Foster) can soon fade while the appeal of male stars (Sean Connery, Dustin Hoffman) stays solid for decades,' went on the magazine's writer Richard Corliss. And of *First Wives Club* he concluded, 'If women can create, star in and see more movies like this one, that will be their sweetest revenge.'

Despite the knockbacks from the major studios, Goldie ploughed ahead with new production ideas. In December 1997 she embarked for India with Jennifer Saunders. Joining the couple was Ruby Wax, who had recently made a hilarious episode of her BBC-TV interview show with Goldie, interviewing her in bed and in the jacuzzi; but Ms Wax was there in her other capacity, as Jennifer Saunders's 'AbFab' script editor.

Two years before Goldie made *The Elephants of India* for the award-winning 'In The Wild' TV series, which had also seen Robin Williams romancing dolphins, Debra Winger traipsing round China after a panda and Julia Roberts hugging orangutangs. *Elephants* had in itself stemmed from an encounter with a half-blind elephant and its baby she and her nephew had encountered in the Kabini animal reserve in southern India seven years before. In a touching and exquisitely made documentary Goldie set off in search of the animal and now found it once again with a baby. As the herd surrounded the baby to protect it she observed: 'There is a lesson about family somewhere in that circle, about how family takes care of each other ... when an elephant is dying, they hold up their sick until they can't any more.' She then revealed to her guide that she held up her mother 'until she couldn't stand any more', adding, 'I took care of her. My seven year old son took care of her. He would roll down the bed in the corners so she could get in. These are things that you give your children, that my mother has given us. The unity of family. Never forgetting where you came from.'

Soon after, shoppers in London's Knightsbridge were treated to the risible spectacle of the film-star being dragged atop a fifteen-feet fibreglass elephant mounted on wheels trundling in the wake of a Dixieland jazz band playing *Nelly the Elephant*. Goldie was opening the annual sale at Harrods; her mission was to draw attention to Flora and Fauna International, which was running a project to save Asian elephants, particularly in Vietnam where fewer than 400 had survived the poachers' guns. Suddenly sensing the absurdity of her situation she declared, 'When you are in love with creatures like elephants you will do anything – but riding on a elephant to Harrods is not something I thought I'd ever do. I have always loved elephants but never understood why. They have made a big dent in my life. We all have to reach out and do something for others in this life – especially the oppressed.' And, so saying, she graciously handed over her £50,000 appearance fee to the charity.

The spirituality, the architecture, the simplicity and the faith of India had left an indelible imprint on Goldie since her first visit during the madcap flight from her responsibilities with Yves Renier in the wake of *Private Benjamin*, and though the affair with Renier was long forgotten, India and its charms were not: she had travelled there on average once every couple of years since. Back at home in Pacific Palisades her twelve-bedroom mansion contained, perhaps self-consciously given the lavishness of their surroundings, artefacts she had collected on previous visits including a white jade statue of

Buddha. There is a Raj Room for meditation, where Goldie chants a mantra given to her personally, she said, by the Dalai Lama. But here in India with Saunders and Wax she visited the holy cities of Rishikesh and Varanasi. India had her in its grip; and memories of many visits, including one with her mother, had triggered a story-idea which had been developed over the previous couple of years with writer Tracy Jackson.

*Ashes to Ashes* was now perceived as the opportunity for a new double for Goldie – not actor/producer, but actor/director. The storyline concerns a woman fulfilling her dead husband's dying wish to have his ashes buried in Katmandu: 'It's about a woman who's reached a certain age, is looking at the second half of her life and wondering what is left.' Now she was handing the project over to Jennifer and Ruby in the hope of turning out a comic script of the magnitude of *First Wives Club*. The trip was not a bundle of laughs, however. Shortly after arriving Goldie's personal assistant was bitten by a dog and as a precaution a doctor had to be called to administer an anti-rabies injection. Goldie, flustered, was heard to utter, 'When the doctor gets here, can you tell him I'm with my astrologer.'

By the banks of the Ganges the trio spent their days wandering the crowded streets, observing cremations and cruising down the river listening to Indian music. They met a holy man on a train and he invited them to his ashram in Haridwar, which they duly visited. But as with so many Goldie projects, a year further on down the line *Ashes to Ashes* had still not been slated for production.

None the less Goldie's passion for things eastern was not to be quashed. She supported a Hollywood protest against the Chinese president Jiang Zemin when he arrived in Washington in late 1997. The protest was to highlight China's occupation of Tibet and the plight of the Dalai Lama, who had been living in exile for more than thirty years. In an unusual move MGM, whose *Red Corner* starring Richard Gere was only one of three current films pinpointing the problem, put out a sixty-second public service announcement in place of one of the five trailers they sent out to cinemas. The clip featured Goldie, Harrison Ford, Julia Roberts and Richard Gere reading from the United Nations Universal Declaration of Human Rights.

Despite an unprecedentedly long career for a Hollywood comedienne, it seemed nothing could quench Goldie's burning ambition to have yet one more hit. Her early promise, largely blighted by poor management, wrong career choices and a bumpy private life, was still there, best evidenced in *First Wives Club*, and ready to be utilised if and when producers called.

Scott Rudin, who made *First Wives*, was so delighted with Goldie's box-office showing that he signed her to co-star with her *Housesitter* partner Steve Martin in a 'non-remake' of Neil Simon's 1970 comedy *Out of Towners*, which originally starred Jack Lemmon and Sandy Dennis. In the new version, filmed on location in Los Angeles and New York, Hawn and Martin play a middle-aged married couple who pack their son off to college and travel to New York to look for new jobs.

Right behind this, Goldie started filming with her old friend Warren Beatty and *First Wives'* co-star Diane Keaton in *Town and Country*, a movie whose storyline is faintly reminiscent of *Shampoo*. Beatty plays an unhappily married man who has a number of affairs before realising his wife is his one true love. Keaton plays the wife and Goldie one of his mistresses, and a large all-star cast includes Charlton Heston, Natassja Kinski and Andi Macdowell. Originally Gerard Depardieu had a role in the film, but fell from his motorcycle shooting early scenes and withdrew; further disaster befell when ten rolls of film were stolen from the back of a delivery van outside a Manhattan film laboratory. The producers put up a reward of $55,000 for their safe return, but in the end the scenes had to be re-shot.

It looked as though Goldie's long-held ambition to star in a big-screen adaptation of the smash-hit Broadway musical *Chicago*, first voiced nearly a quarter of a century before, were finally to be realised. Originally starring Liza Minelli, with whom she hoped to make a screen version, the Broadway show had its roots in a 1920s play, *Gypsy*, by Marine Dallas Watkins. Two filmed versions – *Roxie Hart* starring

Ginger Rogers in 1942 and *Chicago*, a 1927 silent film – preceded this latest adaptation, which was to co-star Madonna as Velma Kelly and John Travolta as a showbiz lawyer. Though through the winter of 1998–9 the film teetered between signature and abandonment, it demonstrated that Goldie's ability to front-line a multi-million movie was as strong as ever.

Or so everyone thought. Then, just a few days before her fifty-third birthday in November 1998 came the news that Nicholas Hytner, the film's award-winning British director, had ordained that Goldie was too old for the part. To make his point, he awarded the role of Roxie Hart to an actress thirty years her junior, Charlize Theron.

Hytner's decision was a brave one, and entirely justified. If *Chicago* could have been made when Goldie and Liza Minelli first conceived it, the film might have had Oscar potential; as it was Hytner saved Goldie from a savaging by critics for being over the hill. None the less it was a bitter pill to swallow, made only slightly sweeter by talk of suitable compensation for this very public snub.

Occasionally now in interviews Goldie would abandon her everything-in-the-garden's-rosy stance and admit that her relationship with Kurt was not entirely blissful all the time: 'Men are really much simpler mechanisms than women. Nothing changes them. Women go through so many different processes in life and they grow and move on. But men ... even when they have midlife crises, they do it in a mindless way. Women do, at least, dig down deep and try to figure life out, but men just go off and have sex with young girls that they can't even talk to. Women have a much longer vision, we are much more nurturing, we understand on a compassionate level the plights of mankind. We're healers and we can work on many different channels at once, whereas a man can only work on a few, then he gets so frightened that he gets angry and then he'll build a bomb and blow everyone up. That's why I think we should let men go off and have affairs with girls and drive fast cars and dream about being virile – and we should run the world.'

This abstract philosophising might be set against another interview at about the same time, given by a friend of Kurt, Sean

McClintock, in which he chose to reveal that the couple's bedroom exploits had become increasingly rare and unexciting and had resulted in them consulting a therapist who 'put them on a renewal program'. It became clear that in the years since the death of Laura Hawn the relationship had gone through a period of hefty readjustment, a fact acknowledged by Kurt. 'We have been through highs and lows,' he confessed. 'Goldie went through a rough time when her mother died. I watched her become a slightly different person, but she came through it and I admire her for that.' Elsewhere he was more specific: 'We had days of fights and total disagreement. At the time it seemed we had unsurpassable differences.'

As the years advanced and she continued to set herself new challenges, some things remained unaltered in Goldie's life, principally her hatred for Bill Hudson, her second husband. At this distance when she compared Hudson with her first husband Gus Trikonis, the anger which had been so much in evidence in 1972 when Trikonis was awarded $75,000 of her money by divorce judges seemed strangely to have evaporated: 'My first husband was a wonderful man; he never took a dime from me. The other one ... yep, he took a lot. The money doesn't matter, but he rarely saw his children and now he doesn't see them at all. He doesn't wish them happy birthday or merry Christmas, and he only lives twenty minutes away. I have cried so often about that. I have helped the children to understand by telling them that he *does* care for them but that he is in a lot of pain.'

As the century reached its close Hollywood could pride itself on its singular contribution to global popular culture; what it would not do is examine with any clear conscience the extent to which it had advanced work opportunities, most particularly equal rights, within its own industry. By the end of the 1990s women were about as important as they had been a hundred years before: as adornments, as icons, as disposable publicity gimmicks. As one commentator acutely observed, 'The female breast is the cheapest special effect there is going' and that, by and large, is where women's contribution to a multi-billion dollar industry stopped. The phallocentric culture, having wavered in the 1980s and allowed women through to positions of real power, closed ranks and forced them out and down again.

To an extent the women who did break through the glass ceiling were victims of their own ambition. Julia Phillips, the Oscar-winning producer of *The Sting*, destroyed herself in a welter of drugs, ego and vitriol, famously describing Goldie as 'dirty' as she walked through the Exit door on her way to obscurity. Despite a promising start Goldie herself failed to advance the cause of the woman producer, and more specifically the woman actor/producer, by blowing it when it came to picking winners. Too concerned with adding a message to the medium, she failed to maximise her unique talent as a comedienne as she might have done by providing her public with comic hit after comic hit. After 1980's *Private Benjamin* when she effectively took control of her own destiny, her career-path meanders from side to side while that of more focused actresses heads more directly towards the target.

There has always been about Goldie a touch of the clown wanting to play Hamlet, as if comedy somehow wasn't enough. With the possible exception of *Sugarland Express* her excursions into the more serious side of drama have proved a mistake; yet as *Benjamin*, *First Wives*, *Overboard* and *Housesitter* continually remind the viewer, she is a matchless comic actress. As a producer she failed to prove to the Hollywood money-men that women should be let through on an equal footing, and despite her continuing comments about producing movies for major studios, during the summer of 1998 it became clear that the retro-jets had been applied to the culture of actor/producer. Disney, who so famously opened their doors to Goldie, producer, only to drop her after one film, took the opportunity to unload a number of other stars including Goldie's *First Wives*'co-star Diane Keaton, Dolly Parton, and Sean Connery. Disney was not alone: Paramount dumped Eddie Murphy who had signed a $15 million deal but failed to produce box-office gold, and Columbia axed Alicia Silverstone, star of *Clueless*, from her $8 million contract.

Back at Disney, deals in development, or 'vanity productions' as they had become known, were cut back from seventy to thirty, at Twentieth Century Fox from fifty-six to forty-four, and at Paramount from thirty to twenty-seven. Disney's boss Joe Roth explained, 'The maths just do not add up, we have come to the realisation that it is just bad business practice.'

If there are stepping-stones for actors wishing to become producers, there is no handrail; and sooner or later they fall. This suits the money-men in Hollywood because, like royalty, they do not like too much light to shine upon their private doings. In the end, however huge a star Goldie is, the Hollywood machine is bigger.

That does not mean she's beaten. Her vitality, her fitness, her mental stamina and her looks are those of a woman fifteen years younger. Her talent has, if anything, deepened. Her universal appeal is undiminished and it is quite clear for Goldie Hawn that the best is yet to come.

Olivia Goldsmith, author of *First Wives Club* sums her up: 'Ageing is different for this generation than it was for previous ones, and Goldie is one of those people who proves you can do it on your terms. She takes her losses, but racks up so many gains she redefines ageing.'

As for the star herself: 'Do I feel more sexual than ever? Yes. Do I feel attractive? Yes. Do I feel strong, energetic? Yes. Do I feel productive? Yes. Do I look back on my life and feel proud? Yes. So what have I got to be unhappy about?'

# Index